Jones's Minimal

SUNY Series in the Anthropology of Work

June Nash, Editor

Jones's Minimal

Low-Wage Labor
in the United States

David Griffith

State University of New York Press

Published by
State University of New York Press, Albany

© 1993 State University of New York

For information, address State University of New York Press,
State University Plaza, Albany, N.Y. 12246

Production by M.R. Mulholland
Marketing by Fran Keneston

Library of Congress Cataloging-in-Publication Data

Griffith, David Craig, 1951-
    Jones's minimal :   low-wage labor in the United States / David
Griffith.
        p.   cm. — (SUNY series in the anthropology of work)
    Includes bibliographical references and index.
    ISBN 0-7914-1309-8 (alk. paper). — ISBN 0-7914-1310-1 (pbk.   :
alk. paper)
        1. Fishery processing industries—Southern States—Employees.
        2. Poultry plants—Southern States—Employees.   3. Alien labor—
        Southern States.   4. Unskilled labor—Southern States.
    I. Title.
    II. Series.
    HD8039.F6752U65   1993
    331.7'98—dc20   91-47584
                                                                          CIP

10 9 8 7 6 5 4 3 2 1

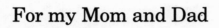
For my Mom and Dad

"I come about the job you got advertise in the paper."

"Yeah?" Lana Lee looked at the sunglasses. "You got any references?"

"A po-lice gimme a reference. He tell me I better get my ass gainfully employ," Jones said and shot a jet of smoke out into the empty bar.

"Sorry. No police characters. Not in a business like this. I got an investment to watch."

"I ain exactly a character yet, but I can tell they gonna star that vagran no visible mean of support stuff on me. They told me," Jones withdrew into a forming cloud. "I thought maybe the Night of Joy like to help somebody become a member of the community, help keep a poor color boy outta jail. I keep the picket off, give the Night of Joy a good civil right ratin."

"Cut out the crap."

"Hey! Whoa!"

"You got any experience as a porter?"

"Wha? Sweepin and moppin and all that nigger shit?"

"Watch your mouth, boy. I got a clean business."

"Hell, anybody do that, especially color peoples."

"I've been looking," Lana Lee said, becoming a grave personnel manager, "for the right boy for this job for several days." She put her hands in the pockets of her leather overcoat and looked into the sunglasses. This was really a deal, like a present left on her doorstep. A colored guy who would get arrested for vagrancy if he didn't work. She would have a captive porter whom she could work for almost nothing. It was beautiful. Lana felt good for the first time since she had come upon those two characters messing up her bar. "The pay is twenty dollars a week."

"Hey! No wonder the right man ain show up. Ooo-wee. Say, whatever happen to the minimal wage?"

—John Kennedy Toole, *A Confederacy of Dunces**

*Reprinted by permission of Louisiana State University Press from *A Confederacy of Dunces* by John Kennedy Toole. Copyright © 1980 by Thelma D. Toole.

Contents

Tables and Figures

Acknowledgments

True to an anthropological tradition, I owe my greatest debt to the many workers, employers, and other individuals knowledgeable about the seafood and poultry industries and about rural southern labor processes, the folks from whom the meat of this study comes. I would thank them all individually, but it would violate a professional confidence.

Others contributed to this study in ways that deserve special thanks. The discussion of seafood processing was based on work supported in part by the National Office of Sea Grants, NOAA, Grants NA85AA-D-SG-022 and NA86AA-D-SG-046 to the University of North Carolina Sea Grant College Program, and the North Carolina Department of Administration. In the Sea Grant office, I am particularly indebted to B. J. Copeland, Ron Hodson, and Jim Murray for their support of my work, and to Kathy Hart, Nancy Davis, and Sarah Friday for comments on my writing. At the national Sea Grant office, Shirley Fiske provided encouraging comments on an early draft of the section on seafood processing and has supported my work in other areas as well. I always find it enlightening and enjoyable to work with and talk with her. I also thank Bonnie McCay and Carolyn Creed for encouraging comments about the work. Bonnie's own work has been inspiring to me in ways that I hope I have done justice here. I thank Barbara Garrity for providing me with some information on the menhaden industry, and for conducting a few interviews with workers. In North Carolina, I am grateful to Katy West and Mike Street, at the North Carolina Division of Marine Fisheries and the Shellfish Sanitation Inspection Division, for providing information on North Carolina fisheries and seafood processing, and for providing me with lists of certified processing facilities from which I drew a sample.

For the research on poultry processing I have accumulated an entirely separate body of gratitude. For project funding as well as for hosting a series of most informative conferences on the impacts of immigration reform and the relations between immigration and labor market dynamics, I thank the Division of Immigration Policy and Research, Bureau for International Labor Affairs, U.S. Department of Labor. People in that office I would like to thank include Demitri Papademetriou, Roger Kramer, B. Lindsay Lowell, Kyle Johnson, and Shirley Smith. I am especially indebted to Shirley Smith. Her feedback and comments on proposals and draft reports have been a great source of encouragement. Another person at the Department of Labor to whom I owe thanks is Rick Mines. Rick's work on farm labor, migration, and Mexican peasant communities represents scholarship at its finest, as evidenced by the extent to which it is cited, and his critical comments on my work, coming from this reservoir of expertise, have been invaluable. For similar reasons, I thank Dave Runsten of the Working Group on Farm Labor and Rural Poverty, Institute for Rural Studies, University of California at Davis. Dave and I co- authored a technical report to the Bureau of International Labor Affairs, and many of his keen insights have informed the present work. To Vernon Kelley, who worked as a research assistant on the project, I offer thanks for his dedication and fine work. In the poultry industry, I thank Bill Roenigk of the National Broiler Council, Bill Satterfield of the Delmarva Poultry Industry, and Bill Powers of the Texas Poultry Federation for their support of the project.

I could not have produced this work without the intellectual and emotional backing of a few key colleagues at East Carolina University's Institute for Coastal and Marine Resources (ICMR). First, as anyone at ICMR will agree, in Bill Queen I have found one of the closest, most scrutinizing, and most intelligent readers and critics of my research proposals, and an excellent director of research activities. I thank Bill for his faith in my work as a social scientist and for all the support he has provided for me over the years. Also deserving my gratitude at ICMR is my friend and colleague, Jeff Johnson, on whom I have relied, from time to time, for methodological advice. Because we operate from different assumptions about the nature of inquiry, we disagree often, but our arguments are usually productive. Others at ICMR whom I cannot thank enough for their work on various administrative and other aspects of this work are Kay Evans, Sandy Bronson, and Cindy Harper. Another colleague who deserves special thanks, though he isn't at ICMR, is Manolo Valdes Pizzini of the University of Puerto Rico. In long conversations with Manolo over the past five years I have had the opportunity to clarify and further develop and refine many of my most fundamental ideas.

Portions of this work have appeared elsewhere. Most of chapter 9 appeared in *American Anthropologist* under the title "Nonmarket Labor Processes in an Advanced Capitalist Economy," 89 (4): 838-852, December 1987. Portions of chapters 4 and 8 appeared in *Urban Anthropology* and *Studies of Cultural Systems and World Economic Development* under the title "Consequences of Immigration Reform for Low-Wage Workers in the Southeastern U.S.: The Case of the Poultry Industry," 19 (102): 155-184, 1989. I thank the editors of these journals, H. Russell Bernard and Jack R. Rollwagen, for their advice and comments on these articles, as well as those anonymous reviewers who reviewed the articles prior to their publication. Similar thanks go to Rosalie Robertson of SUNY Press, and to three anonymous reviewers who provided excellent suggestions for revising the manuscript.

Finally, none of this would have been possible without the constant love, affection, tolerance, and emotional support of my wife Nancy and our two daughters, Emily and Brook. To them I give the kind of thanks they knew on one memorable occasion when, in Jamaica, they fed bread and spiced meat to a starving man.

I
Introduction

The Growth of Low-Wage Labor in the Production of Food

When I was twenty-two years old, I took a job with a construction crew that was building a health club in a rich suburb of Minneapolis. It was a low-paying job with no benefits or opportunity for advancement, earning me enough to rent a twelve dollar a week room owned by a Volkswagen mechanic. Across the hall lived Rudy, an old Latvian with the scar from a Nazi's bullet in his shoulder. He wore sleeveless t-shirts, drank cheap wine, and talked loudly late into the evening, cursing the Russians. Once, on a binge, he threw an end table through my window and then screamed, "Call the police! Call the police! Somebody broke your window!"

The neighborhood supplied Hennepin Avenue's strip joints with Black, Sioux, and Chippewa pimps and whores. Heroin addicts lived in the attic apartment. In the entranceway of the rooming house they begged for spare change and they pilfered food from communal refrigerators. When the mechanic kicked them out they stole a stained glass window, a valued piece of the neighborhood's more affluent past. Into their apartment moved an ex-con who had trouble finding work. For part of his rent he unclogged drains and fixed water damage in the rooming house; for part of his food he hunted cats in the alley with a bow and arrow.

I liked living there. My needs were simple. I had no children, no phone, no charge cards, and I took my meals at a pharmacy around the corner, a block from a school for the blind, where I could get a grilled cheese sandwich served with a pickle and chips for eighty cents. Ketchup was my vegetable. That the blind ate there was a ringing endorsement for someone who earned three dollars an hour driving nails and hauling sheetrock. When the construction crew finished, I stayed on at the health club as janitor. This was an easy job, easier than construction, because from other, more seasoned employees I learned how to look busy and when and where to hide to sleep or read. Whenever I was caught loafing I had to sit through the manager's speech about six hundred other hungry guys wanting my job, about how if I wasn't careful I'd be out on the street with them. But I didn't believe it. From another janitor I learned just how much you could get away with. This guy was a Vietnam veteran who received a monthly VA stipend because of a leg wound. He planned to work only long enough to qualify for unemployment benefits. He came to work, on average, two out of five days a week and never bothered to explain why he didn't show. While at work he spent most of his time casing the joint—estimating values of things around the club, noting concealed doors, paying attention to schedules. When he was finally fired, after nearly six weeks, the club lost a stack of lumber and a few racks of gym clothes and athletic equipment. This was the kind of guy, I thought, I competed against for that job; this was one of the six hundred hungry guys the manager told me about. Eventually, I quit and collected unemployment myself. I was able to stand that job for as long as I had, though, only because I was young, unmarried, irresponsible, healthy, and had, behind me, a thick cushion of family and friends throughout the American middle class.

But most people I worked with had no such psychological relief. Throughout their whole lives they landed jobs like these—dead-end, low-paying, careerless positions, places in the occupational structure of advanced capitalism known colloquially as "grunt work." In every advanced capitalist society,[1] somebody has to haul sheetrock, clean toilets, can fruits and vegetables, harvest crops, cut up and package animals and fish to be trucked to supermarkets. Turks sweep Switzerland's streets. Jamaicans pour concrete in London. In central Texas, illegal immigrant Mexicans carry turkey semen from barn to barn to inseminate female birds. Puerto Rican women working in the tuna canning plants of Mayagüez smell so bad that local taxi drivers refuse to carry them in their cars, and North Carolina women working in crab houses throughout the eastern part of the state acquire a rash they simply call "crab rash" for lack of a medical term.

There isn't much romance in jobs like these. They don't pay well. Often they're dirty, they're hard, they stink, they cause injury and illness, and they earn the people who work them no prestige,

teach them no skill, prepare them for no promotion. In many
regions of the world these kinds of jobs have become associated
with specific ethnic groups, spawning jokes that make fun of a
mythical stereotypic stupidity, further enhancing, further reinforcing, these myths. In other contexts, however, the social
positions of low-wage labor cannot sustain humor. Palestinians
in Israel's occupied territories are revolting against their low-wage-
worker, dispossessed status, as are Irish Catholics in Northern
Ireland. Among the more notorious low-wage workers grappling
their way out of poverty are the black residents of South Africa's
Bantustans.

In each of these struggles, phenotypic, cultural, and ethnic
phenomena have been used to justify and help maintain economic
disparities. In other cases, gender differences are routinely invoked
to justify the differential treatment of workers in labor markets
and economic processes. Workers' responses to unjust treatment
have, as in the above cases, resulted in acts of terror as horrible
as the infamous "burning necklace" of the South African youth,
which consists of a tire set on fire around the neck of a black
who collaborates with the white minority regime. These are,
however, only the newsworthy incidents of the ways workers rebel
against low-wage-worker status. Far more prevalent among low-
wage workers are what Scott, in his *Weapons of the Weak,* refers
to as "the ordinary weapons of relatively powerless groups: foot
dragging, dissimulation, desertion, false compliance, pilfering,
feigned ignorance, slander, arson, sabotage, and so on" (1985:
xvi). To Scott's list we add absenteeism or unreliability, which
interrupts production schedules and hampers planning, putting
a crimp in rationality, as well as the movement out of the formal
labor market and into underground and informal economies
among those who occupy low-wage, careerless jobs.

Theoretical, Methodological, and Empirical Contributions of the Current Work

To address the complexities of these processes, I draw upon
two bodies of literature and apply their insights to low-wage-labor
industries: specifically, seafood processing, poultry processing,
and, to a lesser extent, United States agriculture. One body of
literature deals with labor processes in so-called "advanced"
capitalist societies, especially as current theories explain the roles
of women, immigrant, and minority workers in these processes.[2]

The second deals with the uneven incorporation of peasants and tribal peoples into capitalist labor processes. How can works about peasants and tribal peoples be relevant to the lives of workers in an advanced capitalist economy? Part of the answer lies in the nature of advanced capitalism itself. By advanced capitalism we refer to a phase of world capitalist development characterized primarily by the hypermobility of capital and labor. This hypermobility depends upon subtle and complex relations between capital and the state. These relations draw on ideological constructs that help them seem legitimate and justified. Such an advanced phase of capitalism emerges over long time periods. Relationships between capital and the state must be established, which involves negotiation and compromise and, often, conflict and contradiction. The supporting ideologies must be revised in light of these relations, disseminated to the public, revised again, and occasionally codified into law or incorporated into local "wisdom" or folk knowledge. Most important, however, low-wage labor markets need to *constructed*, reorganized, and maintained. Here lies the relevance of the anthropological literature. As discussed in more detail in the following chapter, recent anthro-pological studies of peasant and tribal communities have focused on the ways these communities have been destabilized and reorganized, or wholly or partially constructed, for the purposes of fueling the expansion of capitalism and its beneficiary states. A crucial component of these reorganization or construction processes has been to establish tenuous yet enduring ties between domestic production[3] and wage labor markets. The domestic sector absorbs much of the cost of reproducing the labor supply, maintaining workers during episodic or seasonal periods of unemployment, and providing for workers during illness and old age. In this way the domestic sector relieves capital of paying living wages, taking responsibility for the unemployed, and establishing health insurance programs and pension funds.

Drawing upon the anthropological literature to understand and explain low-wage labor under advanced capitalism is worthwhile in another way as well. The dialogue between our case material and the anthropological literature provides a platform, a base, from which we can critique current theoretical representations of labor that come to us from economics and sociology. For example, neoclassical economic models view labor as yet another commodity. According to this view, workers are free agents, making rational decisions as they sort themselves among industries, jobs, and positions in occupational hierarchies. The segmented labor market models developed primarily by sociologists and economic historians, however, characterize labor markets as internally fragmented by such factors as gender, ethnicity, and legal status.

While this work draws heavily upon an anthropological tradition, it strays from much of the anthropology produced about U.S. populations in important ways. It is not, I emphasize, a community study, a study of a specific factory, or even a study of a specific occupational group. The book revolves around case studies in the seafood and poultry processing industries, yet is not a study of seafood and poultry workers themselves as much as the ways these workers fit into larger processes of capitalist expansion and development. The work develops four central themes:

1. First, I argue that clear, identifiable relationships exist between the expansion of capitalism overseas, particularly in Third World regions, and the development of capitalism in the United States.

2. Second, the anthropological literature on the expansion of capitalism into peasant and tribal regions has developed theories that apply to the formation, reorganization, and main-tenance of low-wage-labor populations in the United States.

3. Third, low-wage-labor forces in the United States do not just emerge, naturally, as responses to market conditions. Instead, they are constructed, reorganized, and maintained by means of a few common practices. These practices include the use of workers' networks, the reliance on the reproductive labor of workers' households and communities, and the manipu-lation of community institutions to control labor. Each of these practices also depends on the development and use of myths about specific kinds of workers as compared to others, particularly myths about "the work ethic." By looking at these processes of constructing labor forces, we can more fully understand how low-wage industries come to use new immi-grants, minorities, and other workers considered "marginal."

4. Finally, the information presented here leads us to question the application of conventional economic analysis to studies of low-wage labor. This includes neoclassical models as well as the somewhat more accurate split and segmented labor market models.

Besides developing these themes, this work differs from other books on low-wage labor in its approach to the case material as well. The cases of seafood processing, poultry processing, and U.S. farm labor are by no means identical. Instead, they provide informative contrasts. The North Carolina seafood processing industry is, superficially, a "traditional" industry. It is fragmented and technologically simple, where plants are family owned and operated and the work forces relatively small; poultry processing, on the other hand, is ostensibly "modern," composed of a handful of giant corporations whose brands names are known throughout the shopping aisles of America. Poultry firms are highly vertically integrated, employing thousands of workers, and heralded as the model to which modern agribusiness should aspire (Reimund, Martin, and Moore 1981). U.S. agriculture, which provides a smaller share of the case material in this work, includes firms ranging from highly capitalized, corporate-controlled enterprises to small family farms.

While there are clear distinctions between the three, we will see that among their similarities are ways their operations permeate the lives and cultures, the understandings and behaviors, of their workers, organizing the social fabrics by which their workers interact with one another and with people from other cultures. We will see, as well, that the cleanliness of dichotomies like "traditional" and "modern," as elsewhere in the social sciences, cannot withstand much scrutiny.[4] In the most technologically sophisticated operation can be found primitive, authoritarian labor policies, just as in technologically simple environments we find enlightened employers.

My analysis includes interpretations of both workers' views and behaviors and employers' views and behaviors. Examining capitalists' views is something of a novelty in anthropology. Many studies in political economy and anthropology focus too exclusively on the responses of factory workers, peasants, fishermen, and other so-called "local" populations to the vissitudes and impositions of multinational corporations, world markets, political structures and practices, and environmental change. At its worst, such a focus bestows a passivity upon the shoulders of those we study, suggesting that their behaviors are reducible to mere responses to processes originating beyond their communities. Far more accurate analyses focus on the ways that workers actively rebel against the often overwhelming political and economic processes into which they have been incorporated and structured.

Yet even these analyses, fine though they often are (e.g. Nash 1979; Stoler 1985b; Ong 1987), fail to delve too deeply into processes that continually revise the terms by which buyers and sellers of labor come together. Too often, that is, anthropologists fail to examine fully the constraints, opportunities, and political and economic processes that influence *employers'* behaviors and attitudes, and how these influence the trajectories of capitalist strategy and power and, ultimately, capital accumulation.

Methodological Considerations

This work is particularly well suited to examining the perspectives of both workers and employers because it undertakes this examination by means of a dialogue between macro and micro levels of observation. The material on seafood processing derives from a highly localized inquiry. By contrast, the poultry processing and farm labor material comes from several locations around the southern and eastern United States. Constructing an understanding from both macro and micro levels of observation is rapidly becoming the suggested approach to social research questions and problems. Unfortunately, anthropological theory and method has not matured enough to provide all the ideas and tools we need to combine local, regional, and national studies. In order to marshall such an investigation, therefore, I draw upon many disciplines in addition to anthropology, most notably sociology, political science, agricultural economics, and economic history.

In this book, although the lion's share of the material comes from seafood and poultry processing and from the U.S. agricultural labor force, I also draw on other studies. The case material derives from research conducted through the 1980s. At its core are two studies that were conducted for different purposes but that overlapped enough to raise issues critical of current approaches to the study of labor in advanced capitalist society. The first was a study of seafood processing in North Carolina. From January, 1985, to December, 1986, I interviewed eighty-three workers in twenty-two randomly selected seafood processing plants in the four eastern North Carolina counties of Beaufort, Brunswick, Carteret, and Pamlico. These counties were selected for their heavy concentrations of processing plants and their high levels of seafood-processing employment. From the workers I gathered sociodemographic data and information related to their participation in the seafood processing and fishing industries. I supplemented this with participant observations (e.g. fishing excursions), secondary source data collection, and an additional ninety-three open-ended, unstructured interviews with plant owners, other workers, and others familiar with the industry.

The second study focused on the impact of the 1986 Immigration Reform and Control Act (IRCA) on the poultry industry in the U.S. Southeast. From its beginning, however, the study was designed to situate immigration reform within the broader context of relations between labor and capital in the industry. My experiences with seafood processing workers contributed to this design. In that study, I examined coastal developments such as limited entry programs and real estate development in terms of the ways they were influenced by the relations between capital and labor.

The poultry processing study was conducted in two phases. The first phase lasted from the late spring of 1988 until November of the same year. I collected data on the labor practices and labor market behaviors of poultry workers and plant personnel managers. The plants were located in four regions of the southern and eastern United States. The northernmost region was the Delmarva Peninsula. This is the peninsula east of Washington, D.C., including most of Delaware, portions of Maryland, and most of the eastern shore of Virginia. It extends south to the Chesapeake Bay Bridge Tunnel. The two middle regions were North Carolina and northern Georgia, including Gainesville, Georgia, the city whose water tower boasts, "Poultry Capital of the World." The southernmost region was an area comprised by the northwest corner of Texas and the southeast corner of Arkansas. In this work, we refer to these four regions collectively as the "southeast." This is in keeping with Department of Agriculture publications about the poultry industry (e.g. Lasley 1980), despite the fact that this "southeast" region extends west into Texas and north into Delaware and Maryland. Like the seafood processing counties, these areas were chosen because they had heavy concentrations of poultry plants. Also, I assumed they would each have distinctive local labor market dynamics, especially in terms of their access to new immigrant and refugee populations. This research consisted, again, of a survey supplemented by in-depth interviews and visits to each of the areas. The initial interviews, however, were conducted with plant personnel managers rather than poultry workers. The data collected focussed on plant labor policies, such as wage offers, working conditions, plant ethnic and sexual compositions, changes in worker compositions over time, use of new immigrants and refugees, attitudes concerning the work habits of various ethnic groups, and recruiting.

During the second phase of the research, which lasted from April, 1989, to May, 1990, I conducted follow-up interviews with plant personnel managers in northern Georgia and North Carolina. Plant managers in these two areas were engaged in the most interesting labor experimentation, drawing heavily on new immigrant and refugee populations. During this same time, for comparative purposes, I interviewed a sample of meat-packing plant personnel managers, workers, and union representatives in southern Minnesota, northern Iowa, and Kansas. Finally, during both phases of the research, more in-depth, face-to-face, open-ended interviews were conducted with poultry and meat packing workers and former workers in all the regions.

Again, I stress that while seafood and poultry studies form the heart of the present volume, I have necessarily drawn upon other research experiences. These include the meat packing study, of course, but also work on Jamaicans who migrate seasonally to the United States to cut sugar cane and pick apples. It was this research that first introduced me to the complexities of U.S. labor processes, particularly those at work in the U.S. farm labor market. These Jamaicans migrate legally, with H2 or "nonimmigrant" class visas, and work under contract in the south Florida sugar fields and the apple harvests of the east and northeast in a kind of indentured servitude status. The H2 program occasionally attracts the press's attention (e.g. Wilkinson 1988), and annually attracts the attention of organized labor and the U.S. Departments of Labor and Justice (Griffith 1984, 1986b). It is a highly controversial labor-importing program, yet it has been expanding. In the late 1980s, in fact, the program served as the legal mechanism for importing Mexican women to process seafood in isolated counties in eastern North Carolina. In the summer of 1991, the American Civil Liberties Union initiated a lawsuit against seafood processors on behalf of these women, charging such violations as underpayments of wages, servitude, and poor working conditions.

Yet another study that influences this presentation is one that examines relations between wage labor and small-scale fishing in Puerto Rican fishing households (Griffith, Valdes Pizzini, and Johnson 1989). Analyzing life histories of fishermen, we are attempting to determine ways that small-scale producer activities influence participation in wage labor markets. Finally, this study draws on current, ongoing ethnographic research on the United States farm labor force, conducted in farm labor areas in Puerto Rico and the eastern, midwestern, and western United States.

Although the studies may seem only loosely related, all of them involve the mobilization of labor for food production, which itself offers some unifying direction to the analysis. Industries that produce foodstuffs suffer from labor problems that derive, in large part, from their producing perishable commodities under relatively adverse, often seasonal working conditions. Agricultural harvests, seafood processing, and poultry processing plants have difficulty attracting and retaining stable, reliable work forces. This difficulty has been diluted, at certain historical periods, by political mechanisms that assure adequate labor supplies. These have included slavery, indentured servitude, debt peonage, vagrancy laws, or legal programs to import workers from other countries or regions (Daniel 1972). In addition, the basic importance of food has made these industries more immune to high labor standards than other industries. Nevertheless, from the labor demand side, these industries are particularly susceptible to changes in labor processes based on changing local economic growth or decline and changing state or federal labor policy. From the labor supply side, workers in industries like these are often considered "marginal" to the labor force. Their work forces include large proportions of unskilled workers, women, minorities, illegal immigrants, temporary legally imported workers, refugees, students, the mentally retarded, and prisoners on work release programs. Most such workers are considered marginal primarily because they enter wage labor markets seasonally, irregularly, and at a distinct disadvantage. Usually they have little education or inappropriate language abilities and limited employment opportunities. Like the plants themselves, marginal workers are also particularly susceptible to changing political economic environments. They may be forced into unemployment and homelessness by shifts in immigration policy, welfare reform, and the low-wage industrial recruitment policies pursued by local and federal governments all over the world. Also, many marginal workers move among low-wage labor, domestic production, petty commodity production, unemployment, and informal economic activities. This movement further entrenches their status as marginal workers.

Their marginality has made them only a little less elusive to social science than they have been to government reporting systems and modern economic theories of the labor force under advanced capitalism. Many remain unemployed and impoverished, despite their numerical importance. The "food system"— including production, transportation, wholesale, and retail (markets and restaurants) sectors—employs more people in the United States and the world than any other sector of the economy. In the aggregate, food companies spend more money on advertising than any other industrial sector, including the automotive industry. As such, they exert a great influence over the role models we look to for advice on what to put into our bodies. A variety of government programs, subsidies, and legal and political supports are used within the food system to keep food costs low. These programs often have direct negative effects on food system workers. Different segments of the food system have been differentially affected by the growth of labor unions and the struggles among labor, capital, and the state surrounding access to new supplies of more pliant, tractable workers. Within the food system, low-wage workers, legal and illegal immigrants, and refugees tend to concentrate at both ends: in farm work and food processing on the one hand, and in restaurants and other retail outlets on the other. As crucial parts of the food system— production and delivery—these cases provide insight into the ways advanced capitalist labor processes have been changing since the Second World War. Seafood and poultry processing provide particularly compelling examples. In recent years, spurred by increased consumer demand for white meats, poultry and seafood processing plants have been expanding in ways that stress the traditional ways many plants satisfy their labor needs. New labor supplies have been tapped, and old supplies massaged and milked for new workers. Processing plants have relocated and reoriented segments of rural economies and labor markets. In some cases, pioneering labor processes have developed to deal with even more chronic labor supply problems. In others, industry expansion and its associated labor needs have reinforced old stereotypes about workers and work. Still others have reincarnated old methods of labor exploitation in new, and newly disguised, ways, grafting them onto modern organizational structures and supposedly "enlightened" corporate cultures. Finally, a few firms have experimented with involving workers in plant management, product quality, and the operation of the enterprise.

From these case studies, then, emerges an analysis, and a complex story, of low-wage labor in an advanced capitalist economy. It focuses on the ways low-wage labor markets form over time, and how these formative processes both depend on and disrupt workers' homes, domestic producer activities, social networks, and communities. These cases are seated in global political economic processes that influence the currents of world trade and capital accumulation and hence the movement of capital and labor between developed and underdeveloped parts of the world. Within these trends, cases of industries, migrations, employers' attitudes, workers' behaviors in labor markets, and the lifestyles that allow and conform to such behaviors offer critical comment and reflection on the political economics of the last half of the twentieth century.

Seafood Processing, Poultry Processing, and Agriculture Within the Culture and Political Economy of the Rural South

By now, most of us have heard that the U.S. economy is undergoing change, moving from an economy based on manufacturing to a service-and-information economy. This has been accompanied by more integrated ties with international markets for labor, raw materials, finished commodities, and capital. At the same time, reports in the popular media have highlighted employment trends that social scientists and other observers have been addressing for the past fifteen years. At least since the mid-1970s, and arguably much earlier, domestic primary-sector employment (blue collar, unionized, heavy industry) has been losing ground to domestic secondary, service-sector employment and to international labor markets (Frobel, Heinrichs, and Kreye 1977; Gordon, Edwards, and Reich 1982). Population movements in the United States and between the United States and its Caribbean and Latin American neighbors have both reflected and reorganized the new labor processes. While many areas of the middle and northern United States have experienced slow or stagnated growth, the Sun Belt, Mid-Atlantic, and Pacific coasts have experienced steady, at times impressive, demographic and economic growth. Yet the trajectory of economic activity and investment has been anything but even and predictable. Between 1969 and 1976, for example, while 7.5 million jobs were created by new and expanded plants in the South Atlantic states, another 5.5 million jobs were lost due to plant closings or contractions

(Bluestone and Harrison 1982). Throughout this period, the economies of many states in the South continued to grow. In North Carolina, for example, investments to expand and open industries between 1969 and 1976 totaled 4.2 billion dollars, creating 133,771 jobs (North Carolina County Profiles 1985: 16). Since 1976, growth has continued at even faster rates, with industrial investment between 2 and 5 billion dollars per year and more than a half million jobs created between 1976 and today.

Yet other statistics do not provide cause for celebration, lending support to the fact that the performance of the U.S. economy since the early 1970s has been mixed. Most telling has been the slow growth in rates of unemployment, particularly among minorities. Less visible but equally distressing, the reorganization of the economy has caused many of the unemployed, following their last unemployment benefit checks, to return to jobs with lower wages, fewer benefits, and less desirable working conditions. In short, the unemployed have become underemployed. In North Carolina the unemployment rate climbed from 4.3 percent in 1970 to 6.7 percent in 1984, with some years witnessing rates of upwards of 10 percent and some groups—particularly women and minorities—experiencing, at times, nearly 20 percent unemployment. For every 6.7 individuals employed between 1970 and 1984, one person was added to the list of the unemployed, further swelling the pool of available labor and people willing to take low-wage or temporary jobs. While per capita income in North Carolina more than tripled during this period, transfer payments increased six times.

North Carolina's experience is not unique. The recession of the late 1980s and early 1990s has been characterized by economists as "ragged," with areas such as the Northeast suffering while some southern and western regions show signs of lowered unemployment and growth. Even so, pockets of poverty and dispossession can be found in less than an hour's drive in nearly any direction from any point in the South. Small and large communities throughout Texas, Oklahoma, Arkansas, and Louisiana have been struggling through the eighties, reeling from an overdependence on oil during a glutted oil market that benefits most of the rest of the nation. Some counties report unemployment rates of as high as 12 percent for the general population and over 15 percent among blacks (Texas Employment Commission 1988). Throughout the South, while state and regional unemployment statistics suggest an increasingly gainfully employed work

force, discrepancies between rural and urban counties are often
so great that areas less than fifty miles from one another can
have unemployment rates that differ by as many as ten percentage
points (Rosenfeld, Bergman, and Rubin 1985), placing workers
in positions similar to those described in passage after passage
in Steinbeck's classic epic of proletarianization: "They had no
argument, no system, nothing but their numbers and their needs.
When there was work for a man, ten men fought for it—fought
for a low wage. If that fella'll work for thirty cents, I'll work for
twenty-five" (1939: 363-364).

Examples such as these testify to the confusion over the state
of the southern economy and the ease with which we can use
census tracts and other official statistics to paint a portrait that
is alternately rosy and bleak.[5] The general cultural contours of
the South are less hazy. Its racism is legendary, as well as its
paternalism and patriotism and the deepening persistence of its
Evangelical Christian heritage. To some extent, our understanding of southern culture must depend on the way these features
of southern living shape and respond to the economic and social
trends reflected in the statistics.

At the pit of southern culture, of course, is its history of
plantation agriculture and slavery. Despite the very real heterogeneity of the present-day South, this history participates in the
way new immigrant groups—whether bourgeois, petty bourgeois,
or proletariat—become parts of the region. The slave plantation,
that land-labor institution that survived until late last century,
continues to set the stage for social and cultural identity and to
influence hiring practices and southern labor processes. Relations
between Blacks and Whites have improved very little, despite
widely publicized political gains among Blacks. That Atlanta
elects a Black mayor means little, either materially or emotionally,
to hundreds of thousands of residents of thousands of rural
southern communities. The urban, cosmopolitan, seemingly
"enlightened" South has, in many respects, tried to divorce itself
from the Old, the antebellum South. Some of the means used to
divorce urban from rural or new from old are quite conscious,
quite deliberate, such as learning to lose one's drawl or engaging
in aggressive industrial recruitment of Yankee and even foreign-
owned and -managed companies. Others are less within the
spheres of control of southerners or southern communities, such
as the necessity of submitting to interest rates and other fiscal
matters decided in New York or Tokyo.

Yet the Old South has not been excised from Montgomery or Birmingham or Spartanburg or Richmond anymore than the Bells Forks, Nagadocheses, Carthages, or Spivey's Corners have escaped the influence of other regions of the United States, or even the Caribbean and Central and South America. Since the Second World War in particular, the "southern crusade" to change from an agrarian to an industrial power has increasingly confused the distinctiveness of southern identity, though failing to erode some of its most fundamental features (Cobb 1982). The residue of slavery still collects at the center of southern racism. Significantly, it also underlies much of the region's religious tradition, which has, in turn, promoted successful campaigns against organized labor, where local ministers told their flocks that CIO stood for "Christ Is Out" (Cobb 1982). The Holy Trinity of Slavery, Fundamentalist Christianity, and Anti-Unionism is no more coincidental than the relationship between apartheid and Christian Nationalism in South Africa:

> The original cause of Southern distinctiveness was slavery and the society that slavery engendered, an astonishingly complex society whose ruling classes steadfastly maintained that the whole thing was simple, after all, that God had ordained slavery and had ordained a superior class of white men to protect the helpless, simpleminded, innocent black who could not possibly survive as a free creature. As blacks were set so low on the human scale that they were hardly more than beasts, white Southerners—their keepers— elevated themselves to become heirs of mythical and divinely ordained aristocracy directly out of the pages of Sir Walter Scott. (Maurius 1984: 143-144)

More than any other ethnic group, the Black presence has shaped and flavored the southern experience. Political zoning, relations between the federal and state and local governments, labor union activity, housing, entitlement programs—to name only a few—have all centered around the political and economic participation (and nonparticipation) of Blacks. But to assume Blacks in America or the South constitute a homogeneous ethnic group masks the complexity of Black adaptation to institutional and individual racism and the many relations between cities and regions that reflect the Black migrations of this century—from Jackson, Mississippi to Chicago to work in the stockyards; from

Birmingham or Nashville into Gary, Indiana steel mills; from Macon, Georgia to automobile plants in Dearborn or Detroit. Between 1900 and 1930, an estimated 1.3 million Blacks streamed into northern industry, fitting into low slots in the occupational hierarchies and undermining labor organization (Gordon, Edwards, and Reich 1982). These migrations created enduring links between southern and northern Black communities, leading to the formation of migrant networks that still result in exchanges of goods and services, in long-distance visiting and child rearing, and in the flow of information, speech patterns, musical styles, educational goals, political consciousness, economic aspirations.

More recently, the established southern social classes and underclasses—professionals, farmers, rednecks, Blacks, etc.— have been experiencing influxes of legal and illegal immigrants and refugees from the Caribbean, Central and South America, and Southeast Asia. The coastal zones, primarily Florida and Texas, have received the most national attention, but Mexicans, Haitians, Guatemalans, Vietnamese, Kampucheans, Jamaicans, Thai, Cubans, Puerto Ricans, and other immigrant and refugee groups have filtered into rural and urban areas throughout the South. With few exceptions, these groups tend to be incorporated into the low-wage, low-status sectors of local economies, at times displacing native Black and White workers and at other times complementing them. Although they occupy economic positions similar to those of native Whites and Blacks, we will see that the ways they fit into southern ideology are quite distinct from the ways either Whites or Blacks fit in.

Added to the ethnic, sexual, regional, and social complexity of southern labor processes that have emerged from these demographic trends, are the impacts of the new international division of labor (Frobel, Heinrichs, and Kreye 1977; Nash and Fernandez Kelley 1983; Sanderson 1985). It is no coincidence that this new international division of labor has developed along with a renewed southern crusade for low-wage industrial recruitment (Vass 1979; Cobb 1982). Many southern states that were once host to furniture, textile, garment, and other manufacturing industries have been especially hard hit by the flight of cloth and clothing manufacturers to border industrialization programs in Mexico or competition from the garment districts of Singapore, Sri Lanka, Malaysia, and other Third World areas (Rosenfeld, Bergman, and Rubin 1985). While other, both traditional and new industries, including food processing, absorb some individuals thrown out of work by the overseas flight of capital, the composite effect on regions crippled by plant closings has been a general reduction in standards of living and the quality of life. People emigrate and schools stand abandoned. Pigeons roost in the radiators. Businesses close, houses fall down, and even the local roads deteriorate under a shrinking tax base at a time when demand for human services is at an all-time high (Nash 1983). The toll on human mental and physical health and family life is measurable in suicides, lost homes, drained bank accounts, divorces, and all the other consequences of guilt, failure, and loss chronicled by Kathy Newman in her excellent work on the experience of downward mobility in America (1988).

The mid-1970s and 1980s have also seen the erosion of both the powers and public support of organized labor. During these years, the labor unions representing workers in jobs such as food processing have been suffering from attempts to concentrate and consolidate power, expanding their bureaucracies, and operating against a pervasive anti-union climate in the United States, the heart of which was Reagan's firing of air-traffic controllers and the reluctance of traditional supporters of organized labor to support the PATCO strike. According to a recent study of the fired air-traffic controllers, the PATCO strikers:

> ...see the strike as a watershed event that forever altered the landscape of American labor relations. The controllers are hardly alone in this view. Labor defeats as remote as the failed 1987 strike of the National Football League players have been traced to the PATCO debacle. The controllers' strike is an instance of 'original sin' from which the decline of unions, the 'givebacks' in contract negotiations in many industries, and the hard luck of the once-inviolate commercial airline pilots directly followed. (Newman 1988: 170)

More directly relevant to this study, and equally telling of the current problems facing organized labor, labor's weakness relative to the strength of capital came to the forefront during the lengthy dispute between Austin, Minnesota's local P-9, affiliated with United Food and Commercial Workers (UFCW), and Hormel, which ended only after UFCW international withdrew its support of local P-9, dividing the city of Austin and leaving a legacy of continued attempts to form a union that will rival UFCW (Hage and Klauda 1988; *Austin Daily Herald*, April 21, 1989).

The nature of the growth of organized labor in poultry and meat packing certainly contributed to labor's failure at Hormel. Ironically, much of the current weakness derives from the gains made by unions between their early, formative years (1930 to 1941) and their years of growth following World War II. Political and organization successes prior to the 1960s helped legitimate organized labor (e.g. the association between Democratic party politics and organized labor; the Wagner Act; the Social Security Act—see Gordon, Edwards, and Reich 1982), establishing unions and collective bargaining as normal components of many of the larger firms in such cornerstone industries as automobiles, steel, coal mining, meat packing, and, later, clothing and textiles. While making great strides, however, the union movement left large segments of the U.S. working classes and underclasses unrepresented. Union strength and the character of union membership varied regionally, by industry, by size of firm, and by the location of firms in company bureaucracies and production hierarchies. Some union locals were more susceptible to sexism and racism than others; some were more parts of the social landscapes of their home communities than others; some more at peace with management. Despite these variations, the large, umbrella organizations—the American Federation of Labor (AFL) and the Congress of Industrial Organizations (CIO)—grew, the former absorbing organizations of skilled crafts and trades people and the latter absorbing smaller unions composed primarily of unskilled or semiskilled workers. When, in 1955, the AFL and CIO joined hands, the merger set the stage for what current unionized workers view as a level of bureaucratic and organizational complexity that cannot help but engender suspicion and mistrust between national, regional, and local offices and the rank and file. Similar to the corporate mergers that have become common through the 1980s, the large unions have been more concerned with short-term goals (membership increases, dues) than with long-term planning. As a result, they have not been uniformly responsive to the changing demographic climates in the United States.

The principal union representing workers who handle and process food today is the UFCW, which emerged out of a merger between the Amalgamated Meat Cutters and Butcher Workmen of North America and the Retail Clerks' International Association, establishing a union that was 1.2 million people strong but that diluted the relative importance of meat and poultry processing workers in the union as a whole. Workers I interviewed who took part in the Hormel strike held the opinion that the merger significantly weakened the bargaining power of packing house workers. This was considered the worst blow to a united meat-packing work force since the United Packinghouse Workers of America, a more militant union that achieved strength during the 1930s, was absorbed by Amalgamated Meat Cutters in 1968. According to a fifty-two-year veteran of meat packing, the UFCW has become less interested in improving working conditions or wages than in enlarging its membership:

> In Colorado they represented store clerks in a supermarket chain. The first thing they agreed to was to replace full time people with part time people, doubling their membership but negotiating wages down to the minimum. UFCW executives have adopted a corporate image. They fly in jets and have their own dining room. They've forgotten what it means to be on the floor. More members means more dues, and more dues means more gas for the UFCW jet.

The erosion of labor's power and the uneven representation of workers by unions, combined with new immigrations and other demographic developments, has created new opportunities for labor recruitment and labor control. Yet many industries still experience labor supply and retention problems. The paradox of a labor supply problem amidst apparent surpluses of low-wage labor (from plant closings, economic restructuring, and immigration) required at least a generation to develop. Like many traditional, rural industries earlier in the postwar era, the processing plants witnessed their labor forces being drawn away by somewhat higher-paying, year-round, more prestigious job opportunities created when companies fled the unionized, high-wage North for the nonunionized, low-wage South (Wissman 1950; Cobb 1984, 1982). Compared to factory jobs, the sometimes seasonal, spotty, smelly, piecework, processing jobs were far less attractive to new low-wage working women and minorities. During periods of economic growth, work in the processing plants—much like jobs in agricultural harvests—became associated with the least skilled, lowest class, and most marginal sectors of the labor force. Even when plant closings replenished the labor pool, the damage done to the image of processing jobs was too great to assure these new unemployed people would not rather emigrate than hang live chickens, shuck oysters, debone turkey breasts, or pick crabs. In Washington, North Carolina, the small county seat of Beaufort County, I spoke with workers who had recently been laid off from a plant that made small kitchen appliances; they were picking crabs, but they told me they were actively seeking "any other job." While sitting in a turkey plant's personnel office, I watched two men and a woman quit within ten minutes time. The woman was an American Indian who boasted that her Indian status had allowed her to land a better job. Then, as though not wishing to perpetuate any myth of Native American laziness or drunkenness, she added, "It isn't just a matter of quitting. I've got another job." In a small, isolated town in southern North Carolina, three oyster shuckers told me they hoped my questions about their employment histories meant that I would be coming back to hire them to do something else. In the words of one crab-picking-plant owner: "These people would rather do anything besides pick crab." In the words of a chicken plant personnel manager in Georgia: "The work ethic has gone to hell. I wish I could get some boat people."

Yet some personnel managers have, in fact, gotten some boat people, while others have stimulated migrations from half-way around the world and still others continue to draw workers exclusively from local labor pools. What accounts for these differences? How can one firm attract workers from thousands of miles away to cut the wings off birds for eight hours a day? Why does another firm, offering the same wage under similar working conditions, simply dip into a pile of applications for locals to do exactly the same tasks? How do these practices permeate workers' lives, networks, and communities? Just by posing these questions, we express dissatisfaction with current interpretations and explanations of low-wage labor under advanced capitalism. The prevailing theories about labor under advanced capitalism have failed to keep pace with the way capital has changed and adapted to new demographic and cultural developments. By contrast, anthropologists have been working in contexts where capital has been expanding and adapting to new cultural, social, and political economic settings. The insights from these studies, discussed in the following chapter, thus provide a good starting point for reconsidering current theories of labor under an advanced, changing capitalist regime.

Conclusion

In this chapter, I questioned conventional approaches to the study of labor in industries where wages are low, opportunities for advancement are slim, and labor turnover and occupational injury rates are high. I also described, in general terms, the growth of the seafood and poultry processing industries in the context of the South. The more detailed descriptions and analyses of these industries and their labor relations occupy later chapters. Overall, the text is organized into four sections. First, the introduction, consisting of this chapter and the following, outlines the subject matter and theoretical basis of the book. The second chapter discusses anthropological and sociological treatments of labor in the contexts of capitalist expansion into peasant and tribal regions in Latin America, Africa, Asia, and the Caribbean, paying particular attention to the relationship of this body of work to evolving labor practices of "advanced" capitalism in the United States and the developed world.

The second section of the book consists of general descriptions of the seafood and poultry processing industries, focusing primarily on questions of industry structure, the influences of local economic and ecological factors on industry development, and the organization of work. Chapters 3 and 4 thus constitute overviews of the seafood and poultry processing industries; chapter 4 ends with a comparative discussion of the two industries. Chapters 5 through 8 represent the third section of the book. In this section I present and analyze a great deal of information on the two industries' labor relations in the context of family, network, and community, as well as in light of negotiated categories of gender, ethnicity, and nationality. The information shows, in particular, how these contexts and categories enter into processes of labor control, how they affect relations among workers, and how they influence methods of recruitment and the organization of work in the two industries. In addition, these chapters highlight the processes by which one group of workers comes to be preferred, by employers, over another, and how this results in the displacement of one group of workers by another in the local labor market, in low-income neighborhoods, and in communities at large.

Finally, in the two concluding chapters, I return to the theoretical concerns raised here, considering the previous chapters in light of new and old theories of labor under advanced capitalism. Again, I devote particular attention to the roles of ethnicity, gender, nationality, family, community, and social networks in staffing low-wage industries. The extent to which low-wage industries rely on "extra-economic" means to recruit, organize, assign tasks to, and control labor calls into question conventional economic theories of labor. At the same time, these practices underscore the relevance of anthropological and sociological treatments of low-income populations, which have stressed the broader social and cultural contexts of economic activity. It is these treatments that I consider in the following chapter.

An Anthropology of Labor under Advanced Capitalism

I used sometimes to despair that I never discussed anything with young men but livestock and girls, and even the subject of girls led inevitably to that of cattle.

—E. E. Evans-Pritchard, *The Nuer*

An anthropology of labor under advanced capitalism is emerging from the shadows of anthropological work on capitalist expansion around the world. From studies of forced and enticed labor recruitment into plantation agriculture, mining, and industry, anthropologists have become interested in the ways that peasant communities, tribal groups, and other local populations have accommodated the process of proletarianization. The process has been uneven and unpredictable, which is itself telling, but some degree of class formation has occurred in nearly every nation of the world. The process has been neither spontaneous nor incidental to other developments in culture, the family, and political economics. Historically, fairly creative, often authoritarian means have been used to get young women and men to leave their home villages to work under adverse conditions, picking coffee beans, cutting sugar cane, or descending deep into the earth for metals and gems. Anthropologists studying among Latin American, African, and Asian peasant and tribal groups often could not help but address the underlying reasons people came to beg for low-paying, hazardous work at factory gates or hacienda yards. Early observations established that it wasn't simply a question of "maximizing earnings" or having no other economic alternatives, as has been suggested by economic theory (see Borjas

1989). Instead, anthropologists witnessed and documented a variety of ways tribal and peasant groups were being "incorporated" into capitalist circuits of value and trajectories of capital accumulation. Their members were not only entering labor markets, but also commoditizing their labor power in "home work" enterprises or through elaborate subcontracting arrangements. This led anthropologists to question prevailing theories and methods of analyzing peasant and tribal groups, particularly those influenced by classical economic and modernization theory. In his recent volume, global in sweep, Eric Wolf (1982) describes how capitalist modes of production transformed other production modes, with capitalist merchants enlisting the support of local groups to supply such commodities as sugar, fur, and slaves. Similarly, Gerald Sider (1986) has shown how various cultural features of Newfoundland fishing communities contributed to the growth of merchant capital and the eventual inability of Newfoundlanders to prevent the wholesale destruction of their communities and the relocation of the populace to areas in need of labor.

In general, these studies illustrate that capitalist expansion participates in the formation of social groups, rather than simply encounters them. Working from subsequent theoretical developments, anthropologists have begun to contribute to a more thorough understanding of labor in advanced capitalist economies. The applicability of these theoretical developments derives from key similarities between peasants and tribal peoples and certain groups of low-wage workers in capitalist society. The apparent "marginality" of Black workers, for example, and their apparent "otherness" vis-à-vis the dominant cultural group is similar to the marginal positions of many ethnic groups in the national systems of Latin America or Africa. The seemingly passive acceptance of servile status in the labor force on the part of many women and minorities has been encountered again and again among similarly placed women and "others" overseas.

The contributions of anthropologists studying among "others" in underdeveloped regions are also relevant because of their insistence on viewing economic behaviors as intimately tied to cultural, social, and political phenomena. The most influential challenges to neoclassical economic models of labor agree that workers are constrained in their abilities to find and obtain jobs by social characteristics such as race, ethnicity, or gender. These latter studies have not, however, explored as extensively as anthropologists the ties among cultural, social, political, and economic behaviors.

I do not mean to overstate the similarity between low-wage workers in advanced capitalist economies and peasants and tribal workers working in wage labor jobs throughout the under-developed world. Nevertheless, the ways in which such workers are similar may yield insight into the ways capital comes to dominate and then organize populations, families, ethnic groups, and communities. And in some cases, we may be talking about exactly the same people, as in the case of Mexican cyclical migrants, from peasant villages, working as farm workers in California or Florida. This is particularly true with the growth of "transnational" communities (Glick-Schiller and Fouron 1990).

Partially due to the uneven character of capitalist expansion, as well as to the needs of capital for seasonal or temporary labor forces in the face of changing business cycles or longer shifts in economic growth and decline (see Gordon, Edwards, and Reich 1982; Roseberry 1983), many tribal and peasant groups seem to have been incompletely or partially incorporated, existing on the fringes or margins of the labor market. This marginality, however, need not imply isolation or independence from labor processes. Marginal workers can still be recruited to wage labor occupations by means of chains of power relationships between farm or factory owners, labor contractors, ethnic supervisors, and workers' kinship and friendship networks. In the context of international labor migration, such chains of relationships may link small rural villages in Guatemala with Houston, Texas supermarkets (Bach and Brill 1991). In the same way, many low-wage workers in advanced capitalist countries maintain a "stand-by" status in the labor market, waiting to be called during peak labor demand periods or labor supply crises (union problems, expansion of competing industries, restrictions on immigration reform). They do not wait idly, but occupy themselves with activities that generate incomes, including farming, fishing, cottage industry (e.g. cosmetology), taking advantage of social service or welfare programs, and seeking sporadic or seasonal employment in other sectors of the economy (Lomnitz 1977). Such activities may allow them some independence from wage labor processes, yet the uneasy balance between dependence on and independence from wage labor underlies their vulnerability to competition from other, more desperate low-wage workers, particularly new immigrants and refugees. When nonwaged, income-generating activities create scheduling conflicts with wage work, for example, employers may turn to new labor supplies. This may initiate a joint process of replacing and displacing one type of worker (e.g. Black females) with another (e.g. Mexican males).

Far from being incidental, their marginality, and the specific economic adaptations that marginality entails, is a central feature of any explanation or understanding of low-wage labor processes in advanced capitalism. Indeed, one of the hallmarks of advanced capitalism has been its success at the continued reliance on "marginal" workers. These workers are marginal to the labor market either because they are struggling to become independent of wage labor, or because they are forced to seek other means of generating incomes when the jobs they hold fail to meet their consumption needs. Again, peasant and tribal groups also struggle to maintain independent production systems or fall back on such production systems when forced to leave wage labor markets. These similarities among peasant groups, tribal social organizations, and low-wage working classes in advanced capitalist countries constitute yet another reason that studies of peasant or tribal groups (which provide workers to low-wage labor markets) can help us make sense of the behaviors of workers and employers in late capitalist culture. Tracing the theoretical and methodological history of peasant and tribal "incorporation" studies, or the proletarianization of peasants and tribal groups, will be useful to organizing the way we think about low-wage labor processes in the seafood and poultry processing plants and in U.S. agriculture.

Theoretical Background: Relationships Between International and Domestic Labor Processes

Early Conceptual Frameworks

Twenty to thirty years ago, the conceptual apparatus anthropologists possessed to explain the incomplete incorporation of peasants and tribal peoples into capitalist circuits of value were weak. In peasant studies, for example, anthropologists had long called peasants "part societies" or "part cultures." These ideas acknowledged that peasants shared social and cultural space and time with industrial peoples without addressing the question of interactions among peasant communities, nation states, and capitalist economic processes. We tended to ignore the ways capital's representatives reorganized peasant regions and how reorganizing such regions assured continued supplies of labor to capitalist enterprises. We overlooked questions of formation and transformation. Marx (1967) understood the "transformation" of peasants and tribal peoples into rural and urban proletarians as a linear process of separating direct producers from the means of production. Once so divorced, they would have no choice but to sell their labor power. He argued we were witnessing a process of class formation, using the famous case of forcing peasants into the urban work force by usurping common lands and other means of getting them off the land. We now know, however, that the process has not been linear, but uneven. Some regions, some peasant villages, and some tribal groups have been maintained, constructed, or reproduced *as a result of* capitalist expansion.[1] Perhaps nowhere is this more clear than in the Caribbean. There, colonialism and plantation agriculture decimated the indigenous populations, imported new peoples from Africa, China, East India, the Americas, and Europe, transformed the landscapes and adapted ecosystems to sugar, coffee, tobacco, and other crops' production, and constructed entire complex societies. In most Caribbean colonies, viable peasant groups and peasant villages did not exist prior to emancipation in the early nineteenth century.

The foundation for current theoretical development grew out of concrete political conditions following World War II. Most notable has been the sharp increase in the birth of new nations as the world powers, encouraged by the United Nations, dismantled colonialism. The new political and economic forms that followed changed the ways wealthy and poor regions of the world interacted. Until the war, despite isolated "success stories" such as Hong Kong (Bauer 1966), it had been relatively easy to blame colonialism for the poverty, technological backwardness, inequality, injustice, and other negative social features found throughout the colonies. Yet independence failed to stimulate significant change in colonial conditions. Many social scientists began to examine less explicit relations between rich and poor nations and began to make crude, though accurate, connections between economic processes and political developments in the international arena. Lifting the Cold War's hem, they realized that the threat of communism, so mobilizing and justifying a force in the West, was nonetheless a veil behind which capitalists could establish relations of dependence with poor regions throughout Latin America, Africa, and Asia.[2] The recognition of the elaborate and often subtle relations among major capitalist regions and underdeveloped, seemingly "backward" regions, can be traced to the early work of Latin American, Marxist, social scientists from the now well-known (and widely criticized) dependency school. Their primary contribution was to view the apparent technological stagnation, social injustice, inequality, and economic stasis[3] of underdeveloped regions as results of capitalist expansion, rather than as conditions of isolation (e.g. Frank 1967; Furtado 1973). The direct offspring of dependency theory were Wallerstein's (1976) world-system studies, works on global accumulation (e.g. Amin 1979), and the recognition of a "new" international division of labor (Frobel, Heinrichs, and Kreye 1977).

Working from these theoretical developments, anthropologists began documenting the concrete ways capitalist expansion reorganized and restructured regions. This expansion created pools of low-wage workers who could be mobilized for specific projects such as plantation agriculture or the building of oil refineries, and for seasonal jobs. Since these early discoveries, two decades of observers of national and international labor processes have posited progressively more elaborate and more direct relationships between international capital flows and the plight of workers in advanced capitalist economies (Frobel, Heinrichs, and Kreye 1977; Barnet 1981; Sassen-Koob 1985, 1983; Bach 1985; Nash and Fernandez-Kelly 1983). The general framework for much of this work was provided by Froebel, Heinrichs, and Kreye (1979). The "new" international division of labor they describe rests on the hypermobility of capital and the internal and international migrations of labor that accompany shifts in economic growth. Political supports such as open-trade policies and tax-free production zones, and key technological and financial inventions that have made international communication commonplace have increased along with capital's mobility. As I noted in the previous chapter, this mobility of labor and capital is one of the principal defining features of advanced capitalism. As this mobility has been joined by political supports, it has become possible to fragment the production of manufactured goods and to shop for the cheapest, most docile workers the world has to offer. This has negative consequences for workers throughout the world.

Contributions from Peasant Studies

The political and technological capability of major global firms to produce a single product in a number of locations around the world has placed U.S. workers into a global labor pool. Today they compete with workers whose wages are subsidized by formal or informal mechanisms and whose attitudes are anything but militant. The mechanisms by which foreign workers' wages have been subsidized and their docility maintained have generated a great body of literature. This literature has been framed by the general ways peasant communities, tribal groups, and other small, local populations provide seasonal and year-round workers to capitalist labor markets (Wolf 1982; Griffith 1985; Painter 1985; Collins 1988). Groups like these are able to supplement the costs of maintaining and reproducing labor power with small-scale-producer activities such as peasant farming, herding, fishing, and so on. These populations have been *semi*proletarianized. Their small-scale producer activities, though generally insufficient for household survival, nevertheless produce enough income so that individuals can sell their labor power at lower rates than individuals who do not have these small-scale-producer activities to supplement wage labor incomes (de Janvry 1983). At the same time, workers entering labor markets under these conditions may view their wage labor jobs as temporary or secondary to their own small-scale-producer activities. These latter activities may in fact be the true sources of their social identities. Thus, such workers may be less willing to organize or complain about wages and working conditions. This is particularly true of labor migrants, who tend to maintain connections to natal communities and often consider their wage work temporary.

These conditions tend to entail others that, combined, make foreign workers cheaper, more desirable, and more exploitable than native workers in advanced capitalist economies. For example, not only do peasant households absorb many of the costs of maintaining and reproducing workers, but the peasant "condition," historically, has been one of periodic hardships. The history of any peasant region is written in droughts, unjustified taxation, forced recruitment for labor or war, crop failures, and misguided agrarian reforms (de Janvry 1983; Wolf 1969; Scott 1979; Migdal 1979; Popkin 1981). Such hardships both generate suspicion and preadapt people to austerity, which in turn breed fatalism and acceptance of current conditions. Workers with fatalist attitudes tend to be difficult to organize for collective bargaining, if only because they perceive that peasants—or rural peoples generally—tend to be the last to benefit from revolutionary change (Migdal 1979).

Workers with fatalist attitudes will also consent, if grudgingly, to live in cramped and unsanitary housing, to sleep more to a room or a bed, and to behave as though they were *living* in shifts, occupying their homes during leisure hours and surrendering their beds and living quarters to others while at work. Such living conditions cost less than the single-family dwellings U.S. workers are used to, and workers living in such conditions can afford to earn less.[4]

A peasant background also affects attitudes toward child labor. Within the peasant household's independent economic activities, putting one's children to work may be viewed as an obligation to one's ancestors as well as to the children themselves. Child labor may be encouraged as a means to teach one's offspring the technical knowledge and skills required for peasant farming, fishing, cottage industry, or craft production. In such an environment, child labor laws may be either difficult to enforce or, under less humanitarian systems of government, easy to completely ignore. Even child labor opponents living under low-wage labor conditions are sometimes encouraged or forced to put their children to work. Piece-rate forms of payment, where volume of output determines one's pay instead of hours on the job, often encourage women to have their children work beside them, adding to the number of pounds, bushels, boxes, or whatever unit determines how much earned per day.

Finally, these conditions have to be accompanied by understandings and arrangements within and between families and households to accommodate the easy movement of people between wage labor markets and independent economic activities. People must expect to take care of workers during times of unemployment, to care for workers' children, to provide services and food or open their homes to relatives and friends. These arrangements and understandings comprise a social structural context that allows workers to remain absent from their peasant farms or cottage industries for extended periods, while maintaining production in these enterprises through the efforts of family and community members. Over time, these arrangements have a way of becoming institutionalized, thus reinforcing and perpetuating movement between wage and nonwage economic activities. It is as a result of exactly these sorts of expectations that we have witnessed recently the increasing international complexity of households and the growth of transnational communities (Griffith, et al. 1990; Glick-Schiller and Fouron 1990).

Because of these factors, overseas work forces, particularly in underdeveloped countries under authoritarian rule, are notoriously cheaper, less militant, and more responsive to authority than U.S. workers. Women employees in such settings, moreover, are often subject to authoritarian patriarchal rule within their households, ethnic groups, and communities, making it possible for employers to utilize husbands, fathers, and senior village males for recruiting and coming to terms with female labor.

Relevance to U.S. Low-Wage Labor Processes

Using foreign labor around the world may seem unrelated to the labor practices of firms or industries that have not moved their operations abroad. Yet the practice of utilizing overseas labor has defined the technological and organizational parameters of the modern corporation. In particular, under advanced capitalism, modern corporations strive for fragmented production of manufactured goods and services that can be controlled and integrated in a highly skilled service sector. The production itself relies heavily on unskilled or semiskilled labor staffing sophisticated machines or performing simple, repetitive tasks. The highly skilled service sector includes financial, legal, managerial, technical, and intellectual expertise. This division has led to the emergence of what Sassen-Koob (1985) refers to as "global control capability" in major urban centers around the world. This, in turn, entails further revisions of relations between labor and capital.[5] The factors of production needed to produce and reproduce global control capability include, most notably, cost accounting and actuarial expertise. These mathematical operations cannot help but consider labor in terms of accurate, discrete measures such as cost, units of time, and productivity. Such pressures create the need to standardize productive practices to assure accurate measurement for the calculation of profit margins or the reified "bottom line." The very process of standardizing production leads to, and has led to, what Gordon, Edwards, and Reich (1982) call a "homogenization" of labor. This is similar to Marx's notion of classes being defined, fundamentally, by their relationship to the means of production (1967). Because standardization of production encourages class formation, and because class formation engenders class consciousness, modern labor processes have needed to "destabilize" the logical trajectories of class formation. One means of accomplishing this has been to draw upon labor pools peopled by individuals from diverse ethnic and national backgrounds, including peoples coming from peasant backgrounds or living under the conditions described above.

Among the consequences of this process has been the restructuring of the U.S. labor market in such a way that many jobs have been downgraded, relocated, and made available to primarily low-wage, unskilled workers from various ethnic backgrounds and nationalities. A cornerstone of ethnic and national pluralism, which promotes and exacerbates labor market segmentation (Bonacich 1982; Gordon, Edwards, and Reich 1982), has been international and internal labor migration. Yet firms in the United States have also shifted production sites to take advantage of ethnically heterogeneous labor pools, as well as labor environments made favorable by religious or political traditions or by fluctuations in local economies. Finally, companies that cannot or have not taken advantage of the global labor market have subcontracted both social and technical aspects of their production. Each of these practices contributes to the construction of a specific kind of labor force. It is a labor force that has been incompletely drawn into the wage labor market; a labor force composed of interchangeable segments that remain separate from one another because of certain objective characteristics such as legal status, gender, ethnicity, and their ties of family, network, and community.

These developments have been both reinforced and hampered by developments in the state. Legislative initiatives and new policies have been designed to establish greater concert among labor and immigration policy, trade policy, and social welfare policy throughout the world (Bach 1985). Postwar changes in immigration policy have included, most notably, a growth in legal statuses that serve to establish classes of workers with limited access to the labor markets of advanced capitalism (Thomas 1985). This growth in legal statuses within the United States has been grafted onto the growth in nations that has taken place throughout the world since the turn of the century, particularly during the postwar era. This has restricted movement between mother countries and former colonies while laying the political ground-work for multinational corporations to view the entire world as a labor market.

The most obvious example of the growth of legal statuses in effect in the United States today is the British West Indies Temporary Alien Labor Program (U.S. Congress 1978). Annually, this program imports over 10,000 British West Indian workers,

80 percent of whom are from Jamaica, to harvest apples along the eastern seaboard and sugar cane in South Florida. While these workers are in the United States they can work only in the job for which they have been imported. Legally, they cannot move on to jobs they might consider more in line with their skills or personal tastes. Recent immigration reform, known as the 1986 Immigration Reform and Control Act (IRCA), has also created new legal statuses that restrict individuals' free access to the labor markets.

Trade policy continues to draw heavily on capitalist dogma, underscoring the supposed necessity of a free market. These ideologies have successfully blocked a legislative initiative to force managers to give workers ninety days notice before plants are to be closed. At the same time, social welfare legislation has been a major way to appease unions and domestic labor (Bach 1985). On the one hand, unemployment insurance and welfare benefits serve as bases from which domestic workers can choose not to respond to an employer's wage offer. On the other, these programs can also act as subsidies to capital.[6] In yet other cases they reinforce the marginal conditions of low-wage workers.

These national and international political developments are differentially felt at the local level, where the work of anthropologists has become valued for its critical commentary on prevailing political economic theories. While "political" mechanisms are necessary in the structuring and restructuring of labor processes, the management of power occurs outside and inside formal government, in the family, the community, or the ethnic group. Hence, at the local level, it has been necessary to examine relationships between power and the use of labor in capitalist and noncapitalist production. In tribal and peasant societies, power might assume the concrete form of men over women, senior males over junior, or specific lineages over others. Such power, to be maintained materially, involves control over strategic material and social resources such as land, technical knowledge, labor, and the reproductive capabilities of women. Equally important, relations of power depend on certain ideas. Access to resources must be defined jurally, understood as invoking rights and obligations far more complex than the mere fact of possession, and perceived as legitimate by a large enough segment of society that one's claims can be physically protected. As legitimacy develops (or unravels), symbols, myths, and specific methods of interpreting "facts" come into play to disguise the structural consequences and exploitative features of power relations and to reify the rights of those in power. These symbols, myths, and interpretive methods operate as focal points of intellectual inquiry and emotional fervor, influencing sacred as well as profane discourse and diction. They serve as decidedly cultural things by which people orient themselves in relation to others. At the same time, they help justify and make sense of negative social phenomena such as terrorism, inequality, poverty, domestic violence, sexism, and racism. In this way a Pope John II can discourage class struggle in an August 22, 1984, papal message to bishops from Lesotho, Swaziland, Zimbabwe, Botswana, South Africa, and Namibia. A Ronald Reagan can claim that many of the homeless in the United States are homeless by their own free choice. "They say a certain percentage are bound to go to the devil every year," says Dostoyevsky's Raskolnikov, "Bound to, so the rest can stay fresh and healthy. A certain percentage! That's marvelous, isn't it, so fulfilling, so scientific!" (1968: 58).

Whether in the Amazon Basin or a West Virginia strip mine, labor processes depend on complex, flexible, dynamic power relations and supporting symbols and ideologies. Yet the specific manifestations of the relationships between the labor process and its political and ideological supports vary from place to place and across time. They are, in short, historical. Clearly, understanding advanced capitalist labor processes in the United States requires different sources and kinds of information than understanding the labor processes of East African cattle herders. Nevertheless, one purpose of this work is to trace a link between capitalist expansion in traditional anthropological settings and selected labor processes within the United States. I hope to reveal some of the key cultural features of advanced capitalist labor processes as they empower and enrich some and subordinate and impoverish others. A further contribution I hope to make is to show the dynamic features of these relations of power. I acknowledge, first, that those with power over some are subordinate to others. Second, I illustrate that power relations come into play at different points in the labor process and in different social and cultural contexts, factors which are central to their disguises.

Constructing a connection between capitalist labor processes as they operate among tribal and peasant groups and capitalist labor processes in the United States requires working from both within and outside the immediate, concrete context of capitalist production. This method of inquiry derives from the nature of capitalism itself, as eloquently noted by Wolf:

> The growth of capitalism-in-production is a historical, developmental process.... It grew through its own internal ability to reproduce itself on an ever-widening scale; it grew also by entering into working arrangements with other modes, siphoning off wealth and people and turning them into capital and labor power. The capitalist mode thus always exhibited a dual character: an ability to develop internally and branch out, implanting its strategic nexus of relations across the face of the globe; and an ability to enter into temporary and shifting relations of symbiosis and competition with other modes. These relations with other modes constitute part of its history and development. Indeed, as we shall see, the internal dynamic of the capitalist mode may predispose it to external expansion, and hence to interchanges with modes other than itself. (1982: 79)

Capitalist expansion need not involve direct interactions with other modes of production, however. It can be achieved by a general widening of the influence of its various industries, its institutions and state or political supports, and its complex array of myths, symbols, rituals, intellectual arguments, and ideological elements. This may be particularly necessary in the context of industries that have not had the opportunity to expand into overseas regions where they might encounter and utilize other modes of production. In the case of food-producing industries, the very character of their products restricts international flows of the raw materials they use in production, as well as their final products, which can carry disease. Producing highly perishable commodities, these industries possess inherent qualities that inhibit their movement overseas. Yet because they compete against food-producing corporations with access to labor under the conditions outlined above, they have sought to reorganize their productive processes along the lines established by the global corporation. This includes deskilling tasks, acquiring more control over labor, taking advantage of pluralism, utilizing subsidies of the informal and domestic economic sectors, subcontracting, and so forth. Most important, however, they have expanded their influence into the families and communities of their employees by means of both blatant and subtle power relations. This practice in particular contributes to the social construction of the labor force and the terms under which workers sell their labor to capital.

These very developments have parted the veils of many conventional interpretations of labor, leaving an opening for economic anthropology, which focuses on the ways culture and society influence economic behavior. With these research priorities, it has been difficult to follow the lead of neoclassical economics, especially microeconomics. Neoclassical approaches overemphasize market forces and individual initiatives at the expense of illuminating the social and cultural foundations on which such forces and initiatives rest. In addition, neoclassical economists have treated domestic production (production oriented toward the maintenance and reproduction of households) as a second-class economic activity, despite its crucial role in the economy as the principal social arena where workers are born, raised, and eventually groomed to enter training programs or the work force (see Boserup 1971; Beneria and Sen 1981; Griffith 1985; Guyer 1988).

Of all factors of production that circulate through markets in capitalist economies, labor is the most susceptible to social and cultural influences. Its human dimension permeates trade union activity and the design and enforcement of legislation concerning wages, working conditions, and other factors that influence how labor is produced, traded, and consumed in the production process. Its human dimension also affects the ways employers and workers negotiate contracts, or the criteria workers have for training and entering the work force. Thus, for example, the supply of labor depends on factors like the reproductive characteristics of society (fertility, mating patterns, mortality, etc.), immigration policies, and economic alternatives that regulate the opportunity costs of wage labor. Further, different segments of any society's labor force respond to the same economic forces differently. Some workers are more sensitive to fluctuations in wages and working conditions than others. Others are more susceptible to changing immigration policies or to changes in international trade. Some are less likely to organize or join unions. These variations are linked to social and cultural processes that shape the ways workers participate in labor processes. In advanced capitalist societies, in the narrow times and spaces of production, labor is objectified, separated from its living vessel as a "thing" with value or a cost of production. At the same time, it is submerged beneath myths and symbols surrounding such cultural phenomena as the "work ethic," or what constitutes "women's work," or why certain ethnic groups are preferred over others in certain industries or certain tasks. In the United States, for example, it is not uncommon to hear that Swiss make good bankers, Chinese good mathematicians, Germans good engineers, French good chefs, blacks good athletes, Eastern Europeans good steelworkers, Sicilians good criminals, and so forth. These "human" dimensions of labor, because they are mired in social and cultural contexts, create the conditions for capital to establish foundations and "build" their desirable labor forces.

Low-wage workers, such as those in poultry and seafood and agriculture, present additional analytical difficulties because of the often haphazard nature of their participation in labor markets. We noted in earlier passages that people who work for wages in a marginal way (seasonally or part-time, for example) tend also to engage in other social and economic activities that provide supplemental or primary incomes. Like the peasant groups discussed earlier, many are only partially proletarianized. This condition can take place at the individual or the household level, so that even if each household member engages in only one economic activity at a given time, the entire household may be combining incomes, schedules, energy expenditures, etc. from a variety of capitalist and noncapitalist economic activities. The household's total mix of economic activities will influence each member's participation in formal and informal sectors of the economy, including attitudes toward work and class affiliations. Even the time and energy they allocate to tasks that seem explicitly cultural—religious rituals and observances, visiting behaviors, child-rearing practices, feasts and other food events, taboos, and so forth—may reflect economic roles of different household members. Recognizing the household's mix of economic activities is particularly important in understanding the economic roles of female low-wage workers, who devote considerable energies to domestic production, and of minorities, who often organize their social and economic activities around the demands of their ethnic enclaves (Nash 1985; Modell 1985). These behaviors are inextricably linked to broader social and cultural phenomena, including the meanings of ethnicity and sexuality and their roles in a society's productive and reproductive capacities. As such, they come further within the scope of economic anthropology than of conventional economic analysis. Neoclassical economists' attempts to incorporate social and cultural phenomena into their analyses are usually impoverished for their continued emphasis on market mechanisms. When focusing on nonmarket phenomena, they tend to emphasize primarily that which is formally "interventionist" in nature, such as government regulations or labor union strategy (e.g. Sowell 1981).

Recognizing this, the kinds of data we collect and questions we ask assume a new dimension. We care less about income and employment per se, for example, than the ways in which family life, cultural priorities, ethnic categories and cognition, class struggle, and so forth channel *groups* of people into certain sectors of the economy in certain positions. Instead of asking whether a six-hundred-dollar-per-year raise among secretaries will shift the demand curve for panty hose, for example, we inquire into the underlying structural and affective reasons that women in general, in our society, end up in low-wage, careerless sectors of the economy more often than men (Fuchs 1986). Instead of calculating the degree to which wage increases affect profit margins and productivity, we might ask whether or not black and white employees view labor as a commodity in the same way or whether fishermen value family labor differently from labor they hire (see Sahlins 1972; Chayanov 1966; Griffith 1987a). Instead of examining how *individual* economic behaviors affect production, circulation, and consumption, we examine underlying *social relations* (relations of class, ethnicity, sexuality, and nationality) of production, circulation, and consumption. These relations forge and channel individuals' life chances and economic behaviors.

Anthropological studies of capitalism's impact on noncapitalist modes of production have been indispensable to our understanding of capitalist expansion into Africa, Asia, or Latin America. Yet anthropologists have shown considerably less interest in capitalist labor processes within advanced capitalist cultures, particularly in the United States and Western Europe. Instead, enlightening contributions come from economic history (e.g. Gordon, Edwards, and Reich 1982), from sociology and political science (e.g. Sanderson 1985; Portes and Bach 1985; Sassen-Koob 1985), and from economics (e.g. Borjas and Tienda, 1985). These studies nevertheless lack an anthropological perspective, which has grown adept at tracing relationships among political economic processes (including domestic production and reproduction) and the symbols, myths, and interpretive methods with which people conceptualize their roles in advanced capitalist labor processes. Most of these analyses, moreover, tend to be conducted at a national or class level. Less attention had been paid to local levels or the ways in which regional or local developments can mediate national and international processes. At the local level, where anthropologists so effectively study, one can see that relations of power and domination are not, in fact, so clearly relations of class, ethnicity, gender, or nationality. We find that those whom we consider exploited are themselves exploiting others; those whom we see as exploiters are being exploited.

Through these chains of exploitation, response, and rebellion, however, learning, negotiation, and additional symbolizing takes place to modify the character, frequency, and direction of the exploitation and hence alter trajectories of capital accumulation. For example, those who organize advanced capitalist labor processes have learned from capitalist expansion overseas and have adapted some of the characteristics of overseas labor processes to the United States context. They respond to discoveries in business and finance, incorporating new demographic trends into their practices, and they justify their actions based on corporate cultural criteria such as accounting, beliefs in choice, estimations of risk, and fear of competition. Indeed, some of the lessons of capitalist expansion overseas have been carried into low-wage industries in the United States by immigrant low-wage workers themselves, who sometimes teach their employers how to exploit those from their own cultural and national backgrounds. In the same way, low-wage workers learn how to develop new frontiers where the old frontiers have been closed through public and private mechanisms such as fencing the commons, limiting entry into a fishery, or criminalizing food vending along the street by declaring it a health hazard (Pico 1985). As these frontiers develop, too, capital learns how to coopt them and use them for its own accumulation.

It is my contention that, in advanced capitalist societies, these learning and developmental processes can be most vividly seen and documented in interactions between labor and capital that take place in low-wage sectors of the labor market. They can be seen particularly among those workers who tend not to belong to unions and who often hold their jobs seasonally or for short time periods during their lives, and who, I noted earlier, may best be called semiproletariat.[7] It is through dealing with the low-wage sectors of advanced capitalist countries, I argue in this work, that capital experiments with and learns the intricacies of new and old labor, particularly the benefits of utilizing a semiproletarianized labor force and the subtleties by which power relations at the work site can be enhanced and reinforced by power relations in the family, community, ethnic, and other social and cultural settings. And in low-wage sectors of the economy workers learn how to develop new frontiers, new places to hide, new ways to slough off and undermine productivity. Low-wage labor processes in advanced capitalist economies, in short, are both capital's school of exploitation and labor's school of rebellion.

Conclusion

The argument developed in this chapter elaborated the relevance of anthropological work on capitalist expansion overseas to low-wage labor processes under advanced capitalism. Central to this relevance is the notion of formation. Specifically, as part of its expansion, capitalism has participated in the construction, reorganization, maintenance, and reproduction of peasant and tribal ways of life. Equally important, anthropologists have observed that the "underdeveloped" production regimes of peasant and tribal groups, while acting as crucial buffers against periods of economic decline, also serve as subsidies to capitalist labor markets by meeting many of the costs of reproducing and maintaining its labor supply. The cost of producing a key production input—labor—is thus borne by the peasant and tribal sectors themselves. To sustain these relationships, moreover, capitalists rely upon state institutions and ideological supports from political and religious leaders, mass media, and intellectuals.

Under advanced capitalism, we can observe parallel developments within the low-wage sectors of the economy. The similarities are not coincidental. Instead, corporations in advanced capitalist economies have modeled their methods of labor recruitment and labor control on the experiences of capitalist enterprises operating overseas. At the same time, immigrations of workers into the low-wage sectors of the economy have provided forums for the exchange of information about workers' expectations, recruiting techniques, and other aspects of the labor process. These forums "educate" workers and employers alike about the contours of exploitation and the potential for rebellion.

In the following chapters, in the context of a comparative analysis of seafood and poultry processing, we will see that under advanced capitalism, the construction of low-wage labor forces involves practices similar to those found where peasant and tribal groups routinely supply workers to labor markets. Workers in low-wage industries rely on social resources and small-scale production operations to help maintain and reproduce themselves, remaining somewhat marginal to the labor force while still dependent upon low-wage work. As in peasant and tribal production regimes, workers' nonwage income generating activities, or activities that help reduce consumer needs, also constitute subsidies to capitalist enterprises that consume these workers' labor. We will see, too, that control over the time and space of low-wage workers' lives is not restricted to the time and space of capitalist production. Instead, it penetrates social and cultural spheres well beyond the physical walls of the plant. In this the institutions of the state and community willingly participate. Under the guise of free enterprise, backed by the arguments of jobs creation and service to the community, advanced capitalism reaches into the families, the social networks, the communities, and sometimes into the very bodies of workers that low-wage industries employ. Its purpose in such manipulations and invasions of privacy is to construct a labor force that is not only cheap and docile but is also expendable and replaceable, capable of being tossed out the door at the first hint of resistance.

II

Industry Organization:
A Comparative Overview

Anyone shopping in America's supermarkets over the past five years has noticed changes in both the seafood and poultry departments. Not only have seafood and poultry departments gotten larger, they have changed character as well. Commonly, supermarkets now have elaborate, staffed seafood counters or refrigerated sections decorated with fish nets, driftwood, and shells. Often they sell orange roughy from New Zealand or salmon from Norway as cheaply as they sell New England cod or Gulf of Mexico shrimp. Today, even in remote, inland supermarkets, marinated catfish and products made from fish pastes add a variety to seafood selections that would have been difficult to find only ten years ago. Likewise, the poultry sections offer not just more chicken and turkey, but a wide range of boned, ground, fully cooked, marinated, breaded, sliced, spiced, pressed, microwaveable, frozen, or ready-to-eat products. There are rarely individuals in the stores actually staffing the poultry department, but the wide range of products makes one wonder who would not be able to find the poultry product they desired in such a forest of low-fat flesh.

It is quite likely that the changes in seafood and poultry departments of supermarkets reflect actual or perceived changes in the shopper's eating habits, tastes, and ideas about the quality of the food he or she eats. Fueled by aggressive marketing campaigns that highlight the negative roles of fat and cholesterol in the diet, the consumption of white meats in the United States has increased dramatically over the past twenty years, overtaking red meat consumption in the 1980s and continuing to climb into the 1990s. Most of the red meat industry's loss has been the poultry industry's gain, although both the seafood and poultry industries have benefited. Absolute increases in consumer demand for chicken and turkey have been most impressive. The steady increases through the 1970s and 1980s led to poultry consumption overtaking per capita consumption of beef in 1987 (see Table 2.1).

Seafood's gains, although less impressive than poultry's, have maintained steady increases. Between 1970 and the 1987, seafood consumption increased by 30.5 percent, from under twelve pounds per capita to over fifteen. More recent National Marine Fisheries Service estimates now place seafood consumption at over seventeen pounds per capita. These increases

TABLE 2.1

Annual U.S. Per Capita Consumption of Meat,
Poultry, and Fish in Pounds, 1970 to 1987

Year	Beef	Pork	Chicken	Turkey	Seafood
1970	84.4	61.9	40.1	8.1	11.8
1980	76.4	68.1	49.8	10.5	12.8
1981	77.1	64.9	51.3	10.7	12.9
1982	76.8	58.5	52.7	10.8	12.3
1983	78.2	61.9	53.4	11.2	13.7
1984	78.1	61.5	55.2	11.3	13.7
1985	78.8	62.0	57.6	12.1	14.4
1986	78.4	58.6	58.7	13.3	14.7
1987	73.4	59.2	62.7	15.1	15.4
Percent Change	–13%	–4.4%	+56.4%	+86.4%	+30.5%

Source: 1991 U.S. Statistical Abstract

have been reflected in catch statistics. From 1960 to 1988, the value of the total domestic catch of fish increased ten times, from $354 million to $3.5 billion, with average prices per pound (live weight) rising from 7.2 cents to 48.9 cents over the same period. The seafood processing sector has not been an idle participant in this growth. From 1980 to 1988 seafood processing increased from a $4.4 billion to a $5.3 billion industry. Most of the increase, from $2.1 billion to $3.6 billion, occurred in sectors processing fresh and frozen products.

To meet this demand, both the poultry and seafood industries have marshaled extensive expansion and reorganization efforts in product sourcing, production, distribution, and marketing. In some areas of food processing, the two industries have merged to create and promote the variety of highly processed, ingeniously packaged, easy-to-prepare, microwaveable products filling the freezer sections of our supermarkets. The expansion of the white meat industries has had economic and social consequences that reach further into our lives than is immediately apparent. They have, for example, stimulated flows of labor into and through rural communities and urban neighborhoods in a number of locations throughout the United States. They have not only altered the ecologies of coastlines and rural areas, their rates of growth have attracted increased government scrutiny and state inter-vention in the ways they produce and market their products. In the seafood industry, for example, this has caused conflicts in coastal zones among fishing communities, sport-fishing groups, American Indian groups, real estate developers, owners of tourist establishments, and a host of others. In the poultry industry, this has resulted in a constant government presence in their processing plants in the form of U.S. Department of Agriculture inspectors.

The increasing concentrations of capital in both industries, moreover, threaten smaller, independent firms. This process is already far advanced in the poultry industry. Seafood producers, however, remain a heterogeneous lot, although many smaller, independent firms have been threatened in recent years. This has, in turn, driven them towards the regeneration of old and the development of new mechanisms of labor control.

Despite similarities in demand for their products and the increased problems and profits that demand entails, the two industries are far from identical in their structural profiles. I briefly mentioned in the opening chapter that the seafood industry was highly fragmented while the poultry industry was highly vertically integrated and concentrated in the hands of a few large corporations. These differences, it would seem, would lead to extreme differences throughout the two industries, yet this has not been the case. In particular, the two industries share certain features in terms of the ways they construct and access labor markets and organize the labor process. In their processing sectors this is particularly so. Hence, the two chapters in this section discuss the structural differences between producing seafood in eastern North Carolina and producing poultry in four locations in the southern and eastern United States. Chapter three focuses on seafood processing in eastern North Carolina while chapter four deals with poultry processing in the southeast; this latter chapter ends with a brief comparative discussion, drawing out the differences and similarities between the two industries. Later chapters then address, in more detail, the specific similarities between their labor processes.

Seafood Processing in Eastern North Carolina: An Overview

Introduction

The North Carolina seafood processing industry consists of broad and heterogeneous range of operations. Processing operations range in size, for example, from the single fisherman licensed to clean his shrimp or flounder to facilities that can herring and employ more than 250 workers. Some process seafood throughout the year while others process for no longer than six to ten weeks. Some depend entirely on North Carolina marine resources while others buy none or almost none of the local catch. They vary by the ethnic compositions of their labor forces, by the extent of their participation in commercial fishing or overland shipping, and by their dependence on family and friends to process seafood. That each of the industry's component enterprises buys raw marine resources to convert into finished commodities is actually one of the few characteristics they share.

Yet they are an industry—faced with similar problems, regulated by similar government agencies, tied into similar markets, affected by similar shifts in consumer demand. Spread out over thirteen coastal counties, they officially number between ninety and one hundred, fluctuating from year to year. This count includes only licensed processors. It is impossible to know precisely how many more unlicensed establishments exist along the coast, especially if we include such casual forms of processing as shrimp fishermen deheading shrimp to sell along the roads from pickup trucks. North Carolina's coast, blessed with an incredible array of inlets, coves, and marshy backwashes serviced by rutted dirt roads, makes small-scale, illegal seafood processing relatively easy. This is especially true of seasonal operations that shuck oysters or scallops only one or two days per week during the season. It seems safe to say, however, that the official count includes all processors who employ more than five workers, since concealing larger plants from health inspectors or other official personnel would be difficult.

General Contours of the Industry

Species Processed. Data from state licensing agencies reflect the range of species processed in the state, the distribution of plants, and the ratio of processing plants to seafood dealers. Species processed include blue crab, bay scallops, calico scallops, shrimp, oysters, herring, flounder and assorted other finfish, and menhaden. With the exception of menhaden, all are processed for human consumption. Currently, menhaden plants are experimenting with making menhaden seafood products, but the most lucrative part of the menhaden is its oil, which is used in rust proofing and cosmetics. Most North Carolina seafood is sold fresh or frozen to local supermarkets and restaurants or shipped to wholesalers and markets around Baltimore, Philadelphia, New York, and a few southern locations. One blue-crab plant owner described the concentration of their market by saying, "Just like people in the midwest eat potatoes with every meal or people in Louisiana eat rice with every meal, that's how people around Baltimore eat crab meat." He may have been exaggerating, but the fact remains that the market for seafood has been expanding.

Recent licensing data from the North Carolina Division of Marine Fisheries listed 649 business establishments in twenty-eight eastern North Carolina counties that handled finfish or shellfish in some capacity. Five hundred fifty-four (85.4 percent) of these are primarily seafood dealers; these establishments pack, ice, and ship fish, or grade and bag shellfish. The remaining 95 (14.6 percent) establishments, spread unevenly over thirteen coastal counties, perform some form of processing such as picking meat from blue crabs or shucking oysters and scallops.

Plant Distribution. Table 3.1 shows the distribution of processing plants by county and by type of processing. As the table indicates, Carteret, Pamlico, Brunswick, and Beaufort counties host the most and widest variety of seafood processing establishments. Hence, I focus on these four counties in this work. The abundance of crab-picking houses in Pamlico County makes it the largest county for seafood processing in terms of employment. Processors in Carteret, however, handle the most scallops, clams, menhaden, and shrimp, making processing in Carteret County more highly seasonal than processing in Pamlico. Plants in Beaufort and Brunswick probably generate levels of employment comparable to Pamlico, with eight crab-picking houses in the former and seven oyster-shucking houses in the latter. We will see, too, that Beaufort and Brunswick counties are more similar to Pamlico in terms of the ethnic compositions of their labor forces. The short-term, sporadic processing typical of Carteret County draws white women who are related to fishermen, while the longer-term, more regular processing in the crab and oyster houses of Pamlico, Beaufort, and Brunswick counties draw Black, primarily female, labor.

TABLE 3.1

North Carolina Processing Establishments
by County and Type of Processing, 1984

County	Type of Processing					
	Oysters	Scallops	Crab	Shrimp	Fish	Totals (%)
Carteret	2	10	5	6	8	31 (27.7%)
Pamlico	5	4	11	1	9	30 (26.8%)
Brunswick	7		1	3	4	15 (13.4%)
Beaufort			8		3	11 (9.8%)
Hyde	4		3			7 (6.25%)
Onslow		3			2	5 (4.5%)
New Hanover	1		1	2		4 (3.6%)
Bertie			1		1	2 (1.8%)
Chowan					2	2 (1.8%)
Pasquotank			1		1	2 (1.8%)
Craven			1			1 (.9%)
Hertford					1	1 (.9%)
Jones					1	1 (.9%)
Totals	19	17	32	12	32	112*

Source: N.C. Division of Marine Fisheries

*Totals, which do not add up to 100% due to rounding error, include some plants that process more than one species. Total number of plants, exclusive of duplication, is 95.

Plant locations reflect degrees of dependence on fresh, local catches, and the plant's labor needs. Plants that rely mostly or exclusively on local catches tend to be closer to the Atlantic than others. Plants with high labor needs, however, tend to be further inland, closer to poor rural settlements (often Black settlements) from which they recruit workers. The distribution of plants within Carteret County, with its diversity of operations, illustrates the general industry settlement pattern. Most shrimp, scallop, finfish, and menhaden plants in the county are located on or near the sounds, where local fishermen land their catches. Yet Carteret's few crab-picking houses rely more on Black, year-round labor and out-of-state supplies of seafood. As such, they are located either inland or along the inland, estuarine river systems where crabbers string their pots and land their catches. One processor located along the strip of land between Beaufort and Cedar Island said that few labor-intensive plants could be found as far east as the Atlantic because the nearest Black neighborhoods were in Beaufort. Supporting his claim is the fact that Carteret's largest employers of seafood processing workers are located either within the city of Beaufort or just east of Beaufort, along the South River, near Black settlements around Merrimons.

The general logic of plant distribution within Carteret County operates on a regional level as well. The heavy concentrations of crab-picking houses in Pamlico and Beaufort counties reflect those counties' sociodemographic, ecological, and economic characteristics. State government sources consider Pamlico County 100 percent rural, and neither Pamlico nor Beaufort county has a large urban center the likes of Morehead City. Heavily dependent on industries such as farming, forestry, and fishing, the populations of these counties are accustomed to seasonal, low-wage employment. In the past, a few light-manufacturing and textile factories have dotted the eastern North Carolina rural landscape (Rosenfeld, Bergman, and Rubin 1985). Industries directly dependent on nature, however, predominate. Even with its few manufacturing industries, only 26 percent of Beaufort County's labor force are employed in manufacturing and only 14 percent of Pamlico County's workers are so employed. Finally, access to the Pamlico River and sound has influenced the historical growth and concentration of crab-picking plants in the two counties. Today, direct access to the marine environment via the Pamlico River and the sound has become less important, with increased reliance on raw marine resources trucked in from out of state.

Most plants, however, enjoy direct access to one of the big three river systems (Neuse, Pamlico, or Albemarle) to the Pamlico Sound, or to the Atlantic. For those processors who now rely predominately on out-of-state catches, direct access to water is more of a holdover from earlier times than a necessary component of their current operations. Although this direct access is useful and even necessary to such processors as the herring canners on the Chowan River, the crab and oyster plants could be as easily or more easily serviced by well-paved roads that connected them to major north-south or south-southwest interstates. Such a move, however, might place them in direct competition for labor with other industries that utilize low-wage workers. Such competition would likely lead to a constriction of the processing labor supply and to processors pioneering new methods of labor recruitment. In later chapters we will see that this is exactly what has happened in the poultry industry, where relocation and new labor recruitment methods combine to assure continued supplies of labor to, and through, the plants.

Depending on the processor and the time of year, fish and shellfish supplies come from as far north as Maine and as far south and west as Mississippi. With increasing reliance on out-of-state supplies, the industry is bound to become more dependent on eastern North Carolina's highways and other infrastructure of overland travel. In addition, the changing supply sources of seafood force processors must keep abreast of catches and prices in various local and regional locations. One cause of plant closure—temporary or permanent—is an inability to maintain a steady supply of seafood. This problem compounds the labor supply problem in that workers are more willing to work for processors when they know the processors have seafood to process when they need work. Lending support to this, a plant owner cited his practice of catching flounder during the months crab picking was slow, which allowed him to keep his most reliable employees on the payroll, saying, "This is one advantage I have to offer a worker." Wrestling with the seafood supply problem has caused processors to expand their connections up and down the eastern seaboard and along the Gulf coast. Some larger plants send out their own fishing fleets. Many plants that now specialize in only one seafood have, in the past, experimented with seafoods that they have since discontinued. Although it may appear equally simple to process a truckload of oysters or scallops, or to cut spot or flounder, each new seafood implies its own set of supply, storage, marketing, and other problems. Nevertheless, processing a seasonally variable mix of seafoods is slightly more common than processing only one. Of the ninety-five processors listed in the Division of Marine Fisheries list of processing plants, thirty-nine (41 percent) processed only one kind of seafood.

Marketing. Marketing presents its own set of problems. Most processors reported selling only a small proportion of seafood in the state. Picked crab tends to go to Baltimore, New York, or Philadelphia markets, oysters to supermarket chains within and outside North Carolina, and cut fish to New York. Scallops and shrimp tend to be consumed locally more than other species, although this varies within the industry, while menhaden plants target specialty markets for cosmetics, rust proofing, animal feeds, and European margarines. The heavy dependence on out-of-state markets demands that most processors have their own refrigerated trucks and maintain their own sales circuits, which involves phoning buyers and brokers and assessing demand on a daily or at least weekly basis. Maintaining a fleet of trucks demands mechanical abilities and close attention to scheduling, as well as additional personnel. The expertise necessary to locate and maintain markets and marketing connections has led the owners of some larger plants to hire personnel strictly as sales representatives; other plants, such as those jointly owned and operated by brothers, cousins, father-son or husband-wife teams, have divided the labor so that one member of the management team is primarily responsible for marketing. Still others maintain their own seafood restaurants or retail businesses, buying and selling others' seafood along with using their own. Finally, some smaller plants handle the marketing right along with their myriad other tasks.

Perceived Problems: Welfare, Low Wages, and the Labor Supply

In addition to problems arising from coordinating seafood supplies with labor and markets, processors themselves mentioned a variety of problems currently threatening either their plants in particular or the entire industry. Individual plant owners in areas with already high processing plant densities perceived an even greater labor problem than those in low density areas. In areas where four or five small black settlements or neighborhoods provide workers for eight or nine plants, the tensions between plant owners can move from business to a personal dispute. During my interviewing, plant owners in high density regions voiced complaints about plants that were constructed with low-interest government loans and about other plant owners who used what they perceived to be unfair practices to lure workers to picking or shucking tables.

The disdain for government-backed low-interest loans is indicative of a pervasive difficulty processing plant owners have with many local, state, and federal government agencies and programs. Foremost among processors' complaints is their broadly based criticism of the United States social services system. Plant owners throughout the state perceived food stamps, energy subsidy programs, Aid to Families with Dependent Children (AFDC), subsidized housing, and commodity give-away programs as creating disincentives among workers and further undermining the reliability of an already unreliable labor force. Of course, this is an easy, canned explanation—blame the government—yet one given at least some credence by human service employees who report that many AFDC recipients are processing workers and that "98 percent" of the food stamp recipients in the largest seafood processing county in the state work in crab houses. (It does *not* follow, of course, that 98 percent of the crab pickers receive food stamps.) In addition, small black communities and neighborhoods that supply labor to processing plants sport the obvious signs of a partially government-subsidized population: the so-called "projects," or the public housing buildings and community betterment programs. Finally, the processing industry tends to be staffed via female networks, primarily Black networks, and most social services are, in fact, directed toward women and reproduction, a factor which further supports plant managers' claims that they have to compete with county social services offices for their workers.

On the other hand, county statistics show no correlation between AFDC or transfer payments per capita and the size of the seafood processing population. Moreover, social services programs, like the minimum wage, constitute opportunities for low-wage workers to accept or reject plant wage-and-benefit packages, an option that has been legitimized by the very fact that social service and minimum wage legislation are debated and decided at the highest level of government. Utilization of social services sends the message to plant owners and managers that current wage-and-benefit offers aren't good enough. Still, owners continue to blame the dependent attitudes of "second generation welfare" as a major source of their labor problems. The tones of their comments about this were diffuse, ranging from mildly compassionate to downright contemptuous. During one processor's ranting and raving on this point a quote from Saul Bellow came to me. It occurs in the midst of a scene where Augie March is having a weekend fling with his Mexican friend, Manny, and two women. Manny tells of abandoning a wife and daughter in Mexico, and Augie thinks:

> I didn't approve of his boasting that he had left a wife and kid behind in Mexico, but then the tall girl said she had a child too, and maybe the other did also and just didn't say, and so I let the subject pass, since if so many do the same wrong there maybe is something to it that's not right away apparent. (1977: 213-214)

This passage might apply to the processors' constant disapproval of their workers' receiving welfare. What is it that isn't obvious that makes processing plant workers apply for welfare when they could be working? Could it be that they are, truly, lazy? These sorts of folk explanations are often the most obvious but least informative. On one level and for some purposes they are "correct:" if there is, indeed, no social stigma to participating in social programs, if everyone in your personal network does it, if the system has made it available, then, as Augie says, "maybe there's something to it that's not right away apparent." It is difficult to argue that people living under the adverse conditions of poverty I have described above are truly lazy. A more plausible explanation comes from Scott's observations concerning daily forms of resistance among exploited classes:

> Forms of stubborn resistance are especially well documented in the vast literature on American slavery, where open defiance was normally foolhardy. The history of resistance to slavery in the antebellum U.S. South is largely a history of foot-dragging, false compliance, flight, feigned ignorance, sabotage, theft, and, not least, cultural resistance. These practices, which rarely if ever called into question the system of slavery *as such,* nevertheless achieved far more in their unannounced, limited, and truculent way than the few heroic and brief armed uprisings about which so much has been

written. The slaves themselves appear to have realized that
in most circumstances their resistance could succeed only
to the extent that it hid behind the mask of public compliance.
(1985: 34; emphasis in original)

Although most workers denied receiving government assistance,
most likely because they mistrusted the intentions of my data
gathering, those I came to know better told me of receiving some
government subsidy in the form of food, health care, housing,
or job training. Some partial reliance of households on these
programs can be traced to the low wages and the piece-rate
payment systems that prevail in the industry.

Similar to workers in most agricultural harvests in the United
States, the majority of North Carolina's seafood processing
workers are paid by the piece instead of the hour. However they
are paid, according to U.S. labor law, they must earn at least
minimum wage ($3.35/hour during the study period). How much
workers earn per hour thus depends on how fast they can fill
pint or gallon containers or accumulate pounds of meat, factors
which depend, in turn, on a combination of the size of the crabs,
oysters, scallops, etc., and the skill and experience of the worker.
Among crab pickers, a highly skilled crab picker can pick forty
pounds in an eight-hour period, although more commonly, pickers
produce between twenty-five and thirty pounds per day. At $1.25
per pound, the highly skilled picker makes $50.00 per day, or $6.25
per hour, while workers at the low end of the productivity level
earn $31.25 to $37.50 per day or $3.90 to $4.68 per hour. In order
to earn minimum wage, crab pickers need produce only around
twenty-two pounds per eight-hour day. This is below the common
twenty-five to forty pound-per-day range reported by workers,
suggesting most employees earn at least minimum wage; yet I
learned of cases of Department of Labor (DOL) officials imposing
fines on processors for failure to pay minimum wage. Workers
incapable of picking the necessary twenty-two pounds, therefore,
do exist in the labor force. However, most plant owners I met
with, rather than risk DOL fines, lay off workers who cannot
pick at least twenty-two pounds per day. Plant owners express
regret over having to fire such workers. Some processors framed
this issue in terms of a trade-off between providing employment
to willing workers and allowing this labor to go to waste.
Regulations, they say, restrict them from putting willing workers
to work, thus encouraging more burden on existing human services

programs. At times, processors portrayed their having to lay off underproductive workers as an emotionally draining experience; these are often older employees who enjoy working in the plants as a way to interact with others and get out of the house.

Discrepancies between hourly wages and piece rates in other branches of the industry, if they do exist, are difficult to document. I learned of no DOL fines levied against shrimp, scallop, or finfish houses, but my ignorance here does not necessarily mean other processors haven't been charged. Nevertheless, working schedules in these plants, unlike crab and oyster plants, would make keeping track of hours and piece rates difficult, except by workers and owners themselves. Some shrimp processors on the strip of land between Beaufort and Sea Level, for example, reported using housewives sporadically, sometimes at odd hours after the shrimp boats have come in, calling them on the spur of the moment to devein or dehead just a few pounds of shrimp. I visited plants where high school students worked after school, weekends, and summers, and plants that relied almost exclusively on casual labor of the variety one might find outside a private plasma company, waiting to sell blood.

This variability makes it difficult to match earnings with the actual number of hours worked, thus undermining the extent to which the Wage and Hour Division of the U.S. Department of Labor can determine whether or not minimum wages are being paid. In other piece-rate payment contexts, this difficulty has been a continuing source of litigation and investigation, particularly in the case of H2a workers (workers with legal temporary alien labor status) who come to the United States from the British West Indies to harvest sugar cane (Rob Williams, Florida Rural Legal Services, personal communication, 1988). Piece-rate payment systems, as opposed to wages based on time, cause complaints from workers generally. Among agricultural workers, for example, who are often paid by the bushel or pound rather than the hour, charges of chronic underpayment of wages are common (see Griffith 1988; Friedland and Nelkin 1971; Foner and Napoli 1978). Although few workers complained of underpayment in the processing plants, the piece-rate payment system may underlie some of the labor reliability problem. The piece-rate payment system transfers labor productivity from the shoulders of plant owners to plant workers and allows owners to claim that workers are fully responsible for how much they earn. Some owners claimed that their workers could earn $75.00 per day (50 percent more than the highest figure provided by workers). More realistically, annual earnings should probably be based on a daily wage of around $40.00, in which case the average worker, working seasonally, would earn somewhere between $5,000 and $7,000 per year in seafood processing occupations, figures which are well below poverty levels and which underlie the fact that workers earn incomes from a variety of sources. Thus the receipt of transfer payments is but one of a series of adaptations to the poverty and inequality they experience daily. This inequality is reflected both inside and outside of the processing plants.

Influences of Levels of Regional Development on Seafood Processing

Too often, the overwhelming success and technological achievement of the United States masks the many pockets of poverty and other symptoms of uneven development within the nation's borders. Not all areas of the country have participated in the national prosperity to the same degree or with the same enthusiasm. Eastern North Carolina's infrastructure and access to major thoroughfares is indicative of the level of development on which the seafood processing industry must depend to expand and remain competitive.

A recent study of shifting employment patterns throughout the southeast (Rosenfeld, Bergman, and Rubin 1985) ranks and compares 1342 counties in 13 states on the basis of population and infrastructure. Briefly, the counties were ranked on the basis of proximity to a Metropolitan Statistical Area (MSA) or access to an interstate highway.[1] Those counties furthest from MSAs or interstates were classed as Remote, followed by Tier, Corridor, Adjacent, Adjacent/Corridor, and, finally, Metro counties. These latter counties contained an MSA. Although broad and crude, this classification scheme nevertheless reflects general levels of development in a comparative sense. The study noted, in particular, discrepancies between Metro and nonmetro counties in terms of per capita income and levels of unemployment. Income was lower and unemployment higher in the nonmetro South than in the Metro South. Remote and Tier counties also tend to have lower rates of population growth, smaller tax bases, and fewer skilled and professional people than do Metro counties (Rosenfeld, Bergman, and Rubin 1985: 6).

Based on this classificatory scheme, how do eastern North Carolina counties compare with others throughout the southeast? Of the twenty-eight North Carolina counties included in the state's four multicounty planning regions (Regions O, P, Q, and R), only two fall into the Metro category, leaving the remaining 93 percent in the nonmetro class. Fully seventeen of the counties (61 percent) have no direct or easy access to Interstate 95, the major north-south route along the eastern seaboard. The remaining counties are connected by roads of varying quality.

Other indicators of generally low levels of development are presented in the tables below.[2] The particular ethnic and so-called "race relations" history of the United States makes the ratio of Blacks to whites in the counties also an indicator of development. In short, higher proportions of Black Americans generally indicate lower development levels because of racist state expenditure patterns and other discriminatory practices.

Tables 3.2 and 3.3 attest to the generally underdeveloped condition of many eastern North Carolina counties and to the region as a whole. Outside of the counties influenced by urban areas (Craven, New Hanover, and Onslow) most of the indicators of development, as well as figures for income and employment, compare unfavorably to state averages.

Six of the thirteen seafood processing counties experience higher rates of infant mortality than those for North Carolina, a measure long held by development agencies as an indicator of nutrition and health. Infant mortality rates reflect, as well, education, income, and access to health services or knowledge of services available. The people of all seafood processing counties earn lower per capita incomes than the state average, all but two show lower weekly pay, and eight have higher rates of unemployment. Seven of the seafood processing counties have higher rates of unemployment than the state average. Only Onslow County, the home of Camp Lejuene, reports lower figures for transfer payments per capita than the state average. Pamlico County, the biggest seafood processing county, reports the highest of the thirteen seafood processing counties.

Statistical profiles are only enhanced by qualitative portraits. Driving the back roads through some of these counties, at times I felt I had crossed from the First to the Third World. People live in shacks with plastic tarps over the windows and hay bales shored up against the house's foundations to cut down on drafts. Abandoned machinery litters the countryside. Throughout eastern

TABLE 3.2

Selected Indicators of Development:
North Carolina, Twenty-eight Eastern Counties,
and Seafood Processing Counties Compared

Unit   Indicators

	Infant Mortality (per 1,000 births)	Population density	Migration rate	Percent nonwhite	Percent white	Percent rural
State	13.4	126.2	.9%	24.2	75.8	52.0
28 Counties	14.1	85.0	1.1%	—	—	—
Seafood Processing Counties						
Beaufort	11.5	51.8	1.7	31.9	68.1	79.1
Bertie	15.7	30.5	-0.2	59.4	40.6	100.0
Brunswick	11.9	50.5	5.1	23.7	76.3	87.7
Carteret	11.1	89.7	2.9	19.3	89.7	80.1
Chowan	17.5	71.3	1.3	41.9	58.1	57.3
Craven	11.9	110.1	1.6	29.0	71.0	50.4
Hertford	14.2	66.9	-0.1	56.0	44.0	66.2
Hyde	23.3	9.5	-0.4	35.7	64.3	100.0
Jones	16.9	21.0	0.5	43.7	56.3	100.0
New Hanover	11.3	596.9	0.9	22.3	77.7	13.3
Onslow	13.0	157.6	-0.7	24.2	75.8	35.4
Pamlico	15.5	31.9	2.2	31.7	68.3	100.0
Pasquotank	13.2	127.2	0.6	37.3	62.7	50.8

North Carolina, tarpaper-sided tobacco drying sheds tell of a population that has depended on government subsidy programs for generations. These programs have been used as tools of the authority of whites over blacks and of the propertied classes over the propertyless, of rural bourgeois over rural proletariat. In the small towns, boarded-up businesses testify to emigration rates that rival the highest in the state. Much of the land is planted in commercial timber, crisscrossed with dirt logging roads and rented out to hunting clubs during deer season. During a few weeks every year, the pollen from loblolly and longleaf pine trees covers the ground and the roofs of houses. It coats freshly washed automobiles with fine, prolific dust, indicating the drift of the winds coupled with the melancholy summer stillness that un-

TABLE 3.3

Income and Employment for Twenty-eight Eastern North Carolina
Counties as Compared to the State and Seafood Processing Counties

Unit	Income Per Capita	Transfer Payments Per Capita	Rate of Unemployment	Average Weekly Pay
State	$10,852	$1,433	6.7%	$264
28 Counties*	$9,045	$1,593	8.2%	$197
Seafood Processing Counties				
Beaufort	$9,187	$1,534	7.5%	$230
Bertie	$8,405	$1,558	10.2%	$163
Brunswick	$8,212	$1,598	11.4%	$282
Carteret	$9,095	$1,752	6.7%	$192
Chowan	$9,186	$1,777	5.7%	$199
Craven	$10,055	$1,523	5.8%	$242
Hertford	$8,342	$1,618	9.1%	$213
Hyde	$7,451	$1,726	12.2%	$132
Jones	$7,627	$1,623	6.7%	$187
New Hanover	$10,794	$1,676	8.8%	$276
Onslow	$9,512	$1,024	5.1%	$182
Pamlico	$9,262	$1,798	7.0%	$149
Pasquotank	$10,094	$1,755	5.9%	$189

*The twenty-eight eastern North Carolina counties (in multi county
planning units O, P, Q, and R) are Camden, Columbus, Currituck, Dare,
Duplin, Gates, Greene, Lenoir, Martin, Pender, Perquimans, Pitt, Tyrrell,
Washington, Wayne, and the thirteen seafood processing counties
listed above.

evenly distribute the pollen. Eastern North Carolina is no place
for people susceptible to allergies, for along with the pollen come
fertilizers, gravel dust, pesticides, herbicides, and the dust of
pollutants kicked up by phosphate mining.

These are, at times, depressing areas. Yet some people
demonstrate a belligerent independence, reflected in the wide
range of small-scale, independent, domestically based businesses
throughout the countryside.[3] In addition to low-wage and seasonal
work, they sell whatever they can produce with limited means:
honey, duck decoys, farm produce, seafood, ceramic figurines,
lawn furniture. Services they provide include hairdressing and
cosmetology; they are craftsmen, repairpeople, upholsterers,
notaries, palm readers and advisors, and people who prepare
income taxes or stuff and lick envelopes at home for some mail-
marketing firm. Into society such as this, defense contractors

subcontract the wrapping of semiconductors with wire and other detailed and monotonous tasks that don't need security clearances. It is not uncommon to see the equipment of two or three small enterprises littering someone's yard—say, crab pots, a tractor, and a carpenter's pickup truck. Combined with these may be gardens, livestock pens, antlers, cut wood, and fish skeletons, all indicating heavy reliance on the land for food, shelter, and fuel. Along drainage ditches and waterways diverted by the U.S. Army Corps of Engineers, people fish daily with bamboo poles.

Domestic Production and Labor Market Dynamics

These behaviors underlie certain tensions in the labor pools from which rural industries draw their workers. Locating plants in rural areas allows employers to draw upon a labor force that may also engage in the domestic production and independent, small-scale-producer activities mentioned above. Such "informal" economic activities, especially when combined with collecting welfare benefits, undermine the reliability of labor. At the seafood processing plants, such activities contribute to absenteeism when plant schedules conflict with home production schedules. Much of the rural population remains directly or indirectly tied to seasonal economic activities. As such, some individuals move between a variety of jobs—including food processing—during different times of the year.

Informal economic opportunity for workers is not always detrimental to plant labor policies, however. Workers who engage in activities that supplement wages at processing plants are able to pay for a portion of their household subsistence and reproductive costs (however subjectively defined) with these other economic activities. This is similar to the way peasants subsidize capitalist production around the world with cheaply produced food (Griffith 1985; Collins 1988). In North Carolina, as among peasant groups throughout the world, these informal economic activities influence workers' ideas about wage levels. What they consider a "living wage" may be less than the "living wage" of a worker whose household subsistence and reproductive fund comes exclusively from the processing plant. What the plant loses in labor reliability, that is, it may be gaining in the ways workers (or government aid programs) subsidize their household subsistence and reproduction costs. Clearly, this allows plant owners to keep wages low. Similarly, double-income households may be less likely to "need" health insurance and other benefits from both employers if one wage earner's employer provides such benefits for the entire household. In the absence of such need, such workers are less likely to objectify their situations and *interpret* their labor market experiences in political terms. It follows that they are also less likely to view their potential for change as the potential of a community or class of workers. Instead, they are likely to consider their place in the labor market "their own fault." As we discuss in more detail in later chapters, the trade-offs or tensions between workers being unreliable and subsidizing their own wages because of their independent producer activities can effectively disappear as rural industries begin to access new immigrant and refugee populations. Among these groups, similar reduced subsistence and reproductive needs often derive from different subjective notions of acceptable levels of subsistence. This is especially true in the realm of housing, where immigrants are willing to tolerate more crowded conditions than native workers. On the other hand, with minor exceptions such as fishing, the same range of small-scale, independent, producer activities for generating incomes are not open to new immigrants and refugees. Among these workers, there is little chance of a conflict between home production and plant schedules. Processing plant owners thus receive the benefits of lower wage expectations while suffering none of the problems of workers not showing up for work.

Even among natives, however, it is not as though every household has access to a stable income-generating independent-producer activity, nor are the markets for their products sufficient to provide enough income to withdraw from the labor force entirely. Scenes of bee keeping and crabbing might be quaint or romantic if it weren't for their proximity to scenes of dispossession and poverty, for often these domestic producer and income- or subsistence-generating enterprises end in failure. The scars of such failures can be found in almost every cluster of trailers or wood frame houses. Abandoned houses get picked apart for firewood. Abandoned ships rot and swell, and come apart. With their ribs showing they resemble bloated, drowned sea mammals, stuck in the mud. The cycles of use, abandonment, decay, and recycling mirror human concerns about property, community, and the environment, and human involvement in wealth, enterprise, hazard, and poverty. The same cluster of buildings that contains an abandoned, crumbling gas station might include a beautiful new church. Apartment complexes built with government funding sit alongside unused community centers. Throughout the area you see trailers next to or attached to wood frame houses in some ingenious cross-generational symbiosis. Sometimes the community itself fails, becoming like the ghost towns of the west and midwest that the railroad bore and the interstate and airport crippled and finally killed. Human groups are not always the adaptive "systems" we find reified in anthropological literature. One morning I saw a day-care center where the children, dressed in rags, played in a dark house without furniture. It was just an open sore of a home where an old, frightened woman cared for the children of the poor. The isolation of some residents is alarming. Social service employees reported teaching courses in how to use the want ads or dress to go to a job interview. Sometimes they run into people who haven't been more than fifty yards from home in years.

Work Settings

Plant Appearances. How do the processing plants fit into this landscape? What do they actually look like? Like everything else in the industry, they vary—in size, cleanliness, mechanization, location, comforts, etc. Architecturally, they range from small, single-room block or wooden structures to factory complexes. These latter are usually buildings the size of warehouses. Inside they are outfitted with fork lifts and fleets of vans and trucks, conveyer belts, pressure cookers, scales, canning machines, and other factory paraphernalia. Features common to nearly all facilities are long tables at which workers stand or sit before mounds of marine life—shrimp, oysters, steamed blue crabs. The tables are usually made of stainless steel or wood. They are fitted beneath with troughs, in crab houses, or fitted above with chutes, in scallop and oyster houses, for discarding shells and other refuse from production. Usually these disposal systems take refuse outside the plants. Some crab-picking facilities have conveyer belts to carry this refuse away, while others, to dispose of shells, rely on the same men who keep the piles of cooked crab high in front of the workers. Scallop houses often sit high on barnacled pylons at the water's edge. Their chutes lead from inside shucking tables directly down and out the building to small hills of scallop shells. Around most of the oyster houses rise these same hills or mountains of shell, some of them twenty feet high and twenty yards across. The fresh piles attract flies, while the old ones are sun bleached and enormous. Many oyster and scallop houses spread spent shells over parking areas and driveways, making more traversable surfaces that might otherwise consist of clay or muck. In Pamlico County, one plant owner said he had heard of people mixing shell fragments with asphalt to pave country roads. Crab shells, more fragmented, also present disposal difficulties. Most plants truck their shells to dehydration plants where, under intense heat and a powerful stench, they are dried into fertilizers and animal feeds, a fate similar to that of menhaden carcasses after the plants extract the oil.

Disposal problems often leave the outside of these plants looking unkempt and unsanitary, an impression enhanced by the way salty sea air rusts machinery, metal containers, and the bodies of trucks and fork lifts on the premises. If plants seem unsanitary and dilapidated outside, their interiors go a long way toward improving this image. State health standards mandate their cleanliness, and most of them tend to be clean. Workers wear hair nets or plastic or rubber head coverings, aprons, and, usually, rubber boots or shoes like galoshes. These waterproof garments reflect plants' interiors: they are wet places. Not only the shuckers and pickers but also most of the owners and floor help wear lots of rubber. Their outfits normally include white or black boots, yellow jackets or slickers, and yellow, bibbed hip waders or rubber pants with suspenders. In many plants, water runs almost all the time—from a hose to spray the concrete floors or from a tap at a stainless steel sink where people pack seafood in plastic tubs or other containers. Often, strips of clear plastic hang in doorways between work rooms. Working atmospheres vary according to the age of the facility, the seafood being processed, and the organization of work. Somewhat less variable throughout the industry, however, is the character of plant executive and middle levels in the occupational hierarchies.

Plant Management. I have already noted that managers of seafood processing establishments tend also to own them. Under 6 percent of those plants I contacted were not primarily managed by their owners. Generally, plants are family owned and operated, passed down through generations. Family ties permeate the industry, with companies linked not only through lineal descent, but also through collateral and affinal ties of brothers, uncles, nephews, nieces, sisters, and in-laws. In some plants, family members occupy virtually every rung of the occupational ladder, from owner/management to trucking, secretarial/clerical work, harvesting, processing, and sales.

The family basis of plant ownership limits entry into the industry, since ties of kinship can affect access to seafood supplies, prices of seafood, and relations with fishermen. Seafood plants that are linked by family ties sometimes help one another out by trading off labor or seafood supplies when one plant's production schedules have been poorly coordinated. In addition, family-owned businesses have an advantage over nonfamily-owned businesses in the training of new management. Children raised with the business, working part-time as kids, can learn the myriad nuances of the seafood processing business over long time periods, through a variety of economic circumstances and times.

Whether family owned or not, close association with the seafood business in general seems a prerequisite to entering the industry. If one does not come from a seafood processing background per se, new recruits to plant management and ownership might come from the brokering or harvesting sectors. In one plant owned by two men who did not inherit their positions, the men had been crab fishermen prior to opening their own, multispecies seafood processing plant. They purchased their crab-picking facility from a man who couldn't maintain steady supplies of crab because of poor relations with crab fishermen. Working as brokers between crab fishermen and larger plants on the Pamlico Sound, as well as being local residents with good relations with workers in small inland communities, these two men were able to direct their experience and good relations toward establishing a small but successful, expanding operation. In this case, they compensated for the lack of a seafood processing background in their families with their experience as crab fishermen and brokers. Despite the lack of kinship ties in the development of this plant, this case nevertheless further attests to the "home grown" nature of the industry.

Within plants, top management usually consists of a man and his wife or other related male kin, although in at least three plants I visited the primary management decisions were made by women. Whether formally counted among top management, wives of plant owners provide support roles as crucial as those provided by the proverbial fishing or farm wife in rural America. This executive level, daily, is faced with a complex set of tasks and decisions, demanding a high degree of coordination. Processing house managers are, by turns, personnel managers, public relations people, brokers, sales representatives, amateur marine biologists, clerks, mechanics, bookkeepers, engineers, truck dispatchers, quality control personnel, and administrators. They must synthesize vast amounts of information on a daily, weekly, and seasonally variable basis. Again, I point to the fluctuating record the industry has shown over the years as evidence of the difficulties faced by seafood processing plant managers. Coordinating supplies of perishable seafoods with available labor and markets demands close scrutiny and a variety of common and not-so-common business practices. Among their most pressing problems are the way they recruit workers and organize work in their plants.

Organization of Work

Scallops. Many North Carolina fishermen consider scalloping a mainstay of their family's well-being. Scalloping requires few technical or capital requirements. Locating bay scallops presents none of the difficulty of finfishing on open seas, since most productive scallop beds are within sight of shore. The technique involves dragging a weighted net behind a boat over known scallop beds, hauling in the nets, sorting, measuring, and bagging the scallops, trucking them to the scallop house, and prying them open with oyster knives. Low capital expenditures and technological simplicity make entry into the fishery easy.

Ease of entry is undermined, however, when it comes time to process the catch. Scallop openers who will work for the going piece rates (35 percent of the wholesale price per gallon in 1985-1986) are hard to find. Some owners of scallop shucking facilities reported witnessing bushels of scallops rot from lack of openers. Regulations allow scalloping two days per week, on Mondays and Wednesdays, for the nineteen-to-twenty-three week season. Highly perishable and susceptible to bacteria infestation out of water, scallops must be shucked immediately after the harvest. Like most seafood processing jobs, it is stinking, tedious labor. Shuckers sit at mountains of scallops that are still gasping for life, opening them with an oyster knife to strip muscle from viscera, keeping the muscles and discarding the inedible portions. Workers' earnings per hour vary with the size of the scallop meats, since workers are paid by the gallon instead of the actual number of scallops shucked or hours worked. Mobilizing workers under such uncertain, unpleasant, short-term, and seasonal conditions has given rise to a labor process based on kinship.

The shucking houses may employ a few permanent workers who, among other tasks, shuck scallops. Most fishermen, however, arrange to shuck their own scallops, drawing heavily on their kin relations to do so. They pay a set price per gallon to use the certified shucking facility and agree to sell all their scallop meats to the facility's owner. Usually, fishing families own these facilities. Relations between shucking facility owners and the fishing families that use the facility can be complex, involving not only kinship ties but also credit relations. In any case, both the use of a certified facility and the sale of scallops tend to be embedded in a series of other social ties rather than governed by strict market considerations. Although most facilities buy and sell scallops at roughly the price set by supply and demand, the supply of scallops each scallop house receives depends on which, and how many, fishermen use the facility. Use of the facility, again, is usually contingent upon selling one's scallops to that facility. Choice of facility, in turn, may depend on credit relations or kinship ties. Where shuckers actually work thus derives from the social relationships fishing families establish both to harvest the sea's resources and to process them. This is because, again, fishermen rely heavily on kinship to process their catches, using their wives and daughters (often as unpaid workers) and hiring in-laws, sisters, and mothers. Many of these women are willing and available for work during the winter months because they work in tourist related jobs during the spring, summer, and fall months, collecting unemployment while shucking scallops. At the shucking houses, I encountered fishing families spanning three generations who were all shucking scallops together.

As in all the processing plants, the utilization and distribution of time and space in the scallop houses reflects the bases by which work is organized and labor divided. Typically you find small work groups of two to three individuals, mostly consanguineal or affinal kin, hovered around a large pile of scallops that comes from a single vessel's daily thirty-bushel limit. The fishermen members of their households, who are usually male, replenish the pile of scallops in front of the shuckers, as well as make certain the chute for discarding shells is clear. Under this flexible division of labor, the wives, daughters, sisters, and other female kin tend to shuck. The men, who do the fishing, organize the labor process by recruiting kin and nonkin and helping with the actual shucking. Men station themselves throughout the houses, at almost all work locations. These include: (1) sections of the tables along the edge of the main shucking room or rooms; (2) sinks or running water stations to wash the meats; (3) holding areas for scallops still in their shells; and, sometimes, (4) a retail outlet or seafood counter.

In response to a question about securing seafood processing employment, I elicited many statements like, "I'm jes' helpin' daddy," or, "It was my father-in-law got me into this scrape." As the latter of these quotes implies, some kin shuck scallops grudgingly, suggesting they question the legitimacy of the labor process. Towards the end of the season, as the tourist season nears, fishermen whose female kin work in tourist related jobs cannot rely on their female kin to shuck scallops much longer. An owner of one scallop shucking facility told me that many of the women at her facility had been shucking for their fathers "since they were in their early teens," but that few would work beyond Easter. Other respondents, including scallop fishermen, explained that the importance of the fishery in the annual household income made it easier to justify using unpaid household members as workers. Only 13 percent of the respondents at five randomly selected shucking facilities had no direct kinship link to a scallop fisherman. Although dominated by fishing families, scallop shucking also depends on the labor of hired workers, more distant kinsmen, and the crews of the boats. This may have been more common in the past than today, as the slow growth of tourism and the service sector economy in Carteret County have drawn shuckers out of seafood processing. One shucking house owner said, "We used to have fourteen openers when the plant was new (1971). Now we have three old women, people who live around here. We're lucky to have them."

Seasonal, weekly, and daily schedules for shucking scallops can all be described as irregular. Although usually the season lasts from early December to mid-May, the season's beginning and end can both fluctuate from between two to four weeks. Or they may have no season at all, as red tide or ocean pollutants force bed closures. The fluctuations that do occur thus derive from ecological conditions such as microtoxins or changes in scallop populations as well as from social developments such as government policy. This reduces the extent to which shuckers or fishermen make plans around the season's beginning and end.

During the season, weekly and daily schedules are also affected by the character of the catch and by the two-day-per-week law mentioned earlier. If the beds are thick with scallops, vessels can reach their limits prior to noon and begin shucking relatively early in the day. In these cases, sometimes the shuckers can shuck all their vessels' scallops the same day they are landed. On the other hand, when vessels take a full day to reach their scallop limits, shuckers may not begin shucking until late afternoon and early evening, work until around 11:00 P.M., and then finish shucking on Tuesday or Thursday. Thus working hours can fluctuate from late evening to early or late morning and days of the week from two to four. These irregular schedules make the use of family members as shuckers more understandable.

Blue Crab and Oysters. Although the specifics of labor recruitment, mobilization, and organization are quite different from those in scallop shucking, the labor processes behind picking meat from blue crabs and shucking and packing oysters also rest on kinship. The black women who dominate the crab-picking and oyster-shucking labor forces neither come from fishing families nor possess kinship links to owners of the processing houses: North Carolina blue crab fishermen are almost exclusively white, and most of the crab processed in the state is imported from other states to maintain a year-round supply; oyster houses rely almost exclusively on imports. Even with imports, however, crab and oyster houses must phase back operations (and lay off workers) or completely shut down for anywhere from three weeks to two months during the year. Due to seasonal fluctuations and lay-offs, many crab and oyster workers collect unemployment during the winter months, as well as rely on other formal and informal social support systems. This reinforces a general reliance on transfer payments that already characterizes people from these workers' communities (Pamlico County Human Services 1985). As noted earlier, it also contributes to the labor reliability problem. Few men in the black settlements that supply workers will pick crab or shuck oysters, and many plant owners foresee an even greater labor supply problem in the future, since many youth refuse to do the work. Even within the regular labor force, worker reliability is highly variable, with some women showing up every day and others working with extreme irregularity. Processing plant owners cannot afford to be too strict in their demands on workers. Harsh reliability standards carry with them the risk of losing workers to other, nearby plants. One plant owner sum-marized the attitude more or less prevalent among his fellow plant owners: "To keep labor in this business you got to kiss ass *and* smile. Now, I don't mind kissing ass—everybody's got to kiss a little ass in this life—but to have to smile, too, that's rough." These labor supply problems, again, have led to a labor process dependent on kinship.

Despite the lack of direct kinship links between oyster and blue crab harvesters and processing plant workers, kinship permeates labor recruitment, mobilization, and organization. Owners of processing plants exploit their current workers' kin networks to recruit, train, and keep new employees. "For as long as I've been here," said one crab-picking plant owner, "every single new picker that worked out was related to another picker." Many plant owners send vans out to small black settlements and communities to pick up workers. Mothers, aunts, grandmothers, sisters and other female kin who work at the processing plants will often bring young girls to work at the plants during the summer months or after school during the spring months. I encountered girls between thirteen and sixteen years old picking crab or being trained as crab pickers, implying that senior women may draw upon their authority over younger girls (mothers over daughters, aunts over nieces, etc.) to improve their own relations with plant owners. Stated more abstractly, one form of exploi-tation, based on class, may be engendering another form of exploitation based on age. Plant owners encourage their employees to bring in potential workers as soon as they are able to work and owners usually let the person who recruited them handle their training as well. For their part, workers receive training for what is one of the only jobs in these areas, as well as positions that allow them to engage in alternate systems of support. In response to the question about securing seafood processing employment, 60.9 percent reported having relatives who worked in the same establishment, while an additional 32.7 percent responded with statements like, "I was born to this work," or "Everybody I know picks crab." Around 23 percent live with other women who also pick crabs in the same or nearby plants. In a few of North Carolina's small, rural black settlements near the crab-picking plants and large oyster-shucking facilities, it is difficult to find a single household that hasn't received some income from seafood processing.

The lack of direct kinship links between employers and workers, however, makes the organization of work and the distribution and utilization of time and space different from in the scallop houses. The work force tends to be divided into management office personnel, pickers (in crab plants) or shuckers (in oyster plants), and those whom I refer to as "floor help." These latter individuals, usually men, do the myriad odd jobs required to keep the plant running. Often they work alongside plant owners and plant managers, cooking crab, helping maintain or repair equipment, replenishing piles of crab or oysters in front of the workers, unloading shipments, shoveling shell fragments, etc. In the main work rooms, crab pickers sit side by side and across from one another at long tables while oyster shuckers stand at similar tables, prying open oysters with dull knives. Generally, oyster shuckers work closer to one another than do crab pickers, often standing shoulder to shoulder. Each worker has his or her own work station, including the raw seafood (cooked crab or oysters), the tools (knives, shell-cracking implements, etc.), and the plastic tubs or other containers to measure their output. In some oyster plants I visited, workers had small cards pinned to their aprons, usually above and to the left of the heart. After filling a pint container with oysters, they presented this card to a counter who punched a hole in the card. In this situation everyone's productivity is visible at a glance. The worker's wages were then determined by the number of holes he or she had punched in his or her card at the end of the day.

Schedules in crab and oyster plants tend to be more regular than those in scallop-shucking plants. Most crab houses operate full steam from March to mid-December, either closing down completely or phasing back on production from Christmas through February. As noted elsewhere, some plants shift to cutting finfish during these slack periods, keeping on a few of their more reliable or valued employees. Oyster plants' busiest season falls during autumn, especially around the Thanksgiving and Christmas holidays, when consumers demand oysters for stuffing turkeys. Some oyster plants reported remaining open most of the year, closing only during the month of August. In both oyster and crab plants, at any rate, the specific characteristics of the commodities and the practice of importing crabs and oysters to remain open for much of the year make these plants' working schedules more regular than schedules in the scallop plants.

Menhaden. The menhaden industry is the largest fishery in the state and in the United States. It stands well apart from other forms of seafood processing and other fishing enterprises across the country in terms of cultural, economic, and technological features. Its harvesting and processing operations are highly capitalized, vertically integrated, and technologically sophisticated. Its products are not consumed as seafoods but as oils, cosmetics, fertilizer, animal feeds, and European margarines. Its owners typically reinvest more than 5 percent of their profits into new product development (National Fisheries Institute, n.d.), creating a highly skilled research and development segment of the work force that exists in no other branch of the North Carolina processing industry. Finally, its labor force consists primarily of men who have been integrated into the various jobs in the plants along ethnic lines. While management and research and development personnel are usually white, the fishermen manning the United States's largest fishery are black. This may come as a surprise to those whose images of North America's fishermen come from the Portuguese or Italian or Scots-Irish cod fishermen of Georges Bank and the Gulf of Maine, or from Hemingway's novels or Wyatt's paintings.

Generally, most of the fishing crew and low-level factory positions are occupied by black men, while the captain, airplane spotter pilot, and management positions are held by white men. Interestingly, the processing plant positions may be changing from black men to black women under new technologies being introduced to pioneer the use of menhaden as a seafood, primarily in the form of a seafood paste known throughout the industry as "surimi." Surimi is usually made from pollock or lighter, more delicate fleshes than menhaden's dark, oily flesh. It consists of minced, washed, squeezed, and sugar- and starch-enhanced flesh that is artificially flavored and sold as imitation crab, shrimp, or lobster. Inside the menhaden processing plants, workers are organized in a way typical of any modern industry that produces a perishable commodity (e.g., Griffith and Runsten 1988; Runsten 1985a, 1985b). The division of labor by ethnic criteria, of course, has been noted in a wide variety of such settings, ranging from tuna or fruit and vegetable canning (Murray 1972) to agricultural harvests (Friedland and Nelkin 1971). In the concluding chapter, ethnic divisions of labor will be discussed in far more detail.

Shrimp, Other Finfish, and Clams. I have lumped these species together because they represent more or less of a "potpourri" of processing, occupying stop-gap positions in the plants, in seafood houses that are primarily brokerage houses, and in fishing households where one member might sell fish or shellfish to supermarkets or alongside the road. There is actually little "processing" of clams done in the state, although plants along the Atlantic coast, between Beaufort and Cedar Island for example, sort and grade clams to ship out of state or to local markets. Much finfish "processing," as well, consists of little more than sorting and packing, although a few plants whose primary processed species is crab will also, during the slack crab months (December to February), cut flounder, spot, croaker, or some other local species (even eels) to provide work for their best workers. Many scallop houses, in much the same way, process shrimp during the summer months largely to provide work for a few employees. In all these cases, then, the work teams are usually small, consisting of one to three or four individuals, women or men, who work extremely irregular hours, often on an "on-call" basis.

Exceptions to this general pattern are those shrimp and herring processing plants that, once or twice per year, need to mobilize anywhere from 25 to 250 workers for periods ranging from two weeks to two and one-half months. In these plants, the organization of work is similar to that in oyster and crab plants.

Work Organization, Recruitment, and Dependence on the Seafood Industry

The above observations raise questions regarding the ways that the labor processes described above relate to other specifics of the production process. What is it about scallop shucking that forces fishermen to arrange for wives, daughters, and other direct relations to shuck their own scallops while blue crab and oyster fishermen simply sell fresh crabs to be processed by separate economic entities? Why can't crab and oyster processing plant owners rely on labor market forces to recruit, mobilize, and organize workers? What aspects of the production process seem related to differences and similarities with regard to the reliance on kinship and informal social relations in the labor process?

As part of my attempt to address these issues, I developed an index to measure (at the ordinal level) "social interdependence" between workers and between workers and bosses. Respondents' social interdependence scores were determined by assigning them points if they: (1) learned of the job through a relative (two points) or a friend (one point); (2) worked in no other plant or only in other plants owned by the same family (one point); (3) lived with other seafood processing workers or individuals involved in marine resource exploitation (one point for each); (4) worked only in a seafood processing job during the year (one point); (5) had spent at least 60 percent of their working years in seafood processing (one point); (6) had only worked in seafood processing (one point); (7) lived within five miles of the processing plant (one point). Respondents' scores were multiplied by the number of people in their families who were involved in marine resource exploitation. These variables were used to construct the index after in-depth interviews and repeated observations in the processing plants and coastal counties revealed that they were indicative of the presence or absence of informal social relations among workers and between workers and bosses that transcended the work environment. Hence, the higher the respondent's social interdependence score, the more s/he is part of a social network that transcends the work environment and includes seafood processing workers, employers, and fishermen.

In figure 3.1, I have plotted the relationship between social interdependence and the number of months per year the respondent works in seafood processing. The relationship is curvilinear: from one to five months the workers' social interdependence scores increase steadily, and significantly (Pearson's $r=.461$; $df=18$; $p<.05$); comparisons between five-month to twelve-month seafood processing employees, on the other hand, reveal a significant inverse correlation (Pearson's $r=-.573$; $df=54$; $p<.001$) between social interdependence and number of months per year spent in seafood processing. This indicates that attracting workers for either short-term, casual employment *or* for year-round employment presents less of a problem than attracting workers for sustained periods of up to half the year. As measured here, kinship and other informal social relations become increasingly important aspects of the labor process as the number of months per year increases, up to around five months per year, after which they become less important as the processing season lengthens to a year-round operation.

These findings are supported by other observations. As noted above, the North Carolina shrimp and herring fisheries process

FIGURE 3.1

Social Interdependence by Number of Months in Seafood Processing

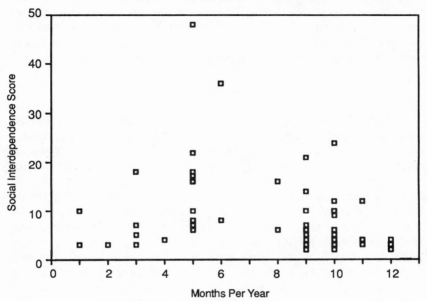

seafood for very short time periods, usually operating for one to ten weeks once or twice per year. Owners of these plants reported that they relied on casual labor consisting of people recruited "on the spur of the moment" by "word of mouth." In some of the smaller shrimp processing houses, employers call up local housewives to come process their product during the short summer and fall seasons. Although most of these have regular employees they call, all owners reported supplementing labor with their own labor and sometimes with the labor of office workers, maintenance men, drivers, etc. The herring processing fishery, which must mobilize up to 250 workers for around six weeks, uses kinship to recruit some workers the same way the crab and oyster processors do, mining female workers' kin networks for new workers. Many workers, however, simply show up at the processing plant during the processing season on an irregular basis, suggesting that a large portion of their workers are casual wage laborers.

Finally, realizing worker reliability payoffs of keeping a plant open all year, owners of oyster-shucking and crab-picking plants operate their plants throughout the year by reducing their reliance on local catches, importing live marine resources when local supplies are unavailable, as well as processing a more seasonally variable group of seafoods. Still, working conditions and reductions in labor needs during a few months of the year make it impossible to rely completely on market forces to assure adequate labor during months of intensive processing.

Conclusion

North Carolina's seafood processing industry, and its coastal fishing villages generally, lend the eastern counties a charm and character that local residents celebrate in a variety of ways. Seafood festivals, seasonally open oyster bars, specialty restaurants, and historic sites such as a mariners museum and exhibits at three state-owned aquariums all attest to North Carolina's heritage of a love of the sea. Small pockets of fisherfolk live in communities with names such as Salter Path, Okracoke, and Harker's Island. They launch skiffs and shrimp boats, they hang their nets to dry, stack crab pots, and land their catch up and down the coast much as their fathers and grandfathers did. In many ways this seems a romantic and noble setting with an *Old Man and the Sea* richness and sense of perserverence and pride. This is not the portrait of eastern North Carolina I have chosen to highlight in this chapter. I could have. I could have followed the tradition of those anthropologists who stress the independence of fishermen, who praise their "entrepreneurial" spirit or their courage at sea. I could have emphasized the sea grasses extending for miles across the wetlands, and how the coastal breeze touches them like so many strings of a piano and the sunlight and shadow play across their surface while juvenile shrimp dance with the currents in the estuaries.

Instead I have focused on the underbelly of this world, outlining the general contours of the seafood processing industry in a local and even somewhat unique setting. I have emphasized the fact that access to a reliable labor supply underlies some of the logic and plant distribution, that the labor reliability issue underlies processors' opposition to most welfare. I pointed out how the region's low levels of rural development enhances the seafood industry's network and kinship-based recruiting methods. While the recruiting methods are effective in part because of the lack of other job opportunities in the region, I also introduced in this chapter a theme that will emerge again and again through this work. One dimension of the effectiveness of these methods is their social and cultural basis. Because recruiting relies heavily on ties of kinship and community, owners of seafood processing houses have been able to bring to their recruitment methods pre-existing rights, obligations, and authority mechanisms based on kinship and community. In later chapters, we will see that this reliance on kinship and community is not, as one might suspect, a function of the size or local flavor of the eastern North Carolina's seafood processing industry. It is, instead, a principle by which low-wage workers in advanced capitalist societies are factored into the production process. This is the case even in the far larger, more technologically sophisticated, more corporate, organized poultry industry, whose general industry contours we define in the following chapter. After describing the poultry industry, I present a brief comparative discussion that highlights some of the similarities and differences between producing poultry and producing seafood.

4

The Poultry Industry in the Southeast United States

Quite different from seafood production in North Carolina and the United States generally, poultry production, particularly the production of young tender chickens known as "broilers," has been heralded as the model for vertical integration in U.S. agriculture, portending what many see as agriculture's future (Reimund, Martin, and Moore 1981). The industry consists of five integrated sectors: egg and breeder farms, hatcheries, feed mills, grow-out farms, and processing plants. Processing plants stand at the organizational as well as the literal center of the industry. Not only do they coordinate production schedules in the other sectors, the industry's rule of thumb is to locate all other sectors within a twenty-five-mile radius of the processing plants.

Unlike many other agribusinesses, poultry grew rapidly during the major farm depressions of the 1950s and 1980s. Since the 1950s especially, the industry has experienced dramatic growth, fueled by the rapid increases in consumption noted earlier (Lasley 1980; Reimund, Martin, and Moore 1981; U.S. Bureau of the Census 1987; NBC, personal communication, June 13, 1988). This growth has stimulated industry restructuring. Capital concentration and vertical integration have progressed to the point that, today, a dozen companies account for two-thirds of the more than 102,000,000 birds hatched, fattened, and slaughtered each week (*Broiler Industry* 1987). Equally dramatic shifts have occurred in locations of production, with firms moving south and west as the industry has become increasingly vertically integrated (Lasley 1980). The most significant changes have been spearheaded by the broiler industry, which has moved primarily to the U.S. South yet which also maintains significant production centers in California and on the Delmarva Peninsula. Relocation and structural changes constitute but two ways the industry has changed. Poultry science has domesticated the chicken into a completely industrial animal, bearing little genetic similarity to the chickens of only a century ago. Aggressive marketing campaigns underlie consumer confidence in chicken. Finally, new low-wage labor markets, including refugee and illegal immigrant populations, have been tapped, new labor processes have emerged, and mechanization continues to modify work environments in what remains a labor intensive operation. Although mechanization continues, the industry is likely to remain labor intensive for some time.[1] This is especially true with turkey production, since poultry science has yet to standardize bird size. In the broiler industry, however, the high-quality boned and further processed products that consumers demand have continued placing pressure on the industry to secure more and more unskilled labor. How these changes came about demonstrate how far an industry's growth, structure, and behavior can reach through the entire economy.

Changes in the Poultry Industry: The 1940s to Today

Beginning in the 1940s, broiler production began to change "from an industry of small, widely scattered, and independent producers selling through an open market into one of the most highly concentrated, integrated, and industrialized agricultural subsectors" (Reimund, Martin, and Moore 1981: 6). Prior to World War II, the poultry industry consisted mainly of a heterogeneous mix of rural egg farms that sold eggs and surplus birds to urban markets. Raising chickens for eggs and meat had been, for decades, a supplementary household or domestic-producer operation, fueled mainly by women and child family labor. One of William Faulkner's images in *Light in August*, written in the early 1930s, reflects the place of egg production in household economies:

Armstid is in bed, his head propped up a little, watching her cross the footboard as, still dressed, she stoops into the light of the lamp upon the dresser, hunting violently in a drawer. She produced a metal box and unlocks it with a key suspended about her neck and takes out a cloth sack which she opens and produced a small china effigy of a rooster with a slot in its back. It jingles with coins as she moves it and upends it and shakes it violently above the top of the dresser, shaking the slot coins in a meager dribbling. Armstid in the bed watches her.

"What are you fixing to do with your eggmoney this time of night?" he says.

"I reckon it's mine to do with what I like." She stoops into the lamp, her face harsh, bitter. "God knows it was me sweated over them and nursed them. You never lifted no hand."

"Sho," he says. "I reckon it ain't any human in this country is going to dispute them hens with you, lessen it's the possums and the snakes. That rooster bank, neither." (1939: 18-19)

Following the war, poultry production began to attract more small-scale producers, though still as a means to supplement household incomes. Investment capital and labor needs were low, with potentially good returns. On the grow-out farms of the East and South, most of which now operate on a subcontract basis, this continues to be the case. As recently as ten years ago, major processing plants on the Delmarva Peninsula were advertising for "part-time poultry farmers," highlighting the supplementary income character of contracting to raise chickens for processing plants.[2]

Increasingly through the late 1940s and early 1950s, the production of young broiler chickens, or "broilers" (six- to seven-week-old birds), became less a mere by-product of egg production than white-meat production oriented toward growing urban markets. During this early phase, most poultry eviscerating and other processing for end consumers was done by grocery store butchers. Poultry processing plants remained in an incipient, disorganized state of development, primarily producing whole birds rather than the wide range of boned, breaded, or fully cooked, products that confront us in today's supermarkets. As with the seafood producers described in the previous chapter, poultry plants' production and handling standards were anything but uniform. Federal regulations for consumer protection against tainted processed poultry products did not emerge until the late 1950s (Reimund, Martin, and Moore 1981).

The industry's disorganization was not to last. Financed primarily by feed companies, which were subsidized by government commodity programs, new organizational forms emerged in the early 1950s that encouraged the growth of the processing sector. Central to the new organization were relations between grow-out farmers and the so-called "integrators"; of particular importance were the production contracts. According to Reimund, Martin, and Moore:

> The production contract at the grow-out stage, which facilitated coordination with other stages of the subsector, was the central feature of the new organizational technology. It made large-scale broiler raising attractive both to the farmers and to feed suppliers, which in turn speeded up adoption of new production technology....
>
> Many chicken producers were small farmers with limited financial resources. They were unwilling or unable to obtain production capital through traditional sources or to bear the substantial financial and market risks inherent in large-scale broiler production. These growers could turn to input suppliers for their financing because production contracts provided them with both an alternative source of production capital and a means of shifting a substantial part of the financial and market risks to the contractor. (1981: 7-8)

In the search for grow-out farmers and cheap, nonmilitant labor, poultry companies turned south. There, minority, uneducated, unskilled workers were abundant and farms were typically smaller than in the northeast or north central regions. In the South, labor could be secured for the plants and farmers could be easily convinced to raise chickens and turkeys for the poultry plants.

The poultry farms tended to be relatively low-labor operations. One person could take care of four to five flocks of around 44,000 chickens per year with little more than family labor. As an economic opportunity, with financing available either through the feed mills themselves or through credit contingent on the contracts, the low-labor intensity of raising birds fit in well with typical southern farm family strategies. Typically families combined farm and off-farm work (Gladwin 1988; Hansen, et al. 1981). Also, guaranteed incomes have always appealed to families whose annual incomes swing between red and black depending, almost literally, on the direction of the wind. Other attractions of the South for poultry production were the relatively low costs of real estate, milder climates, fewer alternative uses for land, and labor (Lasley 1980).

Of particular interest here is the way the industry's move to the South enhanced labor recruitment. During the 1940s and 1950s, labor in the northeast and midwest was growing increasingly organized and militant (Newman 1988; Stanley 1988). Well known, for example, were the gains made by labor unions during the 1940s, which stimulated many meat packers to send labor recruiters into southern states to encourage Black migrations northward (Skaggs 1986; Stanley 1988). During this same time period, as noted in the opening chapter, southern labor remained ardently anti-union, cheap, and accommodating, influenced by community leaders that included prominent politicians and clergymen. The legacy of the notion that unions are communist strongholds or that CIO stands for "Christ Is Out" remains in many southern regions even today (Cobb 1981). That poultry companies moved south to take advantage of this labor environment is reflected in changes in the proportions of broiler production across the nation between the 1950s and the 1980s. From 1950 to 1960, broiler production in the South rose from 421 million birds to 1,433 million, or from 66 percent of the country's total to nearly 80 percent of all birds produced in the United States. By 1980, the southern share had risen to 88 percent (Lasley 1983). These production gains were won at the expense, primarily, of the north central region, whose share dropped from 12.5 percent to just over 2 percent of the nation's total (Lasley 1983). Production in the northeast fell as well. Production gains, while predominantly due to larger labor forces at the plants, were partially the result of technological developments in the plants as well. Dave Runsten (1988) notes that:

> As evisceration came in, more specialized plants were set up close to the grow-out regions. Conveyer belt technology speeded up the processing and created the need for closer coordination with the setting and grow-out of the birds, in order to operate the plants at full capacity. This drove the process of integration.

As poultry became a mass-production industry in the 1940s and slaughter was shifted from terminal markets to specialized processing plants closer to growing regions, there was a shift in the labor force away from male poultry worker in the cities toward more women, minorities, and other marginal groups in rural areas.... (Runsten 1988; quoted from Griffith and Runsten 1988)

Following initial gains, however, for the next twenty years most growth in production derived from enlarging the plants and hiring more workers instead of from raising labor productivity with technological improvements. It wasn't until the 1970s that a new wave of technological, marketing, and packaging changes occurred throughout the industry. These were spawned, in part, by heightened consumer awareness of the health risks of eating red meats and consequent increases in poultry consumption. In marketing, one of the main innovations was to begin branding poultry products. The progressive transfer of packaging from the grocery stores and other retail outlets into the packing plants both encouraged and facilitated branding. Today many companies produce more than one brand, reserving the highest quality products for the principal brandname while marketing lower quality birds and products as other, less well-known brands. Increased attention to marketing led to products that conformed to consumers' lifestyles. In particular, consumers with less and less leisure time desired easy-to-prepare foods. Hence, in addition to promoting brand recognition with national advertising campaigns featuring celebrities such as Dinah Shore, poultry companies began producing complete lines of fully cooked, ready-to-eat, and further-processed products. With brand recognition, companies were forced to pay closer attention to quality control. Of particular concern here have been the bird's size and the color of its flesh. While poultry and food scientists busied themselves with standardizing the bird itself, plant managers had to enforce rigorous bird handling standards in the processing plants. Both were necessary to assure product quality and consistency. At the same time, the new products stimulated new plant layouts, new allocations of time, and new technologies in the plants.

These technological changes in the industry accompanied social and, later, cultural changes in the plants. Most of the new, further-processed products could not be produced without increased demand for low-wage labor in the plants. Machines could perform some cuts, but the more meticulous boning cuts, to assure quality and reduce waste, had to be done by hand. Work organization inside the plants changed to streamline production, accommodate the new products, and address problems of labor turnover. Tasks throughout the plants, never requiring highly skilled individuals, were taught and arranged so people could be shifted from task to task in the event of gaps developing in the line. This was especially necessary for the initial line positions, where the live birds entered the plants and had to be prepared for evisceration and further processing. Live-hanging, or removing the live birds from crates to hang upside-down for the electrified bath and slaughter, was and still is an especially high-turnover job. Making tasks interchangeable necessarily involved either increasing training periods, deskilling tasks, or both. In most plants both occurred, though most of the training concentrated on safety rather than skill, in response to the continuous, if episodic, attention focused on the industry's occupationally hazardous conditions. Deskilling, as we discuss further below, was a general consequence of the transfer of more and more processing tasks from retail outlets to the plants.

All the social and technological changes were occurring in a growth environment, as poultry consumption continued to increase and competition among firms grew fierce. Plants were continually under pressure to assure adequate supplies of workers. This, in turn, set the stage for pioneering new and resurrecting old techniques of labor recruitment. Later, the fierce competition, coupled with the industry's ability to generate cash, would lead to further industry concentration. Major firms became targets of the corporate takeovers that have become a major part of the economic landscape of the 1980s.

Behind the increasing concentration of capital and the deskilling and restructuring of tasks is the redistribution and concentration of labor's surplus value. It has been concentrated in the plants and redistributed, in part, to the machine (Edwards, Reich and Gordon 1973; Braverman 1974). Among the casualties of these changes has been the grocery store butcher, whose demise can be regarded as the poultry industry's contribution to the deskilling of U.S. labor (Griffith and Runsten 1988). Simply, skilled butchering positions have been transferred from the grocery stores to the processing plants, replacing higher paid with lower paid workers.

The Influence of the Local Economy on the Poultry Industry

The transference of butchering from supermarkets to processing plants, with corresponding lower wage rates, is indicative of the mixed blessings poultry firms bestow on their local and regional economies. Processing plants benefit by local economic stagnation and suffer from local economic growth. Of those plant managers who complained that labor supply problems had been getting worse, most blamed local economic growth and new industries as the cause. This is evident in the following responses of plant personnel managers to a question about whether jobs in the plants have been getting easier or harder to fill:

Our labor supply varies seasonally—tied directly to unem- ployment. Been good lately, because of midwest drought and local textiles have had big layoffs.

In our area, unemployment is 4 percent—industrial development is in boom state—lots of competition for the same worker.

Ours aren't the best jobs—they would rather work at Westinghouse, Dupont, etc. Other plants moving in are getting our workers. Chamber of Commerce is partly at fault. They bring in new business, but no new workers. In this area, there's only 4.6 percent unemployment and 2 percent of those wouldn't work in a pie factory.

Those plants that have no problems finding workers are those located in counties with high rates of unemployment and few alternative employment opportunities. In and of itself, this is not surprising. Nevertheless, this observation carries some telling implications for relations between plant management and the communities in which they are located, for the scope of economic processes, and for the geographical mobility of native labor. First, since the success of a community is inversely related to the success of the processing plants, plant managers have a clear interest in keeping local economic growth low. Such practices may result in long-term labor shortages, as younger workers move to areas with more and subjectively better employment opportunities. Many of the labor policies of processing plants, however, are short term in nature.

Second, during the study we were struck by just how *local* the economy could be. It was not uncommon for managers of plants within fifty miles of one another to report opposite labor supply experiences. In one case, a plant manager had such faith in the local labor market to fully staff his plant that he rejected an influx of Mexican workers from the cucumber harvest. He claimed they would be temporary, high-turnover workers. In a county less than thirty miles away, the plant personnel manager was trying to encourage local contractors to build low-cost trailer parks to attract workers to the area, as well as actively directing recruitment toward Mexican populations who worked in the same nearby harvests.

A third point follows from the second: that counties so close to one another experience such radically different labor supplies suggests that native workers are not nearly as geographically mobile as neoclassical economics assumes. According to conventional economics, migration is a principal response to economic disparity (Borjas 1989). In contrast to native workers, immigrant workers are often highly geographically mobile. This is especially true of Mexican workers from migrant agricultural backgrounds, whose existence pivots on the ability to move. In this sense, Mexican immigrants may have an edge over native workers in the labor market simply by virtue of their lack of attachment to home communities. The geographical mobility of immigrants, especially when combined with illegal status and migrant farm worker backgrounds, also entails social units better suited to the migrant lifestyle than those of native workers. Groups of lone males or small family units with few or no young children can move more easily than multigenerational family groups. This facilitates their appearance in the plants and their diffusion through the industry. Work just now emerging on international communication and aid linkages between groups of individuals residing in different countries as migrants have questioned our very notions of household and community (Chavez 1989). While interviewing Guatemalan political refugee/farm workers in South Florida, we encountered a case of a "household" with members in the four countries of Guatemala, Mexico, the United States, and Canada, all of whom kept in regular contact with one another. These contacts involved not only sending money, but also exchanging information about economic, political, jural, and immigrant opportunity in the various countries. These information networks, in turn, influenced the migration, labor market, reproductive, and other decisions of each of the household members.

One tentative observation we can make here concerns the contradictions between large, extended, or in any way rooted (e.g. landed) households and the labor demands of rural industries like poultry processing. The historical works of Immanuel Wallerstein

(1976) and Eric Wolf (1982) teach us that dominant modes of production encourage the development of domestic units of a specific form, or for specific articulations between domestic units and the formal structures of the dominant mode. Under advanced capitalism, the domestic unit has changed from the more extended forms of the late nineteenth century, which provided workers to labor markets as but one of a variety of their functions, into the smaller nuclear forms of today. Clearly, much of the change can be attributed to the changing international division of labor and its extensive reliance on internal and international labor migrations. Such domestic units may or may not conflict with the domestic forms necessary for the success or survival of small-scale, peasant production. In most cases, under conditions of incomplete incorporation, the contours of the domestic unit have approximated the shape of those selected by the dominant mode of production or modified its articulation with the formal structures of the dominant mode. We see this in cases of "international" households in particular, such as the four-nation household described above, where extended families span three separate, yet interdependent, residential units. In this case, the domestic unit has been able to maintain its integrity as an extended family by substituting benefits deriving from residence (e.g., labor, skills, emotional and political support, and technical knowledge) with exchanges of money and information regarding political terror and repression (in Guatemala and in Mexican refugee camps) and economic opportunity.

Such separate-yet-linked households, now relatively common, constitute but one viable social form under advanced capitalism. In addition to its influence over existing domestic units, advanced capitalism also stimulates the emergence and development of other social structures. Social networks have emerged as cornerstones of behaviors ranging from job search to migration to food consumption. Social networks are distinguished primarily for their diffuse characters, consisting of weak and strong ties, as well as for their flexibility, adaptability, and at least temporary resilience to recession or periods of economic decline (Massey, et al. 1987). Indeed, that advanced capitalism "allows" a variety of forms is one of the principal means it disguises its extraction of surplus value from labor (Marx 1967). Such disguise rests on the inability of those social forms to provide theaters for class consciousness. This, quite clearly, affects the concrete features of wages, benefits, and the potential for union activity in the industry.

Wages, Benefits, and Union Activity in the Four Regions

In the above discussion, we noted that low-wage labor markets can become extremely competitive environments, particularly when new industries enter a region. Within such competitive labor environments, with less than attractive poultry plant jobs to offer, wage-and-benefit offers must be higher than those of minimum wage jobs. In 1988 dollars, only in a single north Georgia plant did workers receive minimum wage to start. Average starting pay was usually closer to five dollars an hour, and in no region did workers receive minimum wage after the training period.

As one can see from table 4.1, there are distinctly different starting pays between Texas/Arkansas and North Carolina on the one hand and north Georgia and the Delmarva region on the other. The two regions with higher pay scales also have significantly shorter training periods than the others, indicating that attracting labor to the plants with higher pay may be enhanced by shorter training periods. Shorter training periods, on the one hand, accelerate pay raises and, on the other, increase the potential for occupational injury. After training, pay scales become more uniform across regions, although Texas/Arkansas processors remain at the bottom of the pay scale, while average pay offered by North Carolina processors improves relative to the others. Interestingly, however, North Carolina processors also had the widest pay range between plants, from $3.70 per hour to $6.70 per hour, which further confirms our observations about how extremely local an economy may be.

Union activity has not had a positive impact on wages. Plants in which unions have been or continue to be active (54.5 percent) do not have significantly higher rates of pay, nor do plants that are currently unionized (27.3 percent), as shown in table 4.2. Further, regardless of union activity, almost all plants offer workers comprehensive benefit packages that include life, medical, and disability insurance, sick pay, and pay for holidays and vacations, though often the latter are tied to a worker's work history, particularly his or her rate of absenteeism.

While union activity seems to have little impact on wages or benefits, union activity does vary regionally. Table 4.3 presents figures on the distribution of union representation by region,

TABLE 4.1

Wages and Training Periods by Region

Region

Variables	Texas/ Arkansas	North Georgia	North Carolina	Delmarva
Starting Pay Per Hour for Unskilled Workers (p=.001)*				
minimum	3.75	3.35	3.55	5.00
maximum	5.30	5.65	5.47	5.60
mean	4.52	5.17	4.61	5.12
s.d.	.45	.63	.57	.21
Training Period in days (p=.003)*				
minimum	30	14	30	30
maximum	90	60	90	90
mean	59	35	66	46
s.d.	26	14	25	21
Pay Per Hour After Training Period (p=.065)				
minimum	4.65	4.75	3.70	5.45
maximum	5.40	5.85	6.70	5.60
mean	5.04	5.49	5.36	5.54
s.d.	.22	.33	.79	.06

*=statistically significant (Analysis of Variance)

showing significantly lower representation in North Carolina than in the other regions. This table also shows that union representation was more prevalent in the past than it was when these data were collected (1988), especially in North Carolina and Texas/Arkansas. This seems in line with the current countrywide demise in union representation.

Yet basic statistics on union activity can mislead regarding the extent of union commitment to workers' rights. Two factors are important to consider here. First, although the general, nationwide response to unionization among workers has been, recently, negative and apathetic, the response to unions varies regionally. So, too, does the union's commitment to its members. Some unions were more cognizant than others of the ethnic complexity of poultry plant labor forces, hiring bilingual organizers to work with Spanish-speaking poultry workers. This influenced the extent to which organizers took advantage of the recent "amnesty" or legalization provisions of the 1986 changes

TABLE 4.2

Mean Hourly Wages by Union Representation or Past Union Activity

Status	No	Yes
Currently represented	$5.32	$5.30
Hourly wage (unskilled)		p=.43
Have been represented in the past or are currently represented		
Hourly wage (unskilled)	$5.32	$5.39
		p=.315

Note: probability levels refer to one-tailed t-tests

in the immigration laws. These provisions have been important in the struggle for workers' loyalties in industries that have relied heavily on illegal immigrant workers.

Although many unions in the United States took advantage of these provisions to increase their strength, some poultry companies also took advantage of legalization provisions to generate loyalty among workers whom they helped with the fees and paperwork. Generally, in areas where immigrants have been present in the industry since the 1970s, unions have used the amnesty issue as an opportunity to legalize immigrant workers and increase membership. In these areas, as well, it was common for unions to have bilingual organizers, sympathetic to the needs of Hispanics.

In areas where populations of Hispanic, largely illegal immigrants have less historical depth, on the other hand, unions tended not to seize amnesty as a membership-enhancing opportunity. In one case, changes in immigration laws actually hindered a union drive by generating confusion over legal status issues. Plant managers took advantage of the confusion, telling workers of the possibility of increased attention from the Immigration and Naturalization Service (INS) if workers engaged in union activities during adjustment to immigration reform.

The second point to be made here is that there are sound, viable alternatives to labor unions as means of organizing workers. These new, "grassroots" organizational forms are usually more responsive to workers' needs than the now heavily bureaucratized UFCW. They may also portend future forms of labor organization, which may be based on ethnicity, community, nationality, or gender, as well as one's relation to the means of

TABLE 4.3

Regional Distribution of Union Activity

Region

Variables	Texas/ Arkansas	North Georgia	North Carolina	Delmarva
Current Union Representation (%)				
Yes	50.00	45.45	7.69	62.50
No	50.00	54.55	92.31	37.50
	(p=.048; chi-square)*			
Current or Past Union Activity/Representation (%)				
Yes	66.67	57.14	29.41	75.00
No	33.33	42.86	70.59	25.00
	(p=.069; chi-square)			
% change:	-16.67	-11.69	-21.72	-12.50

* = statistically significant

production. In any case, as labor unions wane for segments of the U.S. working population, we may expect alternative forms of labor organization to develop and influence the paths of both labor and capital. These new organizational forms may be related to other concrete features of the ways industries have developed and become compartmentalized. Among the major ways this compartmentalization or "segmentation" (Edwards, Reich, and Gordon, 1973) has occurred, in the poultry industry as well as in the labor market generally, is by means of gender and ethnicity. These features and others are reflected in the industry's organization of work and division of labor.

Work Organization in the Industry

Early in this chapter I noted that the poultry plants depend on an integrated ("separate-yet-linked") system of breeder/egg farms, hatcheries, feed mills, and grow-out farms. Labor recruitment, mobilization, organization, and labor policies tend to be different in these different industry sectors, based on differences in the labor needs of the sectors. The extent to which the parent companies of the processing plants get involved with the labor problems of the other sectors vary according to whether or not the specific operations are subcontracted or company owned. While only 29.6 percent of personnel managers reported involvement with the labor practices of the grow-out farms, 43.4 percent reported involvement with the breeder/egg farms, 68.5 percent with the hatcheries, and 64.8 percent with the feed mills.

Because all supporting operations tend to be within a twenty-five-mile radius of the processing plant, we might assume that the same sociodemographic features that characterize workers in the processing plants also characterize workers in the other sectors of the industry. Actually, this is not yet the case: except in areas with large new immigrant and refugee populations, the sectors of the industry outside the processing plants rely predominantly on native labor. In the future, this may change in the same way fruit and vegetable packing and processing, once also dominated by native labor, has slowly turned more to immigrant labor. Nearly 70 percent of the plant managers we interviewed reported that labor turnover in the other sectors was less of a problem than labor turnover in the processing plants. This reflects the organization of work in these other sectors, the degree to which operations have been mechanized, and the size of their work forces relative to the processing plants.

Breeder/Egg Farms, Feed Mills, and Hatcheries. With the notable exception of turkey breeder operations, the egg farms and feed mills are nearly fully automated. They can be run with around twenty workers whose jobs consist primarily of monitoring gauges and loading/driving trucks (NBC; PS). Like the grow-out farms, some of the broiler egg farms are operated on a subcontract basis, and most require little labor. Turkey breeder operations, however, may be the most labor intensive sector of the entire poultry industry, since the birds have to be artificially inseminated and the semen, highly perishable, must be hand carried from males to females.[3] Located in isolated rural areas, these farms have historically had trouble attracting reliable native labor and have grown to rely on illegal immigrants in parts of Texas and California (TPF).

From the egg farms the eggs are trucked to hatcheries, where female workers sex the chicks, give them shots, and box them for shipment. Interestingly, the sexing of chickens is a task that was associated with a specific ethnic group early in the industrialization of the chicken: "Since White Leghorn males are virtually useless as meat birds, the so-called chicken-sexer became a key figure in the production of chicks for laying purposes....

The sexing of chickens has been a virtual monopoly of Japanese-Americans" (Smith and Daniel 1975: 281). This early tendency to associate specific tasks in the industry with specific ethnic groups has not been confined to sexing chicks. Three out of four processing plant personnel managers believe that different ethnic groups have different attitudes toward work and different work habits. Walker's (1987) study of Utah turkey processing plants found that these beliefs are reflected in the allocation of tasks in the plants, a practice that occurs in seafood processing plants as well. In the hatcheries, chicken sexing is no longer an exclusive domain of Japanese-Americans, although recently the U.S. Department of Labor has granted temporary work visas to Koreans for the express purpose of sexing chicks. Hatcheries do, however, tend to hire women over men (reinforcing myths of gender rather than ethnicity) since women are perceived to be gentler with the baby chicks.

Although work in the hatcheries is monotonous, working conditions in the hatcheries are less onerous than in the processing plants. The plants can be cold, wet, loud, slippery, and generally unpleasant, with line leaders and supervisors sprinkled throughout the plant. By contrast, hatcheries tend to be quiet, dry, and clean, and employees need no close supervision. Hatchery work forces also tend to be close knit, a factor which may further reduce labor turnover (NBC).

Grow-Out Farms. While the hatcheries and feed mills tend to be owned and operated by the companies that also run the processing plants, most of the grow-out farms (with the exception of those in California) and a portion of the breeder/egg farms tend to be family owned and operated. Some companies mix company-owned farms with those that are subcontracted, but the majority of the farms are owned and run by farm families. On subcontracted farms, the companies deliver the chicks and feed and occasionally send around poultry scientists to check the flocks. Around seven weeks after delivery, company trucks retrieve the fattened birds for slaughter. A farmer's performance is measured by the feed conversion ratio. During years of falling poultry prices, some plants regulate the supply of birds by not renewing less productive farms' contracts (DPI).

The farms themselves are low labor operations. Most of the care of the flock can be done by one person. The common figure cited by cooperative extension personnel and poultry association people was that one individual could care for 44,000 chickens with no more than family labor. The operations consist of cleaning out dead birds daily and making sure the fans and automated feed and watering systems function smoothly. Because the care of the flock is a twenty-four-hour job, however, the farms tend to be run by farm families. Growers on the Delmarva Peninsula and in North Carolina reported using their wives and children to supplement their own labor on the farms.

While daily care requires no more than one or two people, three factors make the farms potentially susceptible to shifting labor circumstances. First, between flocks and during the first weeks of a new flock, when the birds are "bitties" or chicks, the farms require higher labor inputs than during most of the year. In addition, at least a full day of intensive labor is necessary to catch the birds for transport to the plants, though much of this is done by the plants or professional "catching companies." Growers usually tend five flocks per year, with around two weeks between flocks to clean out the chicken houses and other equipment. Some growers on the Delmarva Peninsula reported hiring a professional cleaner during this period; these individuals own equipment similar to beach cleaning equipment that cleans the chicken houses of manure. Others continue to rely on family labor during these high labor periods. Yet some hire casual workers and some of these, particularly in Texas, have relied on illegal immigrants. Mobilizing workers for such short work periods implies using people who are "marginal" to the labor force in the sense mentioned earlier. They are often in the labor market temporarily, to supplement household incomes, and tend to move seasonally or irregularly between different low-wage labor jobs as well as other economic activities. Other contexts in which such sporadic and irregular labor practices prevail include detassling corn in the midwest or processing shrimp or herring during brief, one- to ten-week periods every spring and summer. The marginal workers used in these contexts occupy positions in the U.S. labor market that are structurally similar to illegal immigrants, especially illegals with little experience in the country.

Second, although individual grow-out farms require little labor, their collective labor needs are considerable, especially at the beginning and end of a flock and between flocks. An average processing plant requires between 250 and 350 growers to maintain a constant supply of birds. The daily arrival of birds at the plant thus marks the beginning of a corresponding high-labor period at one or more grow-out farms within the twenty-five-mile radius. Since the plants process birds all year round, there is a need for supplemental labor on the farms all through the year. One worker could move among no more than five or six farms per year, working around two weeks at a time on each farm, and remain employed all year round. An average processing plant's grow-out farms could thus provide between 40 and 70 of these jobs. The entire industry, processing over 102,000,000 birds per week (over five billion per year) must utilize around 23,500 growers (assuming five flocks of 45,000 birds per grower per year), thus generating around 4,300 of these temporary jobs annually.

Third, the poultry industry at times draws upon the same labor pool that supplies U.S. agricultural harvests, which includes minorities, women, illegal immigrants, and others who are marginal to the labor market. Some plant personnel managers reported that during the 1988 summer they saw more Mexicans than usual apply for positions in the plants, citing the drought in the midwest as a precipitating cause of the increase. In other cases employers reported using seasonal agricultural workers after the harvests, attempting to keep them on for more than a few weeks or months. Within this overlap between agricultural labor and poultry industry labor, the grow-out farms seem particularly well situated to locate and utilize those marginal low-wage laborers, especially illegal immigrants. In fact, growers we contacted often hired crews of legal and illegal Mexican workers for their vegetable harvests. In Texas, most subcontracted grow-out and breeder farms used illegal immigrants. Runsten reports, as well, that 70 to 80 percent of the labor on California ranches was immigrant, and most of that undocumented (Griffith and Runsten 1988). I mention this here to suggest that the labor processes developing in the processing plants may be diffusing to other parts of the industry as well.

Processing Plants. The processing plants stand, in both literal and figurative senses, at the very center of the industry. The industry norm of locating all other facilities within twenty-five miles of the plant has far-reaching implications for the populations of counties hosting poultry plants. That the plants have such a complexity of needs results in poultry companies not only influencing local labor markets and other economic conditions, but also in their altering county ecologies. The plants themselves tend to be huge and stinking, generating wastes and surrounded by roads lined with white feathers from endless deliveries. They are generally groups of square or rectangular buildings, often of a kind of ribbed concrete, pumping smoke and commanding the whole horizon's attention. Around the plant itself are the workers' parking lots, receiving areas, and dispatching lots; generally the entire facility is surrounded by chain link fences and guarded.

Cramped into plastic or metal crates and stacked into the backs of open-air trucks, birds arrive at the receiving area on and off all day long. There, during the summer, huge fans keep them cool as well as spread their collective stench well beyond the physical boundaries of the plant. The crates are unloaded onto conveyer belts and taken into the infamous "live-hanging" room, infamous because nearly everyone in the poultry industry agrees that work in this area of the plant is the most unpleasant. The first position actually inside the plant, and often the first given the new employees, it is telling that the live-hanging area suffers from the highest labor turnover in an industry known for high labor turnover. It smells horribly of the chicken manure that spills from frightened cramped birds as the workers, wearing paper gas masks, pull the birds from plastic crates to hang, upside-down, by their claws on evenly spaced stainless steel hooks on which they will ride to their death and then on through the plant. It's dusty and dark; only frosted blue fixtures emit light that is wan and weak by any standards. Supposedly the dark calms the birds.

From live-hanging the birds move into the unmanned slaughter chamber. This is a long, narrow, dark room where the birds are stunned in a charged tub of water just before their throats are mechanically slit. Stunning them with the electric change is supposedly more humane than killing them fully awake. They bleed into the water. Then they are plucked mechanically with rapidly spinning mechanisms similar to the spinning scrubbers at an automated car wash, and semi-gutted; they then enter the big production room on hooks. Still hanging upside-down, but now naked and decapitated, with a little string of guts hanging out over their corpses, they pass overhead through two jets of blue flame that singe the remaining pinfeathers from their bodies. Once through the flames, the birds, still hanging from the hooks, are passed down between two rows of women and men, who pull the guts from their bodies, and quality control inspectors, who inspect the birds. These first line workers after the live-hangers are called "eviscerators." Most of them are women, standing on raised stainless steel mesh walkways, about two feet above the slippery plant floor. The quality control people sit; most of them are men. Like all the other workers inside the plant, with the exception of the live-hangers, these first line workers wear white coats over layers of thick shirts and coats, hairnets, rubber gloves over warm gloves, rubber aprons, earphones, and rubber boots. Compared to the rest of the plant, this first room is relatively warm, though wet, from being constantly hosed down. It's very clean and most of the smell has been washed or singed from the birds, so the room smells only faintly of chicken fat. The eviscerators stand between three and five feet apart; quality control people sit further apart, between about every fourth or fifth eviscerator. As the birds move through the plant, the work stations they encounter become progressively more cramped, as well as colder. According to a spokesperson at the National Broiler Council, "If you see one person processing four pounds on the eviscerating line, you'll see four people processing that same four pounds in further processing. They go from standing three to five feet apart to standing shoulder to shoulder."

From the eviscerating room the birds, still hanging, move to an area where workers sort them, paying attention to any one of fifty-seven imperfections. Birds considered perfect are rehung and shipped out as whole birds. This sorting is a "premium paid" position, where the people get some intensive training (on the fifty-seven imperfections) and then have to take a written test once a month. Those birds not selected for whole fryers get routed to "cut-up," while the whole birds go to a packaging station where workers bag them and a machine sucks the air out of the bag.

The birds that go into the cut-up areas of the plant are machine sliced to go through two lines: breasts, for deboning, where women and men stand shoulder to shoulder with scissors and knives, or into the leg-quarter section. Here they are packaged and shipped on into labeling, where computers weigh, price, and stamp them with labels. From here they are boxed and sent into the big warehouses of the chill rooms, rooms as cold as walk-in coolers, where the boxes are stacked and sorted, awaiting the forty to forty-five trucks per day that leave with full loads.

A tour through the plant yields only a surface appreciation of what it might be like working in the plants. Poultry processing, similar to many low-wage labor jobs, especially meat packing, is one of the most hazardous jobs in the United States. Tasks can lead to the wrist's equivalent of tennis elbow (carpal tunnel syndrome), or to cuts and other injuries; leg and back problems can develop from standing at production lines for eight to ten hours per day. In addition to the physical unpleasantness of the plants, the cold, and the probability for injury, a few features of the plants make them psychologically taxing as well. For example, they are large plants, where managers are pressured to keep output high. Many of them, as well, have experienced influxes of new immigrants and refugees along with constant high turnover. Combined with the practice of moving workers from one work station to another to fill gaps, the influx of new workers constantly reorganizes work groups. Table 4.4 indicates that these features of the working environment do not vary greatly from region to region, but that the variance within regions can be large (as indicated by the standard deviations).

Cold, noisy, wet, monotonous—these factors combine to create labor supply problems (or "reduced applicant flows," in the words of personnel managers) and high labor turnover at a time when demand for further processed products is growing and plants are expanding. Over a third of the plants we contacted (35.2 percent) have added shifts or expanded into new product lines in the past few years, generating new jobs that machines have not been able to perform. "Slaughter is up, up, up!" boasts an industry publication, citing the fact that annual broiler production has climbed from under three to over five billion birds over the past twenty years and turkey production has climbed from 116 million to over 240 million. Only 9.3 percent of the plants in the sample had reduced production, in most cases because they could not find adequate labor. In response to a question about changes in production over time, we elicited responses like:

We added a night shift in 1984.

We used to have a mini-shift from five to eleven; now we have a full second shift.

In the last four years we added four hundred people; in 1985 we started deboning.

We used to kill less. Our goal was 335,000 birds a week and we have increased employment 30 to 40 percent. The plant that was here before was processing only six or eight hours a day.

We added further processing in 1985.

TABLE 4.4

Selected Characteristics of Processing Plants by Region

Region

Variables	Texas/ Arkansas	North Georgia	North Carolina	Delmarva
Number of Processing Shifts				
Percent with 1 shift:	0	21.4	11.8	16.7
Percent with 2 shifts:	100	78.6	88.2	83.3
Average Number of Birds Processed Per Week ('000)				
minimum:	55.00	335.00	95.00	450.00
maximum:	1500.00	1200.00	2200.00	1400.00
mean:	730.75	797.14	756.15	735.71
s.d.:	443.65	280.98	662.46	325.91
Average Number of Workers Per Plant				
Unskilled				
minimum:	194	100	120	100
maximum:	2000	1000	1600	1450
mean:	647	445	636	610
s.d.:	533	288	432	410
Semiskilled				
minimum:	9	0	0	0
maximum:	283	2595	500	300
mean:	91	280	124	50
s.d.:	91	678	136	85
Skilled				
minimum:	5	7	4	0
maximum:	113	100	150	157
mean:	49	32	53	40
s.d.:	38	25	47	42
Total (includes all of the above plus office personnel, supervisors, and managers)				
minimum:	247	279	315	133
maximum:	2428	3366	2210	1276
mean:	820	906	824	677
s.d.:	683	843	592	373

Combined with the information on how plants are affected by local economic growth, increased production in less than desirable working conditions has placed extraordinary pressures on poultry plant managers to secure adequate supplies of labor.

These pressures have translated into plant managers pioneering new, and regenerating old, labor recruitment mechanisms. That seafood processing finds itself under similar pressures, though within a radically different organizational environment, invites some telling comparison.

Conclusion: A Comparative Discussion of Seafood and Poultry Production

The information in this and the previous chapter attest to the fact that differences between the seafood and poultry industries emerge all along the chain from production to consumption. The differences begin with each industry's initial interaction with its raw material. Chickens and turkeys are thoroughly domesticated (Smith and Daniel 1987; Lasley 1980). With the exception of maricultured and aquacultured products, however, the fish and shellfish used to make seafood products are wild creatures, hunted or trapped instead of tamed, corralled, fattened, and raised. From this initial difference derive others.

The Influence of Raw Materials Over Marketing and Production Strategies

First, concerning the raw materials themselves, the seafood industry is confronted with a variety of species. Each has distinctive characteristics regarding the color, fat content, texture, oiliness, grittiness, and other qualities that affect the ways consumers evaluate seafood (Griffith and Johnson 1988; Johnson and Griffith 1985). At this level, the seafood industry is confronted with the problem of how to standardize the quality of seafood, since consistency of taste, texture, and other features are crucial to marketing food. Seafood companies respond to this problem in primarily one or more of three ways. First, they can establish extensive marketing relationships with fishers throughout the world to assure constant access to the same or similar, high-demand species (e.g. shrimp). Second, they can process the sea's raw materials in ways that bring out the qualities consumers desire or that mask or rid the product of qualities consumers find undesirable. Finally, companies can use marketing "tricks," such as calling a variety of fish with similar flesh qualities and flavors by the same name (e.g. scrod).

Poultry firms, by contrast, have bred into their birds the specific qualities of flesh that consumers desire. This has provided a sound basis for developing a marketing strategy of branding and brand recognition. Branding of seafood has proceeded unevenly, associated only with maricultured and aquacultured products, with canned products (e.g. tunafish), and with further-processed and packaged products (e.g. Mrs. Paul's). The branding of fresh and most freshly frozen seafood has not yet been successful or even attempted on a large scale. Similar to growers of fresh fruits and vegetables, who market products with reference to regions instead of actual companies (e.g. Florida Grapefruit), the problem with branding seafood, again, is one of consistency of quality. With seafood products coming from so many political and economic entities, such diverse regions, and harvested with technologies that range from factories-at-sea to handlines, maintaining consistent quality is nearly impossible. Accordingly, seafood companies and restaurants also market fresh and fresh-frozen products with reference to regions as opposed to nationally known brands (e.g. Maine Lobster; Norwegian Salmon).

Industry Structure

The distinctive differences between the two industries' raw materials have had deep impacts on industry structure. As noted early in this chapter, poultry firms are highly vertically integrated, and the industry is dominated by a few large corporate entities such as Perdue, Cargill, and Tyson. Accompanying the standardization of bird size and characteristics, processing plants all employ similar technologies, hire large numbers of workers, and are organized along factory principles whose design and time-and-space allocations maintain line speeds of between seventy-two and ninety birds per minute.

A particularly important component of poultry production is the subcontractual relationship between the grow-out farmer and the processing plant. Because of this relationship, the direct producers' relationship to end consumers of poultry is always an indirect one, mediated by the processing sector. Again, the productivity of individual farmers is measured by feed conversion ratios, and the technology for growing birds is essentially the same from producer to producer. Because most of inputs are provided by the company, grow-out farmers have few incentives to innovate or experiment with production, which might jeopardize feed conversion ratios. This constricts entrepreneurial activity among direct producers. Instead, the structure has created dependent relationships between direct producers and processing plants, with little potential for direct producers to alter this situation through mechanisms that might improve their position in the market (innovation, assuming additional risk with the hope of additional profit, capital concentration, etc.). Growers have, instead, responded to their dependence on the industry through occasional political channels, though with little success (U.S. Congress 1984).

The seafood industry contrasts sharply with this pattern. Instead of similarly positioned growers using similar technology and integrated into a few large firms, direct producers in the seafood industry (e.g. fishers, crabbers, shrimpers) occupy a wide range of positions relative to the processing/retail sectors. They operate a number of different technologies with varying abilities for absorbing capital and creating value, and they are highly fragmented. Vertical integration similar to the poultry industry has occurred in the menhaden, tuna, and salmon industries, but even in tuna and salmon there exist a number of smaller producers.

Further, unlike poultry, the seafood processing sector is also characterized by a vast array of qualitatively and quantitatively distinct entities, from small scallop shucking houses quaintly dotting rural coastlines to the huge tuna canneries of Mayagüez, Puerto Rico, and the freezing and breading facilities for producing packaged fish products.

The heterogeneity of direct producers and processors in the seafood industry has, historically, accounted for a great degree of competition between producers and processors. This creates a fertile ground for incentives to increase productivity and take advantage of niches in the market. The market itself has played a leading role in organizing the industry, sometimes serving as the principal arena where social relations are established that are designed to control direct producers and seafood supplies. These include debt relations, kinship relations, and simple wage labor relations as processing plants purchase their own vessels and construct their own crews. Interestingly, however, as consumer demand for seafood has grown, and the market has expanded to include more international producers, we have seen some linkages between direct production and the processing sector dissolve. An example is the tuna industry, where:

> Prior to 1980, U.S. tuna processors secured tuna supplies by contracting and financing reliable domestic fishermen and, in some cases, by mounting their own fishing operations. But with suitable supplies of low-cost tuna available from many

diverse sources outside the U.S., U.S. processors have revised
their procurement strategy by reducing their involvement with
U.S. fishermen and by increasing their purchases of tuna
on the international market. (Floyd 1987: 217)

State Presence

A further difference between the two industries has been the
character of the state's presence in the two industries. While
mandatory inspection of poultry products began in 1959, the
United States government has not been present in the seafood
processing sector except on a voluntary and haphazard basis.
Under the poultry inspections program, the poultry companies
pay the U.S. Department of Agriculture (USDA) inspectors;
inspectors are recruited from plant work forces, although the
inspectors are, technically, government employees. Currently, one
of the main issues facing the seafood industry is the introduction
of a mandatory seafood inspections program. If this were to occur,
it is likely that smaller, older firms would have difficulty meeting
sanitation requirements and would not be able to pay inspectors,
furthering capital concentration in the processing sector. In
addition, two direct consequences of the imposition of mandatory
inspections in poultry processing were that: (1) the state assumed
control of line speeds, since lines could only move as fast as
inspectors could inspect birds; and (2) the processing sector entered
into a new era of relations with the state that might best be
described as an antagonistic partnership. Losing control over line
speeds immediately caused a struggle within the industry to regain
control. Initially they accomplished this through a variety of
corrupt mechanisms, principally by bribing inspectors (who were
hand-picked by personnel managers). Later, however, they
initiated a series of social and technological changes inside the
plants to facilitate or complement the inspections system. All the
while, poultry firms lobbied the USDA that they should be
rewarded, with streamlined inspection systems, for their paying
the USDA inspectors. Further, rates of contamination fell from
5 to 6 percent in the 1960s to less than 1 percent today. Recently,
regulations have relaxed. In plants that have had records of low
numbers of contaminated birds, inspectors inspect samples of
birds and line speeds have gradually increased.

Increased government presence in the processing sector
would likely have similar consequences in seafood. Most notably,
increasing merger activity, causing an industry shake-out, would

initiate a period of capital concentration and stimulate more vertical integration. It is highly likely that Tyson, Cargill, Perdue, and other large poultry firms—as well as large meat packers such as IBP, ConAgra, and Excell—would participate in this process and subsequently replicate, as far as is possible, the linkage models already familiar to them.

While seafood firms have not yet seen a large government presence in the processing sector, the "common property" component of direct production of seafoods has meant a larger state presence in direct production of seafood than in the poultry industry, particularly in the form of Fishery Management Plans (FMPs), limited entry schemes, quotas, etc. The impacts of these on seafood processing and seafood workers will be discussed more thoroughly later.

Impacts on the Retail Level

Finally, these different industry profiles have resulted in extreme differences at the retail level. In poultry, the further processing of fresh birds (cutting up birds, deboning breasts, packaging, etc.), as well as packaging, weighing, and pricing, have progressively shifted from the retail level to the processing plant, causing a decline in skilled butchering positions in supermarkets. Many may view the demise of the skilled supermarket butcher as a victory for the efficiency of the modern poultry processing plant. Those more theoretically inclined might also consider it a victory, in the Weberian sense, of economic rationality. Others may view it as a regrettable though inevitable development in the way food must be produced and distributed in a country as large and as complex as the United States. And most, in either case, will see the loss of the grocery store butcher as not particularly important to the way they shop or eat.

It is indeed the case that most shoppers can find the poultry products they want without the butcher's specialized knowledge of skeletal structure or tendon or muscle tissue. Consumers may never need to know anything more about the bird than what the package says; they may never need parts the poultry processing plant has not seen fit to produce. Nevertheless, the demise of skilled butchering may reach further into consumers' lives than is immediately evident. First, with the loss of a skilled intermediary between producer and consumer, the consumer exposes himself or herself fully to the information and range of products the producer sees fit to produce. The consumer loses a kind of "second opinion," or an objective third party who makes his or her daily bread by becoming familiar with the full range of meat products available to the public. No longer either a skilled or well-paying position, butchering contains neither the incentive nor the opportunity for the butcher to familiarize himself or herself with the cooking, spicing, and cutting of meat and poultry. More important, few incentives exist for butchers to learn to identify tainted poultry, or to learn about the hormones and other additives in the flesh that might influence a consumer's decision to buy this New York strip or that bird. In the supermarkets of today, the butcher's former job can be filled by a stock boy or, worse, a series of interchangeable stock boys who are more likely to pass along misinformation about a product than accurate, critical appraisals of products. The job, in short, becomes as susceptible to high labor turnover as jobs in poultry processing plants. The business of knowing about cooking, spicing, or the qualities of flesh have themselves become specialized occupations, migrating to the universities and colleges in the form of home economics. This lends support to the idea—suggested by Sassen-Koob's (1985) notion of global control capability—that the international division of labor has led to extremely highly skilled specialists, on the one hand, and large numbers of relatively unskilled, underpaid workers on the other.

A second effect of the demise of the skilled butcher is that the grocery store itself loses the ability to receive turkeys and chickens from local producers—fresher, live birds, fattened on local grains instead of feeds enhanced by pharmaceuticals and developed in laboratories. Many small-scale poultry producers, losing such markets, must themselves participate more fully in the labor market, further establishing the practice of moving between domestic production and wage labor.

Beyond other consequences such as the community's loss of a skilled and higher paid position in the supermarket, if we look at the demise of the butcher in a more abstract light we can better understand some of the effects of capital concentration. Transferring skill from human hands to mechanical parts entails the loss of an individual's ability to improve his or her own position based on his or her own discipline and wits and hard work. When the job itself becomes more important than the individual who fills it, then individual initiative has been usurped by structure. Nothing challenges the employee's intellect; he or she cannot take much comfort in the idea that nearly "anyone" can perform his or her job. Meanwhile, the chasm between labor and management grows. All problem solving, all challenge, increasingly migrates into management's domain and out of the hands of the person on the floor (again, see Sassen-Koob's discussion of "global control," 1985). In the process, the people on the floor of the plant are robbed of the dignity of having an opinion on the way the plant is run or the line arranged.

In contrast to poultry, however, seafood industry structure has made it difficult for supermarket managers to rely exclusively on the processing sector for information about its products. Instead, supermarkets around the country have been training their employees in such things as fat contents, cooking styles, cleaning techniques, and even natural history information about various species of fish. Some supermarket chains have raided state Sea Grant College Programs' Marine Advisory Services for highly trained personnel, or have sought out fisheries biologists or graduates in related fields, staffing their seafood counters with professionals. Many more, however, have been upgrading their own personnel, retrieving some of the skill level lost to the poultry processing plant.

With demand for seafood continuing to climb and most of the value added to products in the processing sector, it is likely that concentration will occur in seafood as it has in poultry. This, in turn, will likely have similar effects on retail-level employment. This became even more probable with Oscar Meyer's recent takeover of Kemp Seafoods and with the further development of aquacultured and maricultured products. Before the staffed seafood counter falls, though, it is noteworthy that industry fragmentation and higher skilled supermarket personnel, if only for a while, go hand in hand.

Summary

We summarize this section with a table that compares seven features of the seafood and poultry industries:

1. The industries' respective raw materials.
2. Their direct production processes, including the nature of the direct producer's link to processors, brokers, and consumers, and the technologies of direct production.
3. The industries' processing (value-adding) sectors.
4. Overall industry structure, from direct producer to end consumer.

5. State or government presence in the industries.
6. Marketing strategies.
7. The state of the industry at the retail level.

TABLE 4.5

Comparisons Between the Seafood and Poultry Industries

Industry Feature	Poultry	Seafood
Raw material	Genetically engineered/ Standardized	Wild/Varied
Direct Production Process:		
a) direct producer's link to consumer	Mediated by processing sector/ Subcontractual	Mediated through the market/some Subcontractual
b) technology of direct production	Standardized	Highly varied
Processing Sector	Factory setting	Highly varied
Overall Industry Structure	Vertically integrated	Fragmented, with some vertical integration
State Presence	USDA inspections in processing plants	FMPs, limited entry, etc. in production sector
Marketing Strategies	Branding and Brand Recognition/Mostly for home use	Fresh market/Primitive branding/Restaurants
Retail Level	Demise of skilled butcher	Increase in staffed seafood counters

In the following chapters, we move from the general to the specific, from the overall industry structures and effects on food marketing and consumption to the roles the two industries play in the histories of communities and the lives of workers. Here, we shall see, the two industries converge along as many lines as they diverge at more general levels.

III

Household and Community in Patterns of Labor Control

Shucking Shellfish, Picking Crab: A Profile of North Carolina Seafood Processing Workers

Within the seafood processing labor force, a clear division has emerged between scallop shuckers on the one hand and crab pickers, oyster shuckers, and finfish processing workers on the other. The division is based on the way labor is organized in the processing houses and plants, the terms of its use and commoditization, and the intimacy of workers' ties to the marine resource. On these foundations have arisen other, more immediately noticeable differences. For example, crab pickers and oyster shuckers tend to be Black and scallop shuckers White. Menhaden plant workers tend to be men while most workers in the rest of the industry are women. These differences underlie the different ways workers may be impacted by various political economic developments. The effects of shellfish bed closures, statewide and local low-wage industrial recruitment campaigns, immigration reform, or coastal gentrification may be cushioned, disguised, or worsened because of the way workers have been integrated into seafood processing production. The different effects of these developments are reflected in differences among workers regarding such things as ethnicity, age, household size and composition, sex, training, and labor market experience. These differences among workers and their households occupy the pages that follow. For theoretical reasons (cf. Deere and de Janvry 1979; Wood 1981; Griffith 1986a), I use workers' households as the primary reference point on which worker participation in seafood processing pivots. In later chapters, I place these households within larger, dynamic processes affecting low-wage workers throughout the United States.

Patterns of Work and Unemployment
in Seafood Processing Workers' Households

As with low-wage occupations generally, incomes derived from seafood processing jobs are so low that other incomes are necessary to raise workers' households above bare survival and poverty levels. In an earlier chapter I calculated seafood processing workers' annual earnings, estimating them at between $5,000 and $7,000. These figures are well below federally established poverty levels (between $12,000 and $16,000 for a family of four in 1986, depending on one's region). Hence, either workers are extremely poor or they come from households with multiple incomes. The reality lies somewhere in between. Many workers are extremely poor, yet low-wage workers often supplement spouses' or parents' incomes, or live under arrangements where incomes from work in the formal sector need not cover all of the individual's consumption needs (where housing is low-cost or free, for example). These latter observations, unfortunately, may be used to justify keeping wages low and simultaneously mask or divert attention from the widespread poverty we inevitably find among low-wage working populations. Households which may seem to be "making it" may in fact be a minor crisis away from homelessness, hunger, ill health, and other conditions of the destitute.

Fully 31.7 percent of the workers I surveyed live in households where the only source of income from the formal economy comes from working in seafood processing. Over a third (39 percent) of the households depend on two jobs in the formal economy, 12.2 percent on three jobs, 13.4 percent on four and 3.7 percent on five. In other words, 68.3 percent of the households depend on more than one job. Also, a large portion of the work force (29.3 percent) comes from households that depend on more than two jobs. This carries social organizational implications. It suggests that processing workers live in households where three or more people might work, living with elderly relatives who still may be active in the labor force, siblings, or grown daughters and sons who still live at home and work. These are creative responses to poverty and labor market discrimination. Because they often influence the quality of housing, particularly the numbers of individuals per room, these responses are also impositions on the ways people organize their space and time. "You learn to survive," said one eastern North Carolina low-wage worker. "You learn to become close to family, to support one another. You just buy food, pay your rent and light bill—you don't buy nice clothes. You don't go out."

In some of the households dependent on more than one job, however, the multiple jobs are held not by multiple persons but by the seafood processing worker, a practice related to the seasonal nature of seafood processing. The survey revealed that, although seafood processing represented the primary occupation for most workers interviewed, workers range from working a month or less out of the year to working all year round. Workers tend to work, on average, 8.6 months out of the year (sd=3.14) and 4.4 days per week (sd=.86) during the months they work. In terms of annual and weekly schedules, then, workers would be able to engage in more than one occupation or economic activity during the week and during the year. In fact, one quarter of the work force combines seafood processing with anywhere from one to four other jobs in the formal economy. The proportion would be larger, of course, if we were to include subsistence activities or domestic production.

The prevalence of holding multiple jobs in the labor force raises questions concerning workers' senses of self, since a good deal of social theory in the United States rests on the assumption that occupation is a cornerstone of identity and social class affiliation. When one holds multiple jobs and engages in multiple informal economic activities, from which job or economic activity might we expect one's identity to come? Under these conditions, occupation often ceases to occupy a premier position in one's identity, becoming superseded by ethnicity, community, religious affiliation, and family. In later chapters we will see that, faced with such shifting bases of identity, employers need to penetrate realms outside the work place, to somehow come to dominate or influence areas of workers' lives from which they do derive their primary identities. Through such influence, employers have been able to stimulate flows of labor into their jobs and enhance mechanisms of labor control.

A brief examination of those workers who hold multiple jobs shows that this practice derives from features of the specific seafood processing job and the alternate job opportunities available near workers' residences. First, over half (57.1 percent) of the workers holding multiple jobs work in plants in Carteret County. Compared to the other three counties in which I inter-viewed workers, Carteret hosts a wide variety of seasonal, unskilled service sector occupations related to the tourist industry; Carteret residents, as well, have easy access to the military facility at Cherry Point. Second, as table 5.1 shows, workers who hold other jobs tend to be White more often than Black, reflecting greater job opportunities for Whites than for Blacks. Third, following from these first two findings, 47.6 percent are scallop shuckers. These workers also tend to be White, to work in Carteret County, and to work only four to six months out of the year and only two to three days per week in seafood processing during the scalloping months. Still, another 42.9 percent work in crab houses, most of which are located in Pamlico and Beaufort counties, where alternate job opportunities are scarce.

TABLE 5.1

Distribution of Those Who Combine Seafood Processing
with Other Jobs by Ethnic Affiliation

	With Other Job	Without Other Job	*Totals*
White	13	12	25 (30.1%)
Black	8	50	58 (69.9%)

Totals: 21 (25.3%)   62 (74.7%)
(x^2=13.493; df=1; p=<.001)

Processing workers who hold second and third jobs besides seafood processing tend to hold similar positions in similar sectors of the economy. Two thirds (66 percent) of those with other jobs occupy low-level positions in the unskilled service sector of the coastal economy, thus being exposed to a range of hazardous occupations. Another 20 percent are fishermen or engage in seafood harvests in some capacity, and the remaining 14 percent have skilled positions in fields such as nursing or carpentry. Yet if multiple jobs support a household, it is usually because more than one person in the household is working rather than because the seafood processing worker holds more than one job. The holding of multiple jobs—sometimes referred to as "occupational multiplicity" (Comitas 1964)—is occurring, in short, more at the household than the individual level.

Despite the heavy contributions to the wage labor market from processing workers' households, unemployed individuals remain in workers' households. While 55.4 percent have two people capable of entering the labor force, and 26.4 percent have three or more people so capable (for a total of 81.8 percent), only 68.3 percent have more than one individual working. Between 12 and 13 percent of the households thus do not supply all capable workers to wage labor markets. This unemployment is usually due to common demands such as childcare, other domestic activities, and independent economic activities such as fishing or farming.

Of those other household members active in the work force, their backgrounds seem more or less in line with those of the processing workers with whom they live. Over half (54.4 percent) of the households possess no individuals with skills or advanced educations. If we look at the distributions of workers by type or class of worker in occupational hierarchies and by sector of the economy, we see that slightly over 70 percent of the other workers in processing workers' households occupy jobs as low-level employees such as unskilled farm or factory laborers or seafood processors. Prior to working in seafood processing plants, most processing workers also occupied low-level positions. This reflects, of course, the general low social status and life chances of members of workers' households. This becomes more clear in a profile of the workers themselves.

When averaged, the survey results show that seafood processing workers are around forty years old, with around thirteen years of experience in seafood processing, possess a tenth-grade education, and live in a household of around four people. Other statistics suggest workers are more likely to be female (75.6 percent) and black (69.9 percent) than male and white. Finally, in the industry, seasonal job offers are slightly more common than year-round job offers, with 56.6 percent working seasonally.

We must keep in mind that these are but statistical summaries. Within each of these groupings, a good deal of variability exists. This variability undermines using statistics as the sole means of classifying workers or understanding their relation to other workers, to capital, to the state, and to the marine resource. For example, although the average age of workers in the industry is around forty, the range of ages found in the seafood processing labor force is highly variable, including young teenagers as well as septuagenarians. Also, this broad age range reflects the depth of processors' labor needs, their often desperate attempts to staff the plants, and their practice of utilizing kinship networks of current workers to recruit new employees. This broad age range implies that all age grades within the low-wage coastal work force have been exposed to seafood processing as an employment alternative. The industry, in short, has pretty well permeated their existence. So thoroughly, indeed, does the industry permeate their communities that federally funded agencies involved in placing workers from agriculture into less seasonal occupations steer women toward either seafood or poultry processing. The most common form of seafood processing is crab picking, in which work 61.4 percent of the sample population. Nearly half (48.5 percent) process more than one seafood, which reflects the tendency of processing plants to process more than one seafood per year.

Seafood processing workers are quite stable with regard to residence. Nearly half (48 percent) of the population live in their natal communities and nearly three-fourths (73.5 percent) live within twenty-five miles of their city of birth. Of the remainder, only 10.8 percent live more than one hundred miles from where they were born. In the field, I encountered only two women who had relatively complex histories of internal migration, leaving their home towns for northeastern cities and returning to North Carolina after a string of jobs. Of those who moved to nearby communities (around 25 percent), the principal reasons they gave for the move were either marriage or that they moved along with their parents. Rarely, in less than 4 percent of the cases, was "to find work" given as their reason for moving, although certainly those who moved with parents or spouses could have been moving for economic reasons.

This residential stability of the work force carries theoretical and practical implications. From a cultural perspective, for example, we can assume that seafood processing workers are carriers of core features of rural southern culture, including beliefs about ethnicity, religion, nutrition, the roles of local and federal governments, and attitudes toward education, job training, and unionization, enclosing their roles in the formal economy in various mythologies of the "work ethic." In the rural South, especially among blacks, these attitudes have become thoroughly enmeshed in ideas about the supernatural and its concrete manifestations in church hierarchies and church-based relationships. "The church has always been the backbone of the black community," said a young black woman who had been active in organizing low-wage working women. "For a long time, the church was the one place Blacks could go to feel relief and talk about your problems. Whether you were rich or poor, you had a voice in church." She went on to explain, however, that both black and white clergymen have been anti-union in eastern North Carolina. Local clergy have labeled any attempt to organize workers—even outside of unions—"troublemaking." Included in rural eastern North Carolinian beliefs, therefore, are ideas about what it is to obtain and hold a job, about expectations regarding work and supervision, and about the legitimacy of protesting your conditions of work.

The residential stability of the labor force, also, may contribute to the problem plant owners have of getting and keeping reliable workers, as long-time residents learn of the myriad legal and illegal, formal and informal ways that coastal North Carolina offers people a living; long-time residence makes it easier to move between seafood processing employment and other activities that provide sources of support, including networks of relatives and friends and social services. The strength of these ties, and their emergence as means to cope with low incomes, clearly contributes to the lack of geographical mobility in general.

A related observation we can make here regards the relationships between human geographical mobility, especially in search of work, and characteristics that are currently "adaptive" in terms of the short-term needs of the international division of labor. Emotional ties to a place—to one's home region, hometown, neighborhood, or community—are out of step with an advanced capitalist economy. Recall that one of the hallmarks of advanced capitalism is its reliance on the hypermobility of both capital and labor. Those willing and able to move to work sites from depressed economic regions generally have an edge over those whose opportunities are forever overshadowed by an allegiance to place. Empirically, too, we have seen in studies of internal and international labor migration that migration itself is often positively associated with such characteristics as innovation, entrepreneurship, risk taking, and achievement, themselves functions of greater wealth, more education, and higher social status (Portes and Bach 1985; Massey, et al. 1987). Seafood processing workers, bound to eastern North Carolina because of community ties, are forever drawn back to the few means of making a living open to them. Picking meat from crab carcasses or scraping oysters out of their shells are among their most readily available alternatives. Survey results confirmed this. Over 40 percent of the workers have had no other wage labor job besides seafood processing (although they may have been self-employed), and over 30 percent have had only one job in the past. The remaining 35 to 40 percent have had between two and six past positions, although it is clear that most of the work force are trained for little besides seafood processing.

Far more telling than the number of past positions workers have had is the nature of those positions. Were they seasonal, permanent, self-employment, unskilled, semiskilled? From my interviews emerged, clearly, employment backgrounds similar to seafood processing: 41 percent of the work force had histories of working in seasonal occupations such as farming, forestry, fishing, or other seafood processing. As we will see more thoroughly in later chapters, the staffing of these kinds of occupations is usually seated deeply in kinship and community ties, which facilitate recruitment, supervision, and task allocation inside the plants. Workers' tendency to engage in seasonal work, moreover, fits in well with the practice of combining a number of income-generating activities, both inside and outside of the formal economy. This practice, in turn, undermines workers' abilities to develop skills that may be applied in other contexts or sold in other sectors of the labor market. The survey clearly revealed that most past jobs held by seafood processors were low-level, unskilled jobs; for 77.1 percent of the work force, seafood processing was as demanding or about as demanding a job as they have ever had.

Nevertheless, at least one in five workers (21.7 percent) have had jobs that demand more skill than shucking scallops or picking crab. Within this group are those who have been self-employed as well as those who have been laid off from eastern North Carolina factories like textile or small appliance assembly plants. If we examine the sectors of the labor market workers have come from, again we find that they tend to come from sectors similar to seafood processing in either skill level or seasonality: unskilled service jobs, manufacturing, fishing, forestry, farming. At the same time, once again, around one in five (18.1 percent) came from skilled service jobs, such as nursing or carpentry, or skilled manufacturing jobs. Certainly others in the farming, forestry, or fishing categories have also occupied more skilled positions than those they occupy in the processing plants. In both past and current positions, the mean number of years workers remain at their jobs is a surprising 10.46 (sd=8.35), suggesting long-term worker stability, even though workers may be unreliable (e.g. often absent) during those years on the job.

Low levels of skilled labor experience among workers both reflects and is reflected in the levels of education they have attained and the kinds of training they have received. As noted above, workers, on average, usually have around a tenth-grade education. Again, this is variable. The work force contains individuals with college educations as well as individuals with no formal schooling at all. Slightly over half of the work force (53 percent) have no high school diplomas, yet 18.1 percent have had some schooling or technical training beyond high school. If we include on-the-job training, which 10.8 percent of the work force claim, in technical training, the percentage who have some post-high school training rises to 28.9 percent. Nearly one-third of the work force, that is, have learned some skill or have more than a high school education. This may, on the one hand, mean that the work force already possesses sufficient raw material for an "upskilling" of workers with the introduction of new technologies, new systems of worker organization, or new product lines. On the other hand, this portion of the work force includes the workers most likely to leave the plants as other employment opportunities arise: comparing skilled and unskilled workers I found that skilled workers change positions more often than unskilled. In their employment histories, skilled workers reported having an average of 2.75 (sd=1.9) past positions while unskilled reported an average of 1.1 (sd=.9) past positions (t=5.226; df=81; p=<.001 level).[1] Because job change often means moving to a new region, moreover, upskilling the labor force might result in more emigration from the seafood processing counties to areas of economic growth. Upskilling, in short, may serve in part to bring workers more in line with behaviors predicted by neoclassical economic thought, where migration is a response to economic disparity between wage offers in different regions or different countries (Borjas 1989).

Because skill and education may contribute to higher labor turnover and emigration, incentives exist for employers to seek out workers with few or no skills besides seafood processing. This would presumably include new immigrant and refugee populations with little experience in the U.S. labor market; indeed, in later chapters we will see that employers in poultry processing plants in some parts of the country already actively engage in recruiting immigrant and refugee populations. Late in the 1980s, moreover, Virginia and North Carolina seafood processors began importing workers from coastal Mexican villages to work in isolated plants located in sparsely populated coastal counties. Further, that employers perceive a need for unskilled labor encourages employers to actively pursue or support policies that contribute further to the deskilling of the work force, such as opposing training programs designed to stabilize workers' incomes or to place workers in less seasonal jobs (i.e., outside seafood processing). Employers might also be expected to oppose the low-wage industrial recruitment policies currently popular among southern chambers of commerce, which threaten to compete for their workers. In fact, among seafood and poultry processors, as well as among other employers of low-wage, largely seasonal labor, I have encountered sometimes vociferous opposition to local chambers' attempts to attract new industry into areas where the locals have traditionally relied on food production and processing employment.

Considered somewhat more abstractly, some of the very foundations of southern racism may be understood in this light. There is a clear material interest among some classes to perpetuate racist assertions of black stupidity and laziness, since such claims would undermine attempts to put in place programs to educate and train blacks for more effective and more prestigious job placement. In any case, from an employer's short-term perspective, it is advantageous to have a labor pool characterized by low levels of education and skill. These factors are fueled by racism. The racist basis of the uneven distribution of education and skill emerges when we compare households by whether or not they contain skilled individuals.

Skilled and Unskilled in Workers' Households: Comparisons of Ethnicity and Seasonality

About half (47 percent) of the households possess skilled individuals qualified to work in more demanding sectors of the coastal economy. I compared households with skilled individuals to households without skilled individuals with regard to seasonality of the worker and his or her ethnicity. The following table shows that the presence or absence of skilled individuals in the household does not seem to vary with worker seasonality but does vary with ethnicity. Black workers, that is, are more likely to live in households without skilled individuals than white workers.

These conclusions, of course, can be deduced from the literature and other observers' accounts of minorities as well as of women in the United States and particularly the rural South (e.g. Fuchs 1986). They confirm that, despite many advances among women and minorities, these groups remain discriminated against in training programs and the labor market.

TABLE 5.2

Households With and Without Skilled Individuals
by Seasonality and Ethnicity

Workers' Characteristics (%):

| | *Seasonality | | **Ethnicity | |
	Seasonal	Year-round	White	Black
no skill	27.71	25.30	6.02	46.99
skill	28.92	18.07	24.10	22.89

*x^2=.723; df=1; p=.395 (not significant)
**x^2=15.652; df=1; p<.0001 (significant)

If we consider the above portrayal of workers and their households from a processual perspective, what emerges is a labor force pulled in many different directions yet continually drawn back to the low wages and unpleasant working conditions of seafood processing. Opportunities to improve skills, to develop small-scale independent-producer enterprises, to move to regions with more diverse job opportunities, and to acquire more education are forever frustrated by the overwhelming "presence" of seafood processing in their lives. While I will develop this argument further in later chapters, that workers are continually drawn back into the industry is a phenomenon enhanced and maintained by the patterns of network recruitment, the recruiting style of choice among employers in low-wage industries.

Recruitment

As in other low-wage and non-unionized blue-collar industries, kinship and informal social ties among workers play crucial roles in recruiting seafood processing workers. Earlier I noted the broad age range of the work force. The presence of extremely old and extremely young individuals reflects the tendency to utilize current workers' networks of friends and kin to locate and draw new workers into the plants. In seafood processing, it is common for mothers to recruit daughters, for aunts to recruit nieces, and for grandmothers to recruit granddaughters. This practice rapidly results in three generations being represented in the processing industry's age profile; we would also see this practice reflected in years of experience in the plants, which also has a broad range, from less than a year to fifty-one years.

Fully 54.2 percent of the work force were recruited to their current positions via a relative or close friend who already worked at the plant that hired them. Of these (N=45), 51.1 percent were related to other employees working in the plant. Many plant owners supplement network recruiting by sending vans to nearby communities to provide workers transportation to and from work, a service most efficiently provided when workers live in the same households and neighborhoods. Even using these measures, loyalty of workers to plants cannot be high, given owners' complaints of high labor turnover and my own finding that 51.8 percent of the workers currently work in more than one seafood house, a practice that wrangles plant owners. An owner in Belhaven, for example, reported that workers who didn't like his operation could easily find jobs at one of the other seafood houses in town. However, as table 5.3 shows, relying on other relatives to recruit new workers does, evidently, slightly reduce the possibility that those individuals will work in other seafood houses. Nearly 60 percent of the forty-five who were recruited with network ties do not work in other seafood plants, while over 65 percent of the workers who were not recruited through network ties do work in other seafood plants.

This is further evidence, too, that the influence of network recruitment extends beyond simply locating and bringing new workers into the plant. That network recruited workers seem less

TABLE 5.3
Workers Recruited Through Social Links
by Employment in Other Seafood Plants

Employment in Other Seafood Houses

Social Links Used in Recruitment	Yes	No	*Totals*
Links not used	25	13	38 (45.8%)
Links used	18	27	45 (54.2%)

Totals: 43(51.8%)   40(41.2%)   83
(x^2=5.488; df=1; p=.019; Phi=.2571)

likely to work in other seafood plants suggests that the presence of related individuals in the plant serves the needs of labor control. As in other industries, workers recruited through network ties must abide by company rules or face the prospect of causing job loss or discomfort on the job for other members of their network. While many have noted the relationship between network recruitment and labor control (e.g. Newman 1988; Burawoy 1976), the other side of this issue is that the presence of networks of related workers in the plant may also empower workers. Industrial sociology has long recognized that workers sometimes decide, among themselves, independent of management, to work at a certain pace and thus establish productivity levels below those they are able to attain. This practice, observed by F. W. Taylor, underlies his "principles of scientific management." Still taught in today's business schools, Taylor's principles led to the many ergonomic studies designed to transfer control over the pace of production from workers to management and machines. Through automation and the joint fragmentation-coordination of tasks in the plants, this has occurred to some degree in manufacturing throughout the United States. Despite changes in the work place, however, workers continue to make agreements with one another regarding conditions of work, even if such agreements remain confined to simple decisions such as changing from one seafood house to another. Network recruitment, and its consequence of the presence of other friends and kin in the plants, facilitates this process. As such, it serves as a source, or potential source, of power among workers. Whether it is a source of power among workers or a source of labor control for owners, however, depends on political, economic, and cultural conditions beyond the plant walls. The nature of economic growth in the area, the rate of unemployment, the ease with which women can dispute male authority or Blacks can question Whites—all these factors affect how much network recruitment empowers workers or becomes yet another tool of labor control. Among these "external" factors that can affect whether network recruitment becomes a tool for labor or a tool for management are the characteristics of workers' households, particularly their size, sex and age composition, and complexity.

Household Complexity

Through network recruiting, household structure becomes a reflection of the household's relation to the processing plants. This can be partially illustrated by examining household complexity. As an index of household size and composition, I focus here on household complexity, by which I mean, primarily, the number of generations present in the household. In my sample, I encountered one four-generation household (1 percent), eighteen three-generation households (22 percent), forty-four two-generation households (54 percent), and nineteen one-generation households (23 percent) (N=82). I call this "household complexity" because, compared to single-generation households, those households with more generations also tend to have more people, to have more jobs or more mixes of employment, unemployment, and underemployment, as well as to represent both sexes, and a wider range of ages, and to contain more lateral kin (e.g. aunts and uncles). Their relations with the industry are correspondingly more complex as well, as various members coming from different age groups become part of the industry's presence in the household.

Considering some basic statistics, first, in three-generation households, the senior generation tends to be active in the work force instead of living with children in retirement. Second, single-generation households tend to be older couples whose children have left home instead of young married couples or workers living alone. Only around one in six (16 percent) of the most complex households consists of old folks living with younger kin in lieu of moving into a nursing home. Not only are senior-generation individuals active in the work force, in over a third (37 percent) of the cases they support older unemployed children. Most support grandchildren as well, and 58 percent of the households contain persons in the middle generation who are over eighteen years old and still live at home; about half of these middle-generation individuals are also unemployed. Not surprisingly, then, although three-generation households contain an average of 2.8 people of working age, they contain only 2.4 working people. Compared to the less complex households this is not a particularly unfavorable ratio (0.85 jobs for each worker in the household), since two-generation households also have around 85 percent employment rates as well. One-generation households, however, actually boast employment rates of greater than 100 percent, with 1.22 jobs for each worker in the household. In other words, people in one-generation households, having no childcare responsibilities, can and do accept more than one job. Single-generation households, in addition to being less complex, usually have access to pension or social security benefits. It should thus come as no

surprise that these households are the least economically dependent on the seafood processing industry. Three-generation households, on the other hand, are the most dependent.

I measured economic dependence by creating an index that
scores respondents on the basis of the number of jobs in the
household, levels of education, skills, and other features that, when
combined, indicate the degree to which the respondent and his/
her household is dependent on the seafood processing industry
as a source of jobs and income.[2] The higher the economic
dependence score, in other words, the greater the household's
economic dependency on seafood processing. Using this measure,
I found that economic dependence on the seafood industry
increases significantly as household complexity increases, with
single-generation households having an average economic
dependence score of 7.9, two-generation households having an
average score of 13.3, and three-generation households having
an average score of 17.0; analysis of variance tests indicated
significant variance, moreover, among the three scores (p=.03).

These findings suggest that those workers who come from
three-generation households are most likely to provide the most
reliable workers, both because of their dependence on the industry
and because their households contain other individuals who can
work in the plants on either a casual or full-time basis, as well
as assume childcare and housework responsibilities. Plant owners
may actually enhance this pattern by specifically targeting three-
generation households as potential suppliers of part- or full-time
workers. In any case, the reliance on network recruitment serves
to create increases in dependence on the industry as more and
more people in the household are drawn into one or another plant.

As a final note to this discussion, I call attention to the
differences between more and less complex households with regard
to seasonality of workers, gender, and ethnicity. It is, to me, telling
that not only does economic dependence on the industry increase
with household complexity, so do those features that correspond
to the most exploited and the least and last rewarded members
of the U.S. labor force. Comparisons between Black and White
and male and female workers revealed that the proportions of
Black workers in one-, two-, and three-generation households
increases from 52.6 percent to 70.5 percent to 84.2 percent. The
relationship between household complexity and proportions of
female workers, however, is somewhat more curvilinear. It
decreases from 78.9 percent in one-generation households to 65.7

percent in two-generation households and increases from 65.7 percent to 94.7 percent from two- to three-generation households.

This should not be too surprising. A wealth of material documents that ethnicity and gender act as key features by which workers are differentially incorporated and treated in the labor market (Bonacich 1982; Gordon Edwards, and Reich 1982; Edwards, Reich, and Gordon 1973). Comparing men and women in the industry, I found that men differed from women in three ways: (1) women processed more seafoods per year; (2) women worked significantly fewer months in the industry per year; and (3) women worked for fewer years in seafood processing than men. Considering these findings, we must be careful to avoid tautological interpretations. In short, while it is clear that women process a wider range of species than men, we should not conclude that they are predisposed to such task assignments. The women have little choice about the tasks they perform in the plants, and task allocation draws upon and reinforces ideas about women being more adept at meticulous, tedious tasks than men. In other words, the underlying myths and traditions guiding processors' decisions to recruit workers and allocate tasks in the plants have been, and continue to be, sexist, as is common throughout the United States and global economies. The rural South has certainly not escaped these influences, and their concrete manifestations in the seafood processing industry serve, if anything, to reinforce and perpetuate sexism and racism. Thus processors tend to use men in more specialized capacities than women, and to keep them on for more months during the year. These features of jobs reflect the fact that they men's jobs are higher in plant hierarchies than the actual line positions held, for the most part, by women.

Further, we should not place full responsibility for these recruitment and task allocation measures on the shoulders of processors: the women themselves, who take the jobs and who often aid in recruitment, are no more immune to myths of gender than plant owners, nor are the men who refuse to take processing jobs at the level of the crab picker or oyster shucker.

The gender differences that exist in the industry reflect, of course, the disadvantaged positions of women *relative to men* in U.S. low-wage labor processes. Again, these differences reflect the general tendency for women in the United States to be channeled into the lowest strata of occupational hierarchies. Myths, as much as by actual hiring practices, contribute to this. An abstract of a recent article addressing this very issue provides a succinct summary here:

> Despite large structural changes in the economy and major antidiscrimination legislation, the economic well-being of women in comparison with that of men did not improve between 1959 and 1983. The women to men ratio of money income almost doubled, but women had less leisure while men had more, an increase in the proportion of adults not married made more women dependent on their own income, and women's share of financial responsibility for children rose. The net result for women's access to goods, services, and leisure in comparison with that of men ranged from a decrease of 15 percent to an increase of 4 percent, depending on assumptions about income sharing within households. (Fuchs 1986: 459)

While a few differences emerged from comparing male and female workers, comparisons of black and white workers demonstrated general uniformity across ethnic groups, a finding with which we introduce the proposition that, in work settings, racism erodes before sexism. Whether by legislative mandate or cultural pressure, men will hold out against granting equal rights for women longer than dominant or hegemonic ethnic groups will hold out against granting equal rights for other ethnic groups. While I discuss this in more detail later, it may be useful to keep in mind that racism and sexism are negotiated processes, not static labels for specific behaviors, and that there exist profound differences between sexism and racism (or ethnocentrism) in terms of the social fields in which they are raised, disputed, or reinforced. The concrete ways in which racism is negotiated include acts of violence, discrimination in courts of law, political zoning, group membership criteria, and so forth. These occur at much more public and more inclusive levels of social participation than the concrete ways in which sexism is negotiated. Sexism is taught, learned, argued, resisted, and submitted to in the privacy of homes as well as in communities, neighborhoods, and federal and state governments. The negotiation of racism is crosscultural, while the negotiation of sexism occurs within cultures, being more deeply entrenched in family and kinship ties, in domestic life, in the different strategies of play among little girls and boys.

But I'm getting ahead of myself, and I don't mean to imply by any means that racism has died out of the seafood processing industry while sexism remains. Black participation in the industry does differ from White, though less than the participation of women differs from that of men. Blacks demonstrate less of a tendency to change jobs (again, reflecting fewer job opportunities), they have slightly fewer years of schooling, and they tend to live in households with fewer skilled individuals—three differences which are, quite obviously, closely related to one another.

Comparisons by sex and ethnicity hint that workers' differential participation in the industry derives from broader features of the United States economy and society. Nevertheless, we cannot understand the industry as merely derived. North Carolina's unique context blurs or confuses the extent to which workers and employers may perceive the social and cultural implications of their hiring, working, task allocation, and task acceptance. Further work shows, in more detail, that the labels of gender and ethnicity are insufficient, by themselves, to illustrate the processes by which workers have been incorporated into seafood processing. The following chapter shows that there are even broader ecological, cultural, and sociological bases to workers' dependence and vulnerability.

Conclusion

Has this chapter contained many surprises? Not really. The social and economic landscapes of eastern North Carolina would lead us to expect to encounter workers of the kind characterized here. Their creative, household-level adaptations to their poverty, their lack of skills, and their low earning potential are paralleled by the equally creative ways that the owners of the plants draw these workers into production schedules and regimes. We have seen a social process in which recruiting operates as a labor control mechanism containing the seeds of worker resistance. People living in households with multiple jobs and multiple incomes, unable to draw comfort from their work experiences, withdraw into church, family, and community for sources of identity and strength. Yet once inside these social and cultural realms, they become vulnerable to the political orientations and ideologies of clergy, business leaders, and even family members who may sift their experiences through outdated or distorted perspectives. Such vulnerability grows as more and more members of workers' households, representing more generations, take jobs in the plants. The entanglements of social relations within households and between households and processing plants attach workers not only to the processing plants but also to eastern North Carolina. As workers become tied to the fates of the eastern counties, the contours of development, unemployment, low-wage industrial recruitment, or other processes help shape and reshape their household structures and lifestyles.

The effects of these multifaceted processes are probably most distinguished by their variability. Just as advanced capitalist expansion is uneven worldwide, its expansion into local areas also affects different segments of the population differently. In the following chapter, I examine the different segments of the seafood processing work force in more detail. I outline the foundations of these differences, as well as the ways such differences figure into the experiences of workers and plant owners in the wake of coastal conflicts and change.

Foundations of Divergence Within the Seafood Processing Labor Force

In the opening paragraph of the last chapter I mentioned that differences in seafood processing workers can be traced, in part, to the intimacy of their tie to the marine environment: simply, some come from fishing households and others do not. Coming from a fishing household influences recruitment, task allocation, supervision, means of payment, and other features of the labor process of seafood processing. Beyond the processing industry, the fishing background influences other aspects of workers' lives, such as settlement and residence patterns, political activity, relations between households, and relations between sexes and generations within the household.

The influence of fishing over other aspects of life is not confined to North Carolina, but occurs in other contexts as well (see Doeringer, Moss, and Terkla 1986). In fact, much of the literature on commercial fishing in the United States emphasizes its tendency to become more of a way of life than a mere means to make a living, similar to farming (see Smith 1977; Acheson 1978). I mentioned in the introduction of this work that I do not wish to contribute to this tradition. While such a portrayal may be generally accurate for some neighborhoods of fishermen, it has a tendency to reify the fishing lifestyle in such a way as to make it seem close knit, homogeneous, romantic, and idyllic. This creates a background against which the tensions and contradictions that emerge from this lifestyle, and are part of it, are perceived to be little more than the isolated difficulties of a few "complainers" or "whiners." Instead, I consider the difficulties of processing workers as key components of the ways families and social groups emerge, relate to one another, and change. The unpleasantness of seafood processing, the impoverished conditions of its workers, and the labor control mechanisms used in the industry are not merely negative appendages to a harmonious occupational community of fishers and processors. On the contrary, they are what Hermann Rebel, in his recent review articles (1989a, 1989b), would call "culturally necessary victimizations."

As noted in chapter 3, fishing in North Carolina is dominated by small, household-organized operations rather than large centralized fishing fleets. Although the menhaden fleet is an exception to this, outside of menhaden two forms of labor mobilization and labor control have emerged in the industry that processes the catch of these fishing households. Both are based on kinship ties, on the use of inequalities evolving out of ethnic and sexual status, and on the ability of processors to penetrate workers' households. In later chapters I discuss the ways in which these features of the labor process manifest themselves in workers' communities. Here I describe the basis for divergence between various branches of seafood processing, and how that divergence affects the responses of various segments of the industry to political and economic developments of the coastal zone.

The Seafood Processing Labor Force: An Exercise in Classification

First, let us consider differences between workers based on the species they process. Clearly, the species workers process influence such things as seasonality of processing, scheduling, the ways plants combine various species during their annual cycle, and workers' abilities to combine processing jobs with other occupations. Tables 6.1 and 6.2 present statistics describing workers by the species they process.

The most obvious conclusion to draw from these comparisons is the difference between menhaden workers and workers in other branches of the industry. Menhaden employees are more specialized, older, more experienced, and less seasonal than most workers in the industry. Other facts about the menhaden industry, mentioned earlier, also set it apart. It is, for example, the only branch of fish processing in the state that does not process fish for human consumption (although some menhaden products are used to make margarines for European consumers). It is highly capitalized and more obviously a "factory" operation. And it is a technologically sophisticated force in both the harvesting and processing sectors of North Carolina fisheries. For a number of reasons, then, the menhaden industry and menhaden workers stand alone from the rest of the processing labor force and industry. It does not follow from this that species constitutes *the* variable to use to differentiate between sectors of the industry, since workers in other branches of the industry are so similar to one another in other ways. Shrimp and scallop workers, for example, are nearly identical in terms of their seasonality. Oyster, scallop, and finfish workers process roughly the same numbers of species. Scallop and shrimp workers are more highly seasonal than others, while crab, oyster, and shrimp work forces have far greater proportions of female workers than do the others.

This variation, again, testifies to the need to combine both qualitative and quantitative information to illustrate the different paths by which the seafood processing industry has developed. Combining the variables presented above with those presented below (see table 6.3), we can see that the North Carolina seafood processing industry has developed along three lines. One segment consists of crab, oyster, and finfish (excluding menhaden) processors (category A in table 6.3). The second consists of shrimp, scallop, and clam processors (category B), and the third, of course, is the menhaden industry (category C).

Most of the differences between the groups of plants can be traced back to the fact that scallop- and shrimp-processing labor and harvesters tend to be members of the same family or the same community of relatives and friends. By contrast, there exist absolutely no close kinship or friendship ties between processing employees, the people who mobilize them to process (plant owners/managers), and the harvesting sector in the blue crab and oyster components of the industry. In short, workers in scallop and shrimp houses are far more directly involved in fishing than workers in blue crab and oyster houses. This basic difference underlies differences in the ways workers in the plants are located, recruited, and organized in the industry. Equally important, however, this basic difference results in differential impacts of various political and economic developments that commonly affect coastal environments. I briefly consider two related developments in terms of how they might affect workers and plant owners in the three different categories outlined above: limited entry or restricted harvesting programs and coastal real estate/tourist development.

TABLE 6.1

Selected Characteristics of Processing Workers by Species They Process (Ratio Level Variables)

Variables	Species					
	Crab	Oysters	Scallops	Shrimp	Finfish*	Menhaden

	Crab	Oysters	Scallops	Shrimp	Finfish*	Menhaden
Number of Commodities Processed:						
Mean	1.8	2.5	2.0	3.3	2.8	1.0
s.d.	.9	1.5	1.0	.4	.7	0
Rank	5	3	4	1	2	6
Number of Workers in Plant:						
Mean	24.6	36.5	19.7	29.3	23.3	19.2
s.d.	8.7	3.6	11.0	3.3	9.6	7.5
Rank	3	1	5	2	4	6
Age of Workers:						
Mean	39.5	51.5	31.1	34.1	33.4	52.8
s.d.	13.9	6.8	6.8	17.1	13.3	13.4
Rank	3	2	6	4	5	1
Number of Years in Seafood Processing:						
Mean	11.7	20.1	9.5	14.1	9.1	26.4
s.d.	11.5	11.9	7.9	12.9	10.4	13.7
Rank	4	2	5	3	6	1
Number of Months per Year in Seafood Processing:						
Mean	8.7	9.1	6.3	6.3	7.9	11.5
s.d.	3.3	.3	2.1	2.8	3.5	.7
Rank	3	2	5/6	5/6	4	1
Number of Jobs Held by Individuals in Workers' Households: **						
Mean	2.0	2.3	2.8	2.4	2.1	1.9
s.d.	1.0	.9	1.4	1.0	1.2	1.3
Rank	5	3	1	2	4	6
Number of Years of Formal Schooling:						
Mean	10.7	8.9	11.6	10.6	11.1	9.1
s.d.	2.3	3.6	1.6	1.4	1.5	3.9
Rank	3	6	1	4	2	5

Note: Doublecounting occurs where workers process more than one species.
*Does not include menhaden workers.
**Includes worker's job.

TABLE 6.2

Selected Characteristics of Processing Workers by Species They Process
(Nominal Variables—Figures are Percentages)

Variables		Species				
	Crab	Oysters	Scallops	Shrimp	Finfish*	Menhaden
County of Plant:						
Beaufort	47.1	50	0	35.7	34.5	0
Brunswick	9.8	50	0	0	0	0
Carteret	0	0	100	35.7	34.5	100
Pamlico	43.1	0	0	28.6	31.0	0
Worker Type:						
Seasonal	45.1	70	100	92.9	57.1	0
Permanent	54.9	30	0	7.1	42.9	100
Sex of Worker:						
Male	9.8	10	26.7	7.1	33.3	100
Female	90.2	90	73.3	92.9	66.7	0
Ethnicity:						
White	11.8	0	86.7	35.7	35.7	44.4
Black	88.2	100	13.3	64.3	64.3	55.6

*Does not include menhaden workers.

Labor Force Implications of Limited Entry and Coastal Development

Limited entry programs usually refer to state and federally mandated restrictions on harvesting certain species of fish, using certain types of gear, or fishing at certain times of the week, month, or year. Ostensibly, limited entry programs arise from concerns for the fishery resource or fish stocks and the perception that too many or too efficient of fishers have entered a specific fishery. In other words, it is believed that entry must be limited to prevent overfishing and the eventual depletion of the resource. These programs are framed as ways to protect the environment, usually drawing heavily on Hardin's "Tragedy of the Commons" model of environmental destruction under conditions of open access (Hardin 1969; Gordon 1954; cf. McCay and Acheson 1989). It is not my intention here to critique Hardin or his many followers. Nevertheless, it is necessary to point out that many studies have

TABLE 6.3

Selected Characteristics that Differentiate Categories of
Seafood Processors in North Carolina

Selected Characteristics	Category A	B	C
Seasonality	Low	High	Medium
Source of supply of processed product	Primarily out of state	Primarily local	Local
Primary Ethnicity of workers	Black	White	Black
Workers' relation to processor	"Conventional" employer/ employee	Family/ community member	"Conventional" employer/ employee
Relation between harvesting sector and labor force	None	Strong	Strong
Workers' control over processed product	None	Full	None
Means of reimbursement for labor	Wage or piece	Unpaid or self-employed	Wage or piece
Labor reliability	Low	High	High

documented ways in which fishers limit entry into a fishery
themselves (e.g. Bort 1987; McCay, Gatewood, and Creed 1989;
McCay and Acheson 1989; Overby 1988). Also, the regulatory
emphasis on environmental management obscures the way
limited entry programs may be used to further the interests of
dominant classes. Sometimes they are developed and implemented
with little or no regard for many of those who depend on the
resource. In northwest Newfoundland, for example, Sinclair
reports,

... licenses to participate in the near shore dragger fisheries
for groundfish and shrimp have been restricted since 1976.

In subsequent years the social structure of the fisheries was characterized by clearly defined groups of fishermen in conflict with each other and with the state. My contention... is that the licensing policy of the Canadian federal government has played a central role in determining the pattern of conflict that has followed. Social divisions based on prior technological innovation were solidified and made impermeable by the imposition of a policy that has protected the social position of a local elite of petty capitalist dragger skippers and their sharemen. (1983: 307)

In the present context we are interested in how limited entry programs might affect the different segments of the seafood processing industry. Initially, then, we need to qualify our discussion by saying that limited entry programs rarely apply to all species. Instead, most commonly, they target specific, usually valued species for "protection," due to perceived biological or economic pressures on the species or the species' role in a food chain upon which an even more valuable species depends. Thus limited entry programs are designed to reduce catches of mackerel, or catches of redfish, or catches of spiny lobster, not to restrict harvesting activities altogether or to close all waters permanently to the taking of all fish and shellfish. Although not usually referred to as limited entry, entry into a fishery also may be limited for public health reasons, such as red tide tainting oysters and other shellfish or the dioxins produced by paper and pulp mills tainting fish in estuaries or other coastal environments where such toxins might concentrate.

Most limited entry programs thus rest on the biological justifications of threats of overfishing or hazards to public health. Yet they tend to have complex origins and equally complex consequences for fishers, their families, and seafood processing workers. In the New Jersey surf clam fishery discussed by McCay, Gatewood, and Creed (1989), limiting entry led to consolidating labor in the fishery by hiring fewer crew members and moving them from vessel to vessel instead of staffing each individual vessel with its own crew. Another strategy that emerged following the regulations included diversifying fishing strategies, seeking a broader range of species. These consequences combined to make it difficult for small, independent fishers to compete with fishers possessing larger and more vessels. This occurred because, first, independent fishers could not keep their labor as productively employed as larger firms, who consolidated crews. Second, diversifying into new fisheries involved pioneering more markets and hence depended on the fishers' relations with the seafood processing/marketing industry. Simply, the larger vessel owning firms were either processors/fish dealers themselves or had close relations, by virtue of their size, with processors and dealers willing to purchase their catches.

In North Carolina, seafood processing in the scallop and shrimp fisheries, we have seen, tends to be dominated by smaller firms run by fishing families and staffed by the wives, daughters, sisters-in-law, and other relatives and friends of scallop and shrimp fishers. This represents a clear case of fishermen attempting to assume control of the market, recognizing, as social scientists have recognized, that those who control markets for seafood products (i.e. merchant capital) control fishers, their families, and their communities (Sider 1986; Valdes-Pizzini 1990; Wolf 1982; Faris 1971; Bort 1987; Antler and Faris 1979). Limiting entry into the scallop and shrimp fisheries would be devastating to these families, as witnessed when the red tides of 1987 and 1988 forced the closure of scallop beds (UNC Sea Grant Program 1988). By the same token, menhaden workers suffer under programs that limit entry or access to menhaden stocks, as occurred in 1985, when state regulators restricted the menhaden fishery in a way that stimulated some of the largest firms to close their North Carolina plants and operate out of Virginia. In this case, some eighty workers lost their jobs, despite the naive claims by those who wrote the regulations that "the menhaden firms were unhappy that regulations had finally come to their fishery, but happy they were not more stringent" (Orbach 1989: 203; cf. Garrity 1991). Evidently plant closures were an expression of this qualified joy.

The menhaden case is instructive in its evolution as well as its outcome. Pressures to limit menhaden fishing arose out of a dispute over the "appropriate" use of public resources—in this case, the ocean, its fish, and the ambience the sea lends to the coastal environment. On the surface of the dispute were typical allegations, arguments, and policy decisions: Sport-fishing groups argued that menhaden served as foodfish for king mackerel and so should be protected to preserve the mackerel stocks. The menhaden industry countered with its status as a traditional industry employing rural Black workers, as well as with biological evidence that less than 5 percent of the stomach contents of mackerel consisted of menhaden. Local tourism business interests argued that menhaden fish-kills repulsed visitors and damaged the coastal environment. Politicians and regulatory personnel expressed concern for their constituencies and declared that any regulation should be "fair" to all parties, reifying the process by which all points of view are considered and weighed in the regulatory decision (Garrity 1991).

Stripped of its many biological and environmentalist arguments and its formal proceedings, however, the dispute was over a more fundamental issue. Beneath the politics, the dispute was over whether this public resource should be used as capital, as a productive resource, capable of generating wealth, or whether it should be used as a consumer good, a resource whose only participation in the generation of wealth becomes indirect, as the principal attraction of tourist and real estate development, leisure activities, and sport fishers. In more abstract terms, this process is an attempt to rewrite the "cultural biography" of the coastal zone. This is similar to the process of singularization described by Kopytoff in his discussion of slaves: "What we see in the career of a slave is a process of initial withdrawal from a given original setting, his or her commoditization, followed by increasing singularization (that is, decommoditization) in the new setting, with the possibility of recommoditization" (1986: 65). Kopytoff is talking about rewriting the cultural biography of the slave. In the menhaden case, the participants involved were engaged in a collective revision and debate over the cultural biography of the coastal zone. In the one biography, the coastal zone plays an integral role in the economic and social reproduction of those engaged in commercial fishing and related industries. It doesn't just "have" a human component; it is defined, in large part, by its human component. In the other cultural biography, the coast exists apart from any specific process of social and economic reproduction. It reproduces itself for its own sake.

This latter biography emerges despite the fact that both uses of the coastal zone have concrete social and economic implications. Whether used as capital or as a consumer good, the coasts will continue to generate value. Yet the two uses involve distinctly different circuits of value and hence distinctly different trajectories of capital accumulation, enriching different social segments. Seen in this light, the implications of the dispute for fishing families (including seafood processing workers with close ties to fishers), become quite clear: as the sea becomes less of a productive resource and more of a consumer good, as it loses its status as capital (being channeled from one circuit of value into another), it loses that value that is created, by fishers, when their labor power interacts with and transforms nature, the value to which the labor of seafood processing adds (Marx 1967; Kopytoff 1986). Fishing families lose, in short, their ability to use the sea to generate wealth; the coastal community becomes the carpenter selling his hammer for a meal.

Of further interest in the menhaden case was that the dispute was, essentially, between competing segments within the same class instead of between different classes. Despite this, members of fishing communities, fishers' households, processing workers, and rural black workers were drawn into the dispute in both material and symbolic (i.e. biographical) ways. The menhaden industry includes corporations backed by major oil companies as well as smaller corporations run by families, yet throughout the dispute they attempted to focus attention on their history as a "traditional" industry upon which entire rural black communities had depended for generations. During interviews I conducted with menhaden industry plant managers and executives, what emerged were portraits of benevolent, family-owned businesses whose elders captained vessels as Hemingway's Old Man had and established thriving seafood processing businesses, generated revenues and employment, only to be driven out of business by foreign (Soviet) competition and government regulation. That these companies had no long-term interest in the welfare of black communities became clear when they cut back their North Carolina operations, laying off whole neighborhoods.

On the other side of the dispute were extremely politically powerful, well-funded groups of sport fishers. Although clearly representing capitalist interests, these individuals also attempted to play down their wealth and power in favor of presenting an image of the environmentally-conscious weekend fisherman concerned that the leisure activity he shares with his son was being undermined by big corporations.

While the black menhaden workers and the solitary recreational fisherman were both relied on as symbols of the dispute, the eventual regulation was no victory for the individual, but a victory for a segment of the capital-accumulating class and a loss for fishing families and communities in general. While this consequence may have been unforeseen or imperceptible to regulatory personnel, local agencies given the task of enforcing the regulations may have understood their essential logic. Most of the enforcement personnel have ties with the fishing community, or at least local society. Their initial response to the dispute and its outcome was in the form of a silent protest: simply, they ignored the new law, failing to fine vessels that didn't comply in the first few months following its passage.

Regulations such as those emerging from the menhaden dispute, in short, pave the way for leisure-oriented capital to increase its control over a public resource—the coastal zone—by changing it from an essentially productive resource into a consumer good. This involves rewriting its cultural biography as well as entails material consequences. Once the cultural biography of the coast has been rewritten or revised, leisure capital can restrict access to the coast in the well-known ways of tourist traps: exclusive resort development, privatized beaches, restricted parking, high costs of living, etc. To the extent that similar regulations occur in all coastal regions of the United States, limiting entry will further the concentration of capital in fish and shellfish processing and promote the location of processing facilities offshore (e.g. tuna in Mexico or factory vessels). These developments are likely to drive out of business those firms that rely on local catches, as well as provide a competitive edge to those set up to process imported marine resources, whether those imports come from other states or other countries. Thus, fishing families involved in the North Carolina scallop industry are likely to suffer, since their production operations involve harvesting and processing primarily local catches.

By contrast, limiting entry into the blue crab and oyster fisheries would probably have little if any impact on processing workers in the blue crab and oyster houses, since they process primarily imported marine resources. Because the range of species in such seafood houses include finfish such as flounder, workers in this segment of the industry may be productively employed with one species if another happens to be in short supply due to closures. The flexibility of this group of seafood processors carries important implications for the seafood processing labor process. It is in this sector of the processing industry that capital concentration is most likely to occur. Processors in this sector need not depend on either local catches or local fishers. Instead, they are well situated to create dependent relations with local fishers as they, the processors, assume more prominent roles in local economies. Thus, increasing the concentration of capital will increase the power of fish processors and merchants relative to fishing families. At the same time, it will place increased pressure on plants like blue crab and oyster plants to locate and keep workers, causing them to further penetrate workers' households and communities and, ultimately, to experiment with new labor recruiting methods and new sources of labor. Elsewhere I have mentioned that some crab and oyster processing plants in isolated counties in North Carolina have already begun importing Mexican women. In this capacity, they use special immigration provisions (H2b visas) which establish contractual arrangements between workers and employers similar to indentured servitude. During the summer of 1991, this labor importing program received media attention when the American Civil Liberties Union filed a lawsuit against processors on behalf of fifteen Mexican crab workers. The suit contends that the women experienced "sub-minimum wages, sub-standard living conditions, racial discrimination, and were held in virtual involuntary servitude" (*Raleigh News and Observer*, August 8, 1991: 1A). Such examples reinforce the idea that the impacts of developments in the local and national economies are differentially received by different industry sectors based on each sector's internal characteristics. The sector's internal characteristics, in turn, relate directly to the ways in which they interact with the coastal environment, the commodities they produce, and the local labor force.

Conclusion

While many similarities exist among North Carolina seafood processing workers, this chapter has shown that such unifying features as gender, ethnicity, and class may be either enhanced or undermined based on the extent to which production and family life become interwoven. That interweaving is itself a reflection or component of the various economies and ecologies of scallop, shrimp, blue crab, oyster, and menhaden fishing. These factors influence patterns of work organization, labor recruitment, labor control, and the potential for the industry to reinforce myths of gender and ethnicity. Equally important, the extent to which production and family life are interwoven affects the vulnerability of various industry sectors to capital concentration, competition from larger firms, and the ability of the firm to survive conflicts. The susceptibility to the increasing concentration of capital is particularly important in terms of strategies of labor control. In the short run, of course, capital concentration is liable to lead to unemployment among those attached to family-based harvesting and processing enterprises. In the long term, however, it is likely to lead to increased pressures to maintain more comprehensive levels of labor control. This translates into heavier reliance on marginal workers, new and illegal immigrants, refugees, and others who may be perceived to be particularly docile and easy to control. The recent use of H2b workers underscores this rather blatantly. Yet it is doubtful that this will be a uniform process. In the following two chapters, comparing poultry workers in four different regions of the southeast United States, we will see that labor control mechanisms vary according to the ways local and regional economic and social developments have contributed to their construction.

Family, Community, and the Construction of Labor Markets in the U.S. Poultry Industry

In the examination of seafood processing, I documented some of the key ways capital penetrates workers' households, as well as how different kinds of penetration underlie the susceptibility of the industry to political and economic developments that seek to control resources currently within the industry's grasp. Yet the problems experienced by the industry and its work force, its sexual and ethnic complexion, its patterns of growth and change, and other features, derive in part from unique local circumstances. These circumstances might include North Carolina's unique estuarine system, its historic animosity toward labor unions and labor organization, or trends in North Carolina demography. Thus the possibility remains that the findings presented above apply only to North Carolina. Such a possibility seriously undermines our claim that seafood processing labor processes are indicative of the general path by which advanced capitalism travels. With the material on poultry processing, however, I draw on a more regional and comparative study, focusing on plants in northeast Texas/southwest Arkansas, North Carolina, northern Georgia, and the Delmarva Peninsula.[1] There are distinct advantages and disadvantages to this. On the one hand, it hasn't been possible to conduct a survey of randomly sampled poultry workers. This is because, first, no complete list of workers exists and, second, the distance between plants and suspicion of plant managers prevented the cluster sampling approach we used in North Carolina. Because of this, we focus initially on the processing plant.

On the other hand, the regional perspective contains advantages all its own. The poultry industry has experienced much more ethnic and national heterogeneity than the seafood processing industry; in short, poultry plants include among their labor recruitment strategies the use of new immigrants and refugees. Considering the poultry industry allows comparisons that can help place both the seafood and poultry industries in a broader empirical and theoretical framework. It will also allow us to focus more explicitly on the ways in which local circumstances interact with regional, national, and international developments affecting low-wage workers.

Sexual and Ethnic Compositions of Plant Work Forces

Sexual and ethnic compositions of work forces in different regions lie at the heart of processing plant labor policies. Each region, to be sure, has its own distinctive ethnic mixture, as well as distinctive distributions of the sexes within ethnic groups. In all regions, however, work forces tend to consist of half women and half men. As shown in table 7.1, the two ethnic categories that most distinguish regions from one another are Blacks and Hispanics, and there is a clear break between the two more southern regions (Texas/Arkansas and Georgia) and the two more northern regions (North Carolina and Delmarva) in terms of the percentages of these groups in poultry plant work forces. Simply, the southern regions rely more on Hispanics and the northern regions rely more on Blacks. The similarity between the two southern regions is more than mere coincidence. Links between the two regions developed as the Texas economy declined during the early 1980s and Mexican/Mexican-American workers moved to the poultry processing region of north Georgia. In some cases, workers were referred to Georgia by Texas state employment service personnel; in other cases, they were drawn through network ties to those already there. Our interest in this regional distinction is all the more notable because the presence of Hispanics in the work force is correlated with lower wage rates for unskilled workers (Pearson r=-.296; p>.05). This compares to positive, though statistically insignificant, correlations between the presence of White (Pearson r=.083; p<.05) and Black workers (Pearson r=.166; p>.05) and wage rates.

TABLE 7.1

Sexual and Ethnic Compositions of Plant Work Forces by Region

	Texas/ Arkansas		North Georgia		North Carolina		Delmarva	
	W**	M	W	M	W	M	W	M
Percent of Workers Who Are:								
White (p=.143)								
minimum:	2.00	3.00	2.00	2.00	3.00	2.00	3.00	5.00
maximum:	49.00	36.00	47.00	51.00	49.00	49.00	15.00	32.00
mean:	17.25	16.67	22.75	24.92	16.07	18.79	8.18	12.64
s.d.:	15.98	12.42	15.43	15.24	15.22	16.50	4.33	7.78
Black*** (p=.020)*								
minimum:	0.00	0.00	0.00	0.00	2.00	5.00	20.00	16.00
maximum:	50.00	46.00	54.00	42.00	76.00	46.00	72.00	54.00
mean:	25.25	18.33	22.17	17.00	35.07	25.14	39.09	33.36
s.d.:	18.26	13.77	19.00	14.45	21.60	11.89	16.14	10.81
Hispanic (p=.036)*								
minimum:	0.00	0.00	0.00	0.00	0.00	0.00	0.00	0.00
maximum:	50.00	40.00	14.00	45.00	8.00	9.00	5.00	11.00
mean:	10.00	12.25	3.00	8.58	1.07	1.86	1.18	2.64
s.d.:	15.82	14.37	3.98	13.04	2.06	2.85	1.40	3.07
Asian (p=.056)								
minimum:	0.00	0.00	0.00	0.00	0.00	0.00	0.00	0.00
maximum:	1.00	1.00	5.00	5.00	2.00	1.00	5.00	7.00
mean:	.33	.42	1.00	1.17	.57	.36	1.54	1.72
s.d.:	.49	.51	1.35	1.75	.64	.50	1.57	2.24
Native American (p=.418)								
minimum:	0.00	0.00	0.00	0.00	0.00	0.00	0.00	0.00
maximum:	5.00	5.00	1.00	1.00	14.00	15.00	1.00	2.00
mean:	92	.83	.17	.08	1.86	2.14	.09	.27
s.d.:	1.73	1.47	.39	.29	3.94	4.86	.30	.65

Mean percentage of women per plant:
    49.00   50.69   53.79   48.00

Mean percentage of men per plant:
    51.00   49.31   46.21   52.00

Mean percent of workers who speak no English:
    6.33   3.92   3.68   2.64

*=Statistically significant (Analysis of Variance); probability levels refer to total percentages; percentages do not always add up to 100 due to rounding error.

**W refers to women, M to men.

***Includes Haitians.

Other notable differences between regions include the relatively high percentage of Asians (both Vietnamese refugees and, increasingly, Koreans) in the Delmarva plants compared to the other regions and native Americans in North Carolina plants. Interestingly, although Asians occupy a small place in most work forces, they occupy a revered position, in many processors' minds, as embodying the quintessential work ethic. This point will become more important as our analysis deepens.[2]

Finally, in all regions, plant managers reported that small portions of the labor force speak no English, although during a restudy of plants conducted in 1989 we found that non-English speaking workers had increased in the industry. In addition, plant managers usually clarified their answers here by saying that the workers had some "limited" knowledge of English, and that to characterize them as speaking no English at all was inaccurate. During site visits to regions, we found that English abilities among Mexican workers were, for the most part, restricted to the basics of purchasing food, using money, exchanging greetings, etc. Most commonly, if other languages are spoken in the work place, the language is Spanish or Spanish and Korean; languages cited by managers included, as well, Vietnamese, French (Haitian Creole), and Thai. Between 50 and 60 percent of the plants in each region have individuals who speak no English.

Changes in Labor Force Compositions Over Time

Somewhat more interesting than current ethnic mixtures in the plants are the ways that the ethnic compositions of plant labor forces have changed over time. Examining changes in ethnic composition—as reported by processing plant personnel managers—can give us some idea of the process by which various ethnic groups displace others in certain jobs or stimulate new recruitment strategies. In response to a question about how sexual and ethnic compositions of plant labor forces have changed over time, eleven categories of change emerged. Most readily apparent here is the extent of ethnic change that has taken place in the industry. While relatively few employers noted any change in the sexual compositions of their work forces, a relatively high percentage (at least 40 percent) in each region noted that their work forces had changed ethnically. Most notably, Hispanics and Asians have been taking up larger portions of labor forces in recent years. This is particularly the case for Hispanics and particularly in Georgia, where changes have had a far greater impact than in other regions.[3]

TABLE 7.2

Ethnic and Sexual Changes in
Plant Work Forces Over Time by Region

Region

Categories of Change	Texas/ Arkansas	Georgia	North Carolina	Delmarva	Mean
No change:	58.4	7.2	58.8	58.4	45.7
More women:	0.0	0.0	0.0	8.3	2.1
More men:	8.3	7.1	11.8	0.0	6.8
More Hispanics:	16.7	50.0	11.8	8.3	21.7
More Hispanics and Asians:	0.0	7.1	5.9	25.0	9.5
More Blacks:	8.3	7.1	0.0	0.0	3.8
More Whites:	0.0	0.0	0.0	0.0	0.0
More Haitians:	0.0	7.1	0.0	8.3	3.8
Fewer Asians:	0.0	7.1	0.0	0.0	1.8
Fewer Hispanics:	8.3	0.0	0.0	0.0	2.1
Unspecified change:	0.0	7.1	11.8	0.0	4.7

Between 1988 and 1989, the process of ethnic change assumed new dimensions, as Hispanics populations grew in plants that used them in 1988 as well as began moving into the work forces of other plants. Asians, however, have tended to leave the plants, being more upwardly mobile, taking advantage of refugee services to improve English skills, and moving into better paying jobs. Examining the character of the changes in more detail will provide more insight into how labor policies in the plants have been affected by immigration policy. Along these lines, a selection of plant managers' discourse, elicited in response to questions about ethnic change in their work forces, is telling:[4]

We've had more Koreans and Hispanics; drastic increase this last month in Hispanics. Probably due to drought.

Six months ago the work force was 65 percent black, 15 percent white, 15 percent Hispanic, 5 percent Asian, but now it has changed to 49 percent black, 11 percent white, 33 percent Hispanic, 7 percent Asian. The reason for the change was that the Midwest drought has brought them here looking for work. The available labor was not here (we have 2.6 percent unemployment in the area and were having problems filling jobs). We needed the workers, but we didn't recruit them. They just came to the area. But since then, they have proven to be such good, stable workers that we've been recruiting more Hispanics to stabilize the work force.

We've seen more Hispanics—they just moved into area; friends or relatives recruit them.

We haven't had much change so far, but it will change soon— we're involved in Korean program, soon will have two hundred new Koreans; they will end up replacing blacks because of high black turnover.

Over the last three months, Mexicans have replaced Vietnamese, almost entirely.

We needed the Hispanics and have worked hard to keep them. In 1986, Hispanics started to come looking for work in Texas, North Carolina, Georgia; they filtered down.

We've hired more Hispanics out of necessity; this season they're coming from the fruit and vegetable harvests, but we used to have some permanent workers.

We keep getting more and more Hispanics and more Koreans. (A local vegetable grower has always had Hispanics). Mexicans come in for the vegetable harvests, work for the season there, then we hire them and try to keep them. Now we also have thirty convicts on work release programs.

Three themes emerge from these statements. First, employers recognize strong relationships between agricultural and plant work forces, drawing direct correlations between increases in Hispanic applicants and decreases in agricultural employment (due to droughts of the tail ends of vegetable harvests). This hints at dynamic connections between various segments of rural labor markets, suggesting that the poultry processing work force possesses a wide range of labor market experiences in low-wage, unskilled, and hazardous jobs. Second, the ethnic change is recent, having taken place primarily since 1980. The plants, in short,

are drawing upon *new* immigrant populations. Finally, and most
importantly, once employers become familiar with Hispanics and
Asians, they make active attempts to recruit them, through
network ties, sometimes at the expense of black and white native
workers.

One further, notable feature of ethnic change concerns
Asians, primarily Koreans and Vietnamese: plant managers tend
to have mixed or ambivalent feelings about them. On the one
hand, managers perceive Asian workers as hard-working, good
employees; on the other, they question their loyalty to the plant
and perceive them as working their ways out of poultry processing
and into either better or higher paid jobs or independent economic
activities (e.g. shrimping).[5] Nevertheless, some plant managers,
particularly on the Delmarva Peninsula, have been actively
pursuing a program of importing Korean workers. Even this
program, however, received mixed reviews: one plant personnel
manager said that their plant had not pursued this alternative
because the imported workers were not bound to work at their
plant any longer than the first few minutes of the first day. This
same personnel manager told of a case where one plant in the
area imported some Koreans and they worked only until they
found out that another nearby plant paid 5 cents per hour more.
In the words of another plant manager:

> We're looking to bring in Koreans and people from lower
> Texas, and to expanding our recruiting, moving people,
> helping them find homes and pay their deposits. This is a
> mess, because we bring them in and have to put them in
> [nearby town] because we don't have housing here. They
> usually end up getting a job in [the town] or going home
> after we have wined and dined them.

Plant managers' experiences with a variety of different ethnic groups have influenced their attitudes about different work
habits based on ethnicity. Overall, 72.5 percent of the personnel
managers (N=55) interviewed said that different ethnic groups
had different attitudes toward work and different work habits.
Regionally, 66.7 percent of personnel managers in Texas/
Arkansas agreed with this, 84.6 percent in Georgia, 70 percent
on the Delmarva Peninsula, and 68.8 percent in North Carolina.
Again, plant managers' discourse here is particularly telling:

Koreans and Hispanics are very hard workers—but Koreans are probably the best. The white and black work ethnic is sinking.

I have been in the industry eight years and have worked in areas that have used many different ethnic groups. Cambodian and Loatian women are best workers—Hispanic men good workers, but when one leaves, they all leave. Oriental population is great in Atlanta. They have worked hard to educate themselves and better their position in society. Take a group of black and white workers and bring in Asians or Mexicans and the others (blacks and whites) will start to work harder and have less absences.

The Mexicans work every day every hour they can—we used to have a problem filling orders, but not since we got the Mexicans.

Vietnamese and Spanish start working hard when they first get here, but after a while they must get Americanized, because their productivity and attendance fall off.

Vietnamese kept their heads down and elbows flying; I would like to have some back.

Asians are very conscientious, have very good attendance— blacks have high turnover.

Koreans have an excellent work ethic. We have problems with blacks—30-40 percent do not care if they work or not.

Our experience is that the Hispanics are very conscientious and grateful for nice jobs; we have very few problems with Hispanics. I came from a different area of Texas and at first, my attitude was that Hispanic workers should be sent back; but after working with the Hispanics, I found that they are hard workers with a good attitude and they are working to make a better life.

We had difficulty at first keeping Asians and Hispanics on line—they were used to taking breaks when they get tired. Have overcome this now. I'd like to bottle their work ethic— work ethic is good and some have moved up.

Vietnamese will work for 50 cents an hour. There's a lot of opportunity there.

Hispanics—finest workers, on time, work hard, very organized. Often grant one month leave to go home and grant them status back, because it would be greater hardship to lose worker completely. He will come back because of benefits.

Immigrants work hard and show up. Work ethic has gone to hell; wish I could get some boat people.

A lot of blacks don't work as hard as Hispanics, but the legalized Hispanics tend to not work as well as when you could hire illegals.

The clearest theme to emerge from these statements is the belief that Hispanics and Asians have superior work habits at the same time the work ethic among blacks and whites has been deteriorating. Coupled with the information on ethnic change, this theme is significant in that Hispanics and Asians have been more prevalent in the work force in recent years. Interesting other comments further suggest that plant employers have developed a preference for new immigrant and refugee populations, whether Hispanic or Asian. This suggests that they have developed a preference for those most likely to be illegal aliens, unused to or unfamiliar with U.S. working conditions, patterns of authority in the plants, or the U.S. labor market. For example, the managers who said that different work habits were a result of "more the level of society than maybe the race"; or "Vietnamese and Spanish start working hard when they first get here, but after a while they must get Americanized, because their productivity and attendance fall off"; or "the legalized Hispanics tend to not work as well as when you could hire illegals" hinted that the newness of the ethnic group was more of a factor in work habits or work ethics than ethnicity itself.

Also of interest in these comments is that ethnicity has been associated with specific tasks in the plants, as evidenced by statements such as the following:

Asians like to do more skilled jobs (deboning and cutting); Hispanics don't care which job they do. Hispanics like to work overtime and Asians feel the same way. Not as loyal to company—they will leave for 5 cents more somewhere else.

Mexicans are hard workers; Vietnamese do any hard-working job, but can't communicate; they hate live-hanging. Would work day and night, money oriented, good with knife. They live in shacks but drive Trans Ams, live with a lot of people. We use white women for interpreters; they won't do rework— very loyal to company.

Asians are very good cutters. Haitians are good at gut pulling.

This is important because plant tasks are coordinated, integrated to the extent that when certain key tasks are understaffed the entire plant's production schedule suffers. This is especially true with jobs associated with receiving or live-hanging—the place where the birds are initially prepared for killing and their subsequent passage through the plant. Over 45 percent of personnel managers cited these jobs among the jobs with high labor turnover. In his study of Utah processing, Walker (1987) found that key tasks such as these, with traditional high labor turn over, were occupied by illegal immigrants. Their presence, in this case, was thus complementary to native workers' tasks in the plants, rather than a threat to native workers. Processors we interviewed, in north Georgia primarily, also indicated that Hispanics were occupying positions in the plants that natives refused to take; many workers and community members we interviewed in Texas saw Hispanics as complementing the native labor force as well. Most commonly, in Texas and the other regions, workers and community members stated simply that few native workers wanted to work in the plants.

At the same time, though, some workers in Texas perceived Hispanics (some of whom were illegal) as threats to their jobs at the plants because, they said, the plants were actively attempting to hire Hispanics over other ethnic groups. According to one worker, "The bosses don't want any more whites or blacks. If there is a Mexican there they will hire them first." In Arkansas, a July, 1988, inspection at a processing plant by the border control and immigration officials resulted in indictments against three people at the plant for providing illegal aliens with false documents. In yet another plant in that region, workers reported that, in the past, some of the office/clerical staff had been jailed for driving Mexicans over the border. These comments, in combination, suggest that plant involvement with illegal immigrant populations has been great in the Texas/Arkansas region. Indeed, with the exception of eastern North Carolina, interviews with workers and others in the industry in the other three regions (including western North Carolina) indicate similar penetration of plant work forces by illegal immigrants. By the summer of 1989, moreover, this practice had diffused even into eastern North Carolina. Combining this information with comments of plant personnel managers regarding work habits of ethnic groups raises an interesting question: If, early in their experience, plant labor policies target new immigrants to work in tasks that native workers will not perform, might they later use them in an expanded capacity, given an apparent preference for Hispanics and Asians over native whites and blacks? Their potential for expanding the use of new immigrant Hispanics and Asians at the plants, moreover, is facilitated by current patterns of recruitment.

Network Recruitment

Network recruitment, or the recruitment of friends and relatives of current workers, is an industry norm. Table 7.3 presents some of the basic parameters of network recruitment by region.

TABLE 7.3

Network Recruitment by Region

Region

Variables	Texas/ Arkansas	North Georgia	North Carolina	Delmarva
Percent of processors who use network recruitment with a bonus:				
	0.0	50.0	29.4	58.3
Percent of processors who use network recruitment without a bonus:				
	66.6	35.7	70.6	41.7
Percent of processors who do not use network recruitment:				
	33.3	14.3	0.0	0.0
Percent of work force recruited with network recruitment:				
minimum	1.00	5.00	3.00	1.00
maximum	99.00	85.00	80.00	65.00
mean	51.67	36.00	33.83	24.45
s.d.	36.15	26.65	26.73	22.23

While only 36.4 percent have a bonus system, in which workers receive payments for recruiting friends and kin, fully 89.1 percent of the plants utilize current workers as labor recruiters. Regional differences in network recruitment are interesting in that there exists an inverse relationship between the pervasiveness of network recruitment and the percent of workers recruited in this way. In other words, while the smallest percentage of processors in Texas/Arkansas use this technique, those who use it use it more intensively than processors in other regions. By contrast, Delmarva processors use paid network recruitment more than any other regions' processors, yet smaller proportions of workers in that region are recruited in this way.

These differences seem related to the ethnic mixes in plants in each region, suggesting that certain ethnic groups practice ethnic recruitment more readily than others. Although table 7.4 shows no direct correlation between extent of network recruitment and a specific ethnic group, it does rank the three ethnic groups in terms of network recruitment and shows that Hispanics rank first, blacks second, and whites third.

TABLE 7.4

Correlations Between Degrees of Network
Recruitment and Ethnic Groups

Degree of Network Recruitment

	Pearson score
Percent Hispanic	.238 (p>.05)
Percent Black	.038 (p>.05)
Percent White	−.237 (p>.05)

Network recruiting does not exist in isolation from other developments in the local economy and society. In some cases, for example, it has been used as a tool to *construct* labor markets by initiating migrations into communities and regions. This has been accomplished in combination with formal recruiting mechanisms as well, such as enlisting the aid of local employment offices and other federal and state programs (the Job Training Partnership Act, Association of Farmworkers Programs, and Targeted Jobs Tax-Credit programs).

The above comparisons among ethnic groups also suggest that network recruitment programs may be most effective among populations with the most tenuous of positions in the U.S. labor market: refugees and illegal immigrants. In this case, poultry processors rely not only on informal authority of the ethnic group, they also, indirectly, rely on the formal authority of the United

States government. This is because U.S. immigration policy confers various tenuous legal statuses on illegal immigrants and refugees, statuses that influence their behaviors in the plants. This point is particularly significant in the wake of recent immigration reform laws, which have resulted in new legal statuses (e.g. Seasonal and Replenishment Agricultural Workers—SAWS and RAWS) as well as the expansion of temporary worker programs. These laws have introduced more diversity into U.S. labor market structure and hence more potential for using workers from different circumstances against one another. In my discussion of union activity in poultry processing plants in chapter 4, I noted that attempts to organize workers in some plants met with limited success because employers were able to generate confusion over the legalization provisions of IRCA.

The ease with which employers use these legal status issues to confuse workers may be enhanced by the new immigrants' and refugees' inexperience with life in the United States. This inexperience often includes a lack of skill with the English language and no direct access to information that might contradict or clarify information coming from the employer. As Keesing notes in a recent article (1987), drawing on Foucault and others, the distribution and control of information and knowledge has long been a source of power. Also, the use of language as a tool of isolation and exploitation is significant in the tendency for many low-wage labor settings in the United States to be dominated by Spanish (Algren de Gutiérrez 1987). With the proliferation of legal documents printed in Spanish, however, some Hispanic workers— primarily Puerto Ricans—become more enlightened and simultaneously less preferred. As this occurs, employers move on to other, more recent ethnic groups. In the poultry industry this has included new immigrant Hispanics, Koreans, Southeast Asians, or monolingual speakers of Indian languages (e.g. Kanjobal) from Central America. The newness of an ethnic group facilitates more effective network recruitment, because new ethnic groups have fewer contacts outside their networks. In the Massey, et al. (1987) study of migration between the United States and Mexico, researchers found, not surprisingly, that the number of friends outside one's immediate ethnic group increased along with one's experience in the United States. The speed with which one establishes these ties also varies by the historical depth of the ethnic group itself in the United States, since new immigrants can take advantage of previous immigrants' network ties. Both the pace of network formation and experience can be modified by the nature of an ethnic group's incorporation into U.S. economy and society. Refugee groups, more subject to government resettlement programs, may be less adept at forming ties outside their ethnic groups than illegal immigrants who settle and percolate through society differently than refugees. Thus the state has not been merely a passive or instrumental participant in the construction of labor markets, but has provided various legal and institutional mechanisms for their construction.

In addition to network recruitment, processors also enhance recruitment in three ways: (1) by providing workers with transportation to and from work, sending vans into both rural and urban areas; (2) by expanding their recruitment efforts to wider and wider areas; and (3) by using new recruiting tools such as bilingual poster campaigns and radio announcements. Many of these attempts have been added in the past few years. We noted above that 48.2 percent of plants had seen their labor supply problems worsen in recent years; processors perceive an even greater labor supply problem in the future. Again, this varies regionally, with only 17 percent of Texas/Arkansas processors fearing future labor problems, compared to 73 percent of North Carolina processors, 86 percent of north Georgia processors, and 92 percent of Delmarva processors.

Nearly all Delmarva and a substantial portion of north Georgia processors foresee labor supply problems in their futures. Fears of future labor supply problems has a positive impact on wages. Those who foresee labor shortages pay an average of 32 cents per hour more than those who foresee no labor problems (t-test p=.028). Moreover, the presence of Hispanics in a labor force seems to quiet processors' fears concerning future labor problems: those who foresee problems have an average of 15 percent fewer Hispanics in the labor forces (t-test p=.003).

Recruitment campaigns and labor relations have undergone revision in light of past and present labor supply and retention problems and in the shadow of future problems. Among the alternatives being considered, only 20 percent of processors are planning on enhancing processing jobs themselves by offering childcare services, paying higher wages, increasing benefits, or even using the "quality circle" type of modifications recommended by Peters and Waterman in their book on excellence in U.S. business (1982). Somewhat more popular (among 42 percent of processors) are solutions such as increased mechanization, increased labor supplies (as opposed to retention) via imports of workers from other states or other countries, expanding current recruiting efforts with vans and low-income housing, or promoting bilingual speakers to supervisory positions to aid in recruitment and training. These latter methods are in line with recent trajectories of advanced capitalism. Instead of creating a work setting in which long-term, stable, loyal workers feel comfortable working, more processing plant managers are capitalizing on the geographical mobility of workers and the use of workers over which they have ever greater control. Such labor practices rest, ultimately, on the use of new immigrant and refugee workers or other workers who exist on the margins of the labor market. Workers who meet these criteria often, out of necessity, maintain complex social linkages to support systems beyond those provided by capital or by the state. These social linkages derive from, as well as facilitate, network recruiting and the labor control mechanisms that network recruiting entails. Because new immigrant and refugee populations seem to engage in network recruiting more than native minorities, women, or white workers, it should come as little surprise that poultry processing plants are pioneering new labor processes based on accessing new immigrant and refugee populations.

North Georgia and North Carolina Revisited: 1988 to 1989

As noted above, during the first phase of this study we discovered that poultry plants in north Georgia and western North Carolina had been recruiting heavily among Hispanic populations. In particular, they targeted new immigrant, largely Spanish-speaking, monolingual populations, often drawn from the farm labor market. These recruiting efforts were quite consciously designed to assure a continued Hispanic applicant flow (Griffith and Runsten 1988). They were enhanced by aggressive network recruiting, employing Spanish-speaking personnel office workers, and promoting bilinguals to supervisory positions. At that time, neither all of the north Georgia plants nor all the western North Carolina plants were hiring from Hispanic populations, and practically none of the eastern North Carolina plants were tapping into new immigrant Hispanic networks to recruit workers. Yet by the spring and summer of 1989, this practice had diffused to virtually all the north Georgia plants, throughout western North Carolina, and into eastern North Carolina. This recruiting, moreover, has not been confined to Mexican Americans or Hispanic U.S. citizens. Only five (19 percent) of the twenty-six firms we revisited had no green card workers in their plants, and two of those anticipated hiring green card workers in the future. We tend to use the size and character of the Hispanic population in the plant as a barometer of the plant's susceptibility to immigration reform. While this may seem discriminatory, the qualitative and quantitative information we have received from various sources suggests that, in fact, such things as green card workers, INS raids, and so forth increase along with increases in the Hispanics in the plants.

Change has also occurred in the extent of Hispanic hiring both within the plants themselves and, as noted above, within the total population of plants. Currently, 92 percent report Hispanics in their work forces, up from 85 percent in 1988. Inside the plants, Hispanics have grown by anywhere from 3 percent to 80 percent, judging from comments such as the following. This sampling represents responses of 58 percent of the plant personnel managers to a question about changes in their plants labor forces from last year to this:

We just had five Hispanics last year, now twenty. They just show up.

Whites are the same; blacks same; but we had two Hispanics last year, and now have fifteen.

We have two hundred more Hispanics now. Asian men and women are decreasing slowly, moving to bigger cities.

Maybe we have 1 or 2 percent more blacks. We had seven Hispanics last year, but we've seen an 80 percent increase; now they make up 12-13 percent of seventy-three workers.

Whites and blacks—same. Had ten Hispanics last year, twenty-five now.

Last year: 9 percent (62) Hispanics. This year: more than 20 percent (140) are Hispanic. This has been our only change.

We've had an increase in Hispanics: from 16 percent last year to 30 percent now.

We added Hispanics: thirty-five-forty now, mostly due to changing our location.

One of the key question to arise from the growth in Hispanic workers is whom are Hispanic workers replacing, or displacing? In an industry with as high labor turnover as we find in poultry processing, the line between replacing workers and displacing workers blurs as plants adopt recruitment policies aimed more at one group of workers than another. Clearly, plant personnel managers prefer Hispanic workers to other ethnic groups—Black, White, American Indian, even Southeast Asian. The Southeast Asians were initially seen by poultry industry personnel as hard working, valued employees; this positive attitude has become shrouded with ambivalence. Many plant personnel managers expressed concern that the Southeast Asians would not last long in the industry, perceiving them as more educated than Hispanics, more ambitious in the job market, and more oriented toward saving and opening their own businesses. Revisiting poultry plants a year after the original survey, we encountered this ambivalence again. From an in-depth interview with a plant personnel manager, I recorded the following:

He [the personnel manager] has seen many more Hispanics with work permits in the past year than in previous years... The Hispanics have pretty much displaced the S.E. Asians, he said, as well as many of the blacks... During this part of the conversation he also began comparing ethnic groups— S.E. Asians tended not to last, because they were more "education-motivated." "They work here only until they can save up enough to get to technical school, where they can learn about computers." A lot of them have parents and other relatives in Vietnam whom they send remittances. "The Mexicans, though," he said, "are more in it for themselves. They want to work a couple of years to get money to buy a little piece of land, and they don't care much about becoming legal citizens, as do the Asians (the Asians have no choice— they can't go back)." Also he said the Asians were more educated prior to coming to the U.S., where many of the Hispanics ("a high percentage," he said) are illiterate even in Spanish. (Griffith's field notes, spring, 1989)

While these views are not held by all personnel managers, others reported "cutting Orientals" from their labor forces or observing that "Laotians are hard workers, but they save money and go into business for themselves." A union official in Kansas, speaking of meat packing instead of poultry processing, said that the industry had "already used up the Southeast Asians. They went right through them. Now they're going through the Hispanics." He was referring, of course, to the tendency for tasks in some (not all) meat packing plants to literally wear workers down until they are crippled by carpal tunnel syndrome or other occupational hazards.

As further evidence that Hispanics are being hired more than other ethnic groups, the following comments of the plant personnel managers concerning ethnic recruitment are notable in their overwhelming focus on Hispanic recruitment and the fact that most other ethnic groups receive no mention whatsoever:

> We've been satisfied with Hispanics. We have a lady who married a Hispanic and she is helping us now by letting us know when some more are coming. We are expecting a few more in the next few days.

> They [Hispanics] have better quality work and are dependable. Would hire more if good. They always want to work.

> We're enthused with work ethic of Hispanics. Wish we could bottle it. It is not unusual to have a Hispanic come up after working eight hours and want more work. The Laotians are hard workers, but they save money then go into business for themselves.

> Biggest difference since last year is our Hispanics. They don't mind working and working on a regular basis. Our work force is stable, but if it changes, I will consider all options.

> We've had real good luck so far with Hispanics—real motivated, always show up. Would like 10 percent Hispanics in work force: advertising and word of mouth will get us the 10 percent.

> We're working with job services in Gainesville where there are lots of Hispanics. The Department of Labor is helping us get organized to recruit them.

> We're looking into the Gainesville population of Hispanics and I am looking into establishing a mobile home park. Then we can go into Texas area.

We don't anticipate changing anything. We have steady flow. Hispanics are outstanding workers. They do a great job.

Hispanics have better work ethic. All our recruitment of them is word of mouth—we don't promote. We've got no game plan for recruiting.

Right now there just aren't many Hispanics who are migrating—they come one at a time. When they come in groups, if one's late, they're all late. One quits, they all quit.

Probably the principal group the Hispanics are replacing in the poultry plants are the Blacks. Again, there exists a fine line between displacing and replacing, and many Blacks still work in the plants; however, some personnel managers openly reported hiring Hispanics to replace what they called their "sorry Black workers." An issue directly related to the displacement of Blacks by Hispanics in the plants is the displacement of Blacks by Hispanics in the social and cultural spaces of places like Gainesville, Georgia, a town known for its poultry plants (indeed, one of its water towers reads "Poultry Capital of the World"). As one would expect, the Hispanics have moved into the low-income housing/ghetto areas of Gainesville, areas previously inhabited predominantly by Blacks. Outside of the subsidized government housing, they compete with Black families for living space, as well as share the same social space during leisure hours, flavoring local culture with Hispanic music, food, odors, etc., that may be perceived by Blacks as an infringement upon their own cultural space. Reports concerning Black-Hispanic relations in this section of town were mixed, with some saying tensions ran high and others reporting no troubles at all. The Hispanic presence in the Black community has, however, raised the general level of hostility and hatred directed toward minorities in general in the South. At a Ku Klux Klan/Skinhead march on September 2, 1989, in Gainesville, a march billed in the news paper as being "in protest of the immigrant community," (*The Gainesville Times*, p. 1), most of the placards carried by the marchers focused on Blacks and Jews instead of Hispanics, suggesting that their very presence serves as a rejuvenating force among groups and individuals given to hostility toward Blacks, Jews, feminists, and homosexuals. Again, quoting from my field notes:

As a response to the growing Hispanic community, the KKK & skinheads, along with assorted unsavory characters, marched through downtown Gainesville today. It was a clear, hot day, and shortly after noon they began to congregate in a parking lot across from a group of municipal buildings. All around were police—state, county, city, in different colors, helmeted, with gas masks hanging from their belts.

The KKK, skinheads, and others occupied the central portion of the parking lot, milling around, trying to organize enough to march. Surrounding the lot, facing the onlookers with their backs to the marchers, were police without colors, wearing all black uniforms, helmets, and bullet-proof vests in the 86-degree heat. They were to lead the parade, in a quick march step, carrying these blond wooden night sticks that were as long as baseball bats but thinner, sleeker. On the other side of their human wall were the spectators—the disorganized, detached ones like me and the organized ones, members of a New York-based outfit called THE ALL PEOPLES CONGRESS. They came with their own bullhorns and chanted anti-KKK slogans like, "Jews, Blacks, Women, Gay—we don't need the KKK." In response to this, among other things, an old man, in his seventies at least, thin, lily white, wearing a Panama hat and open-necked blue shirt like a country barber's, raised a sign above his head that read, in crude lettering, PRAISE GOD FOR AIDS.

When the march began, led by the goosestepping police and three long, white cars with Klan markings, carrying fat old white men, the police made us line up along a white line on the street and guarded us with their long night sticks. A Black woman standing near me said, "I think it's interesting that the police always face us." Another woman near me recognized one of the riders in the second car. It was J. B. Stoner. When I asked who he was, she said, "He's the one who burned that Black church in Alabama."

The marchers on foot were segmented into KKK first, wearing their silky robes and pointy hats like elegant dunce caps—some black, some white, some white with green trim, as if saying if they had to look like a confederacy of dunces, they were bound to be dunces with a sense of style. Behind the Klansmen walked the skinheads, and behind the skinheads were a cluster of loosely organized marchers without uniform dress, some of them young mothers with infants, all carrying rebel flags.

The rebel flag was the principal flag of the whole march. Klansmen and skinheads carried it alike, along with placards bearing racist slogans. A rebel flag flew from the grand wizard's long Buick, and some of the younger women and children carried smaller, hand-held flags. Among these were their banners and placards. Both the All Peoples Congress and the marchers carried them, of course, but those carried by the skinheads were by far the most hateful and vivid: "Immigration is Jewish," read one. Another had a picture of a caricatured Black man, Sambo-like, with the exaggerated features of the old cartoons, and read, "Equal to What?"

The people roaming in and out among the marchers were also interesting. They seemed to be security people, of sorts, for some wore combat fatigues and others wore scary looking black uniforms with armbands. The armbands bore Nazi emblems—swastikas, iron crosses, the twin SS lightening bolts. These guys had a very paramilitary look. Walking around and through the entire march, carrying a bullhorn, was a woman in Klan garb that couldn't have been much over four feet tall. She shouted orders to the others about how to arrange themselves, while the men in fatigues led White Power chants and said things like, "We don't need no Gook nor Taco vendors neither."

Conspicuously absent from the crowds, however, were Hispanics and Southeast Asians. I say conspicuous was their absence because in a town the size of Gainesville, Georgia, a substantial population of Hispanics stands out. Here, at night, in the grocery stores and fast food restaurants, sharing the same space with the Blacks, the Latinos and Southeast Asians tend to stand out.

The KKK march illustrates not only the depth and character of the fear and hatred of nonwhites in the South, but drives home, quite blatantly, the notion that perceptions of various "others"— minorities, new immigrants, homosexuals, feminists—are continually negotiated and revised in public and private spheres of social action. While the KKK strategy is to lump all "others" together, poultry processing plant personnel managers distinguish among ethnic groups as part of their developing ideas about the work habits of various workers. In the words of one personnel manager, "Not many Hispanics come. Not many farms around and no housing—some were coming sixty-five miles one-way. So right now we can't bring them in easily. Management is split as to whether Hispanics are reliable and will stay. So it's tough to decide if we should recruit." In this case, obviously, the personnel mangers have been discussing Hispanics as a component of plant labor policy, considering whether or not they should embark on an active recruitment campaign or rely on labor market mechanisms. One of the cultural characteristics of Hispanics—their attitudes toward work—is a point of discussion, negotiation, and revision in the closed and private discourse of personnel managers. At the Klan march, considerations of non-white culture are anything but private. Indeed, they are designed to generate and spread fear, hatred, and terror through the community. Such public reinforcement of so horrifying of ideas is sure to yield intimidation, violence, murder, and other atrocities. The existence of these sentiments in the community represent a resource which plant managers can draw upon in one of a number of ways. On the one hand, they may use the institutionalized hatred as a foil, against which they can set themselves up as a protector of a new immigrant group. To Hispanics and Southeast Asians they can portray the plant as a sanctuary; to Blacks they can portray the plant as a microcosm of the wider community of hatred and terror. Finally, the two uses of institutionalized hatred need not cancel one another out: both may be used in the same plant and even on the same individuals, episodically, varying on a situation-by-situation basis.

While hostility toward Blacks may not be as acute as that presented by the Klan, in the plants we encountered, again and again, the attitude that Blacks are lazy, have a propensity toward absenteeism, and are content to collect welfare payments and deal drugs. From this attitude, together with the deeply racist heritage of the South, we may infer that plant personnel managers are likely using Hispanics to replace Blacks in the plants.

This alone, however, doesn't account for why the hiring of Hispanics has generated such an enthusiastic response in the industry. It is not merely a question of using Hispanics to keep wages low. Since 1988, 85 percent of the plants have increased their base wage by an average of 20 to 30 cents per hour. As we mentioned earlier, employers perceive Hispanics as having a work ethic superior to most American workers, Black or White. In a plant in north Georgia, where the Hispanic presence was relatively young (most had been hired since February and all since November of 1988), on a tour of the plant the personnel manager invited me to watch the Hispanic workers and compare them to the others. He pointed out that the Hispanics hustled back to their work stations after breaks, but that the other workers would saunter and stop to talk to everyone on their return to work. My own observations went along with this—the Hispanics did appear to be working harder. Thus it seems that explaining the enthusiasm over Hispanics is neither difficult nor surprising: new immigrants do tend to work harder or at least give their employers that impression.

Yet this explanation is only partial. At least as important as "hustle" on the job are the characteristics of reliability and docility. Commonly, employers characterize their work forces as consisting of a "core" of solid, long-time, native employees "who have been with the plant forever," and another groups of "sorry" workers, characterized by high absenteeism and a reluctance to follow orders. Many also report that the "sorry" component consists primarily of younger workers (under 25 years old) and that, in fact, their core workers are retiring out of the plant. Hispanics, obviously, are replacing those of the high turnover group; while they may be high turnover themselves, they tend to hustle while on the job, show up for work, and they possess cultural and linguistic characteristics that make them appear more docile than native workers. The lack of English-speaking skills in particular may underlie their apparent docility, since this not only reduces their ability to complain; it also encourages plant personnel managers to delegate to bilingual workers many supervisory tasks that might otherwise involve their participation. The practice of promoting bilinguals to supervisory positions on the plant floor is common. While in the field, I learned of a case in Delaware of a Puerto Rican who was promoted to supervise a group of Mexican women who had come into the plant from the work in the harvests; in this case, the Puerto Rican brokered all the complaints of the Mexican women in a way that the women felt did not accurately represent them. The women also reported some hostility between them and the Puerto Rican, and finally they quit because they had no one to whom they could effectively complain. This case illustrates that the hierarchies based on linguistic ability as well as citizenship status may be complex. There may exist in the plants a dominance of bilingual Hispanics over monolingual Hispanics, whether legal, half-legal (i.e., with temporary work authorization), or illegal, that is similar to the dominance of Mexican-American and black-American crew leaders over Mexican crews in agriculture. As bilinguals are promoted to supervisory positions, as they become brokers of complaints, they may be softening the appearance of other Hispanics in the plants since their success as supervisors depends, in part, on workers being docile. Hence, employers may perceive Hispanics to be "better" workers because their complaints are defused or altered by their bilingual supervisors. Network recruiting further facilitates the development of these "social buffer zones" between plant managers and workers.

Conclusion

This chapter opened with regional comparisons of work forces and ended with a discussion of hatred, terror, and labor control. Is it insignificant that the comments of plant personnel managers ferried us from comparative analysis to hatred and terror? I don't think so. Often without design, plant managers develop and revise their own and others' ideas about what it is to be Black, Hispanic, Asian, and female. In developing these ideas, these stereotypes, they stitch observations and behaviors inside the plants to developments in the community. The resulting fabric constitutes their actual interaction with workers on the shop floor and clothes their overall strategy of accessing and controlling the most willing, reliable, hard-working, and docile workers they can. In chapter 8, we will see how these labor control strategies are enhanced by a variety of mechanisms inside the plant and in the community.

8

Swollen Hearts, Swollen Hands: Labor Relations in the U.S. Poultry Industry

Our understanding of changing labor relations in the U.S. poultry industry depends on our placing the industry in the more general context of changing relations among labor, capital, and the state in the low-income sector of the U.S. economy. This may be best accomplished by considering the issues of occupational safety and injury inside the plants, since low-income households face a variety of unhealthy living and working conditions. In particular, what are the implications of occupational safety and injury for labor turnover, worker loyalty to plants, labor control, and the intense pressures on workers to maintain high productivity?

The presence of injury in poultry processing and related industries such as meat packing is so pervasive that nearly all workers we interviewed mentioned swollen hands, cuts, slips, and the high incidence of carpal tunnel syndrome (repetitive motion disease). Occupational injury lies at the heart of a grassroots organizational effort among workers in eastern North Carolina. Both workers and the USDA inspectors link occupational injury to increasingly more rapid line speeds. From management's perspective, occupational injury is emerging as one of the two top problems facing the industry today, second only to USDA inspections. Understanding how workers, employers, and the state deal with occupational injury in the plants provides a portrait of the essential features of labor relations in the industry.

Occupational Injury as a Reflection of Labor Relations

Officially, food processing occupational injury rates are sixteen per one hundred, around four times rates in other industries. This is, however, only the *reported* rate. Plant managers and workers both contribute to underreporting, for reasons that reveal aspects of labor relations inside the plants.

First, workers will tolerate minor injuries when plant nurses are reluctant to acknowledge that the injury derives from work on the line. Common conditions such as carpal tunnel syndrome, swollen hands, and lower back pains, because they are not *obviously* linked to the job, become points of contention with plant nurses. Supposedly skilled medical personnel, resting on the authority of their positions, plant nurses tend to treat these complaints symptomatically (e.g., with Ibuprofin and vitamin B12) and blame their causes on the workers' own health history. In one case, a woman who complained to the nurse that her hand needed surgery, because of carpal tunnel syndrome, was told that the condition was probably hereditary. Suspecting the nurse was saying this as a way of putting her off with medical jargon, the woman quickly said that no one else in her family suffered from such a condition. After this, the nurse claimed that the woman, who was thirty-eight years old, was going through menopause, to which the woman responded, "You better go ask some of those nineteen year olds out there with swollen hands if they are having menopause." The behavior of plant nurses is in line with the industry position that no conclusive study has been done that links carpal tunnel syndrome to work in the plants.

Another reason workers underreport injuries stems from fear. Workers are afraid that they will be fired for complaining too much or will lose pay due to lost time from work. Again, they are willing to tolerate minor injuries because of this. In the same way, workers also fear that other workers will reprimand them for reporting injuries. After the fashion of labeling unpatriotic people communists during the McCarthy era, poultry processing companies are quick to label disgruntled employees "troublemakers." They reinforce this with threats that the company, if too pressured, will leave the community. This strategy is particularly effective in small communities, where a poultry or meat packing plant might be among the largest employers. Further, companies reinforce community sanctions against worker complaints by donating to local United Way campaigns or to local churches. Donating to Black churches has been a particularly effective gesture in areas where the principal labor source is Black, since the church has long been a backbone of Black culture in the rural South.

From the industry side, underreporting of occupational injury rates is sound from the standpoint of keeping insurance and legal costs down, maintaining a low profile in the face of government inspections, and keeping workman's compensation claims to a minimum. Incidents of underreporting are documented in OSHA violation files, as in the examples that follow, copied from citations at two plants in eastern North Carolina:

13 NCAC 7B.0302(a): The log and summary form of *occupational injuries and illnesses* (OSHA Form No. 200 or its equivalent) was not completed in the detail provided in the form and the instructions contained therein:

The following cases which were recordable under the recordkeeping requirements were not entered on the 1989 OSHA 200 Log:

17 cases where medical records were available were *not recorded* on the 1989 OSHA 200 Log. (N.C. Department of Labor 1989a, emphasis in original).

13 NCAC 7B.0302(a): The log and summary form of *occupational injuries and illnesses* OSHA Form No. 200 or its equivalent) was not completed in the detail provided in the form and the instructions contained therein:

(A) 1989 OSHA 200 Log.
   (a) 1 recordable injury or illness case was *not recorded* on the log.
   (b) 3 cases of underreporting of days away from work due to a work related injury or illness.
   (c) 13 cases of underreporting of days of restricted work activity due to a work related injury or illness. (N.C. Department of Labor 1989b, emphasis in original)

Particularly telling in terms of labor relations and occupational injury is that employee health benefits are among the first points of negotiation to arise during times of fiscal crisis. An example of this comes from meat packing, an industry that is becoming more intimately related to the poultry industry as corporate mergers occur. During a recent crisis in the Albert Lea,

Minnesota, and Cedar Rapids, Iowa, Farmstead Foods plants, initial reports focused on cutting insurance benefits: "The company wants to cut workers' compensation costs. It is proposing greater emphasis on safety, drug and alcohol testing after accidents, and the possibility of a program where injured workers, if able, are placed in productive jobs to suit their situation" (*Cedar Rapids Gazette*, February 16, 1990: 7A).

This passage not only reaffirms the importance of occupational health in meat packing, it points to the common strategy among companies of minimizing the severity of job-related injuries by keeping injured workers working in the plants. This practice, which occurs in poultry plants as well as in meat packing, contributes to the underreporting of injury because workers who remain at the plants don't file workman's compensation claims. These claims are a principal index of occupational injury at the plant. During interviews with North Carolina poultry workers, we encountered cases where workers were injured so badly that they couldn't work, at least temporarily. Despite this, they were encouraged to come to the plant. One woman had to sit all day in the cafeteria after an injury rather than stay home. "They would rather pay full salary to a worker who couldn't work than let them receive workman's compensation," said one poultry worker.

Injury, Worker Productivity, and Labor Control

The high rate of occupational injury in poultry processing derives most directly from the constant pressures to increase or maintain high line speeds. According to an ergonomist familiar with the poultry industry, "the current nationwide rash of reported cases [of carpal tunnel syndrome] is a by-product of the country's pursuit of higher productivity in the last decade. 'What we're seeing is we're wanting more and more from everybody,' he said. 'We're pushing people closer and closer to their limits'" (*Raleigh News and Observer* Sunday, April 9, 1989, p. 1.).

Similar conclusions may be drawn from the OSHA documents cited earlier as evidence of underreporting, which underscore the number of times per shift that debilitating tasks must be performed, suggesting that the speed of production underlies injury:

During the period from April 4 to July 31, 1989, each *knicker in the Deboning Department* used a knife to cut in excess of *12,000 chicken breasts per shift.* Postures included reaches below the waist, ulnar deviation, palmar and dorsal flexion, and wrist supination. Forces were induced by pinching and grasping the knife and cold meat as well as by force necessary to cut the cartilage. (N.C. Department of Labor 1989a)

During the period from April 5 to July 31, 1989, each *drawhand* in the Evisceration Department pulled, twisted, and placed viscera of chickens *in excess of 10,000 times per shift* in postures that included palmar flexion, wrist supination, reaches below elbow height, and reaches outward at or above mid-chest height. Forces were induced as a result of gripping, twisting, and pulling slippery viscera as well as by repetitive arm extensions. (N.C. Department of Labor 1989b).

Pressure to keep line speeds high has always shadowed industry labor relations. This pressure underlies not only high injury rates but also creates an environment in which control over workers' time and movement is central to production. Labor control inside the plants is designed to keep workers compartmentalized, their attention trained on a single task. Their movements through the plants are restricted to a designated range of places and times. Inside some plants, workers wear different colored helmets that tell where in the plant they are supposed to work (Erickson and Stull 1988). This approach to labor control extends beyond the plant floor, into the families, networks, and communities of workers.

In the context of such rigid controls over workers' space and time in the plants, antagonism arises when plant supervisors infringe upon the small windows of free time granted to workers during the work day, such as breaks and lunches. Among workers at an eastern North Carolina poultry plant, for example, one of the principal gripes concerned lines at the bathroom during break times. Employees reported spending their entire breaks in line, unable to use the bathrooms during production time because of strict rules regarding leaving work stations. Sometimes these rules are so rigorously observed that employees urinate while standing at the line, or vomit if sick; they are afraid leaving their positions will cost them either their job or a portion of their pay (Goldoftas 1989). "They have people who write down how many times you leave for the bathroom," said one worker. "At one time, they had on the board we could only go to the bathroom twice, but took it down. We used to have a pass and everybody started to complain. They did away with it."

Such rigid control is established and maintained through a variety of direct supervisory and more subtle and indirect methods. First, direct supervision, extensively relied on, is based on the internal differentiation of the work force. Plants have anywhere from two to six levels in their hierarchies. At the low end are the new production or line workers, who are trained and closely monitored by line leaders. The amount of direct supervision practiced by line leaders over line workers varies more by individual characteristics rather than the dictums of plant labor policy. The line leader works the line alongside the production workers. Above the line leader is the line supervisor, who was described by one worker as, "the one who pops the whip." Others confirmed that most direct supervision falls to these individuals. In some plants, line supervisors keep the same position throughout the day, standing over the line, watching production, taking notes on workers and work habits, driving the workers to keep up their speed, and granting or denying requests for breaks. "They (line supers) are sneaky," said one worker. "They will get you working steady, slip away and speed the line up." Another reported: "Supervisors are all right. Nag you if you stay out. They want a doctor's note. They send you upstairs and write you up. Three warnings and you're fired."

Line supervisors are themselves subject to direct supervision, driven by department supervisors who roam through their departments. Department supervisors, in turn, report to heads of supervisors. Although these heads usually have no direct supervisory contact with the production workers, they roam from department to department through the plant. They come under the control of the superintendent of the entire plant.

Not all plants conform to this pattern, but in every large plant the work force is internally differentiated hierarchically for supervisory reasons. Work forces are also differentiated laterally, with distinctions between jobs and positions in the plant, although these distinctions have little direct relationship to the system of labor control. Production workers differ primarily by the relative difficulty of one job over another. How workers are moved around inside plants varies from company to company and from plant to plant, although the practice of rotating and cross-training workers among a variety of jobs is widespread, serving purposes of safety and efficiency. Rotating workers, on the one hand, relieves them of the same repetitive motions and thus cuts down on their chances of developing carpal tunnel syndrome. Cross-training workers allows them to move to different work stations as bottlenecks develop because of worker absences or injuries.

While these practices are beneficial for both employees and managers, neither rotating nor cross-training workers is easy to practice on a regular basis. First, the range of jobs in the plant is not diverse enough to continually move people from job to job. Second, the efficiency of dealing with bottlenecks by cross-training is balanced by the efficiency of keeping workers at one location to maintain peak line speeds. Workers reported that it wasn't necessarily advantageous to perform well at your job, adding statements like, "They hold you back or won't move you. They promote and move the ones who can't keep up. It's actually a hold back to do your job well."

The specific criteria by which workers are allocated tasks in the plants are unclear to most workers and haphazardly applied. In a plant in eastern North Carolina, for example, workers complained of women getting promoted or moved to "easy" jobs simply because they were perceived as "pretty." In addition, workers reported that pregnant women received preferential treatment. After an ammonia leak incident at one of the nation's largest poultry plants, for example, the pregnant women were sent home while the others, despite lingering fumes, were directed back to their work stations. Finally, there are indications of task allocation by sex and ethnicity, and perhaps by legal status. Specifically, most workers report that women are promoted less often than men, and that few supervisory positions are occupied by women. Similar claims used to hold true regarding Blacks, said some older workers, although this was perceived to have been changing.

It was reported that monolingual Spanish-speaking Hispanics were treated differently, though not uniformly better or worse. For example, some workers perceived Hispanics to be allowed more absences and given more warnings than native workers. At the same time, workers reported that the company took advantage of the inexperience of the Hispanics by paying them less and deducting outrageously high rents for company-provided housing. And most workers agreed that Hispanics concentrated in less desirable second shift tasks than native (U.S. citizen) workers.

Control over workers' space and time inside the plants is mirrored in more subtle mechanisms of control beyond plant walls. Workers' lives are constrained by such activities as drug testing, network recruiting and its implications for harnessing resident authority, and, in some cases, control over workers' housing. Plants also influence the attitudes of local clergy, police, politicians, and businessmen to keep workers in line. The industry presence in workers' lives beyond the plant floor is diffuse enough to be a component of contemporary labor relations inside the plant. Whether this industry presence is used as a tool of labor control or a tool of worker resistance, however, depends largely on developments in the local economy and society. Most important among these developments is the community's receptivity to new immigrant or refugee populations. In general, in areas with a declining native labor force and little or no alternative labor force, the fact that employees recruit and work alongside their relatives and friends empowers workers, since firing one worker may lead to others leaving. One worker, for example, reported a marked positive change in supervisors' interactions with her after her sister quit; others said that Mexican workers were given more warnings than native workers because they are hired in groups and tend to quit in groups as well.

Nevertheless, the ability of plant owners to use network recruiting as a tool of labor control increases with the firm's increasing penetration of workers' lives and communities. Two illustrations detail how this may occur. First, this may be seen in an eastern North Carolina poultry plant. Mexican workers who now live in company-provided housing have been recruited to the region from Florida and Texas, primarily from the agricultural labor force. In this case, the firm originally introduced the Hispanics to the area and provided them with housing near the plant, building a trailer park for them. The industry's initial control over these Hispanic workers' lives derives from the firm *representing* their entry into the community and thus establishing the terms of their incorporation into local economy and society. Many native workers at the plant resent their being provided housing (one worker said plant management wouldn't have done the same for Black workers). Yet the community merchants accept and welcome them. Beyond this, the control over these new immigrants' lives is somewhat more explicit. The Hispanic workers in this case are recruited into the plant in "bunches." Entire networks are brought into the plant at the same time, as well as into the trailer park, establishing an initial basis of network dependence on the plants. The provision of company housing carries further implications for worker control, however, in that the housing is assigned and occupied on terms dictated by the company. Rents are deducted from workers' paychecks and couples may occupy trailers together only on the condition that both work at the plant. The plant reserves the right, moreover, to assign new workers to already-occupied trailers. In one case, the company assigned two workers a trailer that was occupied by a couple. The woman worked the day shift and the man worked the night shift; the two new workers were also assigned one day shift and one night shift. The man complained to company officials that he couldn't leave his wife alone with a strange man at night, but the company refused to modify the arrangement, forcing the couple to quit.

That the company is able to use housing as an instrument of labor control further enhances the desirability of a new immigrant work force. Bringing a "fresh" work force into an area implies providing housing and other basic needs to immigrant workers and thus increasing workers' feelings of gratitude and loyalty toward, and dependence on, the labor importing firm. Two further pieces of information support this. First, poultry processors in North Georgia and on the Delmarva Peninsula, currently getting involved in a Korean worker import program, reported that loyalty to the plant was secured by assuring sponsorship for not only one wave of Korean workers but for successive waves as well. The Koreans are contracted to work for a year; they are discouraged from breaking these contracts by the company's promise to import more Koreans, their relatives among them, every year. By such mechanisms, we know from Mexican case material (Goldring 1990), entire overseas villages may be emptied of their most productive citizens. In the Korean case, those recruited tend to be middle class and educated, with some working capital and upwardly mobile outlooks, likely to spend no more than a year in the plants. The industry simply serves as a conduit or funnel for an international migration.

Second, a statement by the National Turkey Federation (NTF), published in a major industry magazine, hints at similar or heightened use of immigrant labor programs, as though paving the way for H2b labor provisions:

> NTF adopted a resolution during the annual convention which supports amending the Immigration Act permitting the expeditious importation of willing foreign born workers into low-skill or no-skill positions. This, of course, would be contingent upon a demonstrated shortage of ready, willing, and able American workers.
>
> This action is a result of a current serious unavailability of American workers to work in poultry processing plants. (*Turkey World,* "Washington Update," March/April 1990 p. 34.)

Our second illustration of the ways companies may penetrate workers' lives and communities focuses on the grassroots organization called the Center for Women's Economic Alternatives of Ahoskie, North Carolina. The center developed out of a number of struggles, primarily by women, over various unfair and sexist treatment in low-income occupations. Early organizing efforts included hosiery mill workers, nursing home workers, convenience store clerks, and seafood processing workers. More recently, the center has focused on poultry workers. In the present context, however, more telling than their accomplishments has been the nature of opposition to their organizational efforts. The difficulties encountered by the center's attempts to organize poultry workers, in other words, offer a somewhat different perspective on the extent and nature of poultry companies' penetration of workers' communities. Most notably, while the center has been successful in organizing and educating over two thousand women regarding their rights as workers, their efforts continue to be frustrated by the community's dependence on poultry jobs. Under too much pressure, workers fear, the company will close the plant.

This "scare tactic" strategy reflects strategies of cultivating fear among workers inside the plants. Threats to close the plant have been supplemented with threats to replace the current work force with imported Mexicans. Workers do not take these threats lightly. This very tactic was used during the summer of 1989, when native chicken-catchers for the plants refused to work under oppressively hot conditions in the chicken houses. Mexicans were brought in and housed in local motels and used as replacement labor during the dispute. This option, moreover, becomes both visible and viable to the company annually, as Mexican migrant labor crews move through the eastern North Carolina cucumber and tobacco harvests.

These strategies, of course, are reinforced by whole families and networks working in the plants. One member's fear may infect other members of the network. In this way, too, the plant may benefit by the authority of older members of the network over others, insofar as that authority may be tapped and exercised through other forces of authority in the community that support the industry. Again we point out that the clergy's role against organized labor has been important in the rural South. Despite Martin Luther King and other church-based civil disobedience and protest movements in the South, many clergymen remain conservative forces, preaching patience, in both black and white communities. The church is, as well, an institution with a great deal of authority over its members. In any struggle, even its attempt to maintain neutrality must be interpreted by its members as conservative. In the present case, according to individuals familiar with the center's organizational efforts, the poultry industry has been able to enhance this "neutrality" with contributions to the church. Also, the center's emphasis on women assuming leadership roles may be seen by clergy as potentially undermining their own authority in the community. Activists in the movement have been labeled "troublemakers" by both the company and others in the community. In some cases, members of activists' families, still working in the plants, have been interviewed by plant officials concerning the activists' organizational activities. This suggests that maintaining an effective intelligence network among workers is a crucial component of labor control in the poultry industry. In similar fashion, when we circulated a brief questionnaire among meat packing workers in Sioux City, Iowa, a personnel manager at one of the largest plants there contacted us to object to our interviewing "his" workers. Indicating our surprise that plant officials knew about the questionnaire, the personnel manager said, "You wouldn't believe the intelligence network we have."

The Developing Role of New Immigrants in Industry Labor Control Strategies

The above assessment of contemporary labor relations in the poultry industry emphasized the multifaceted ways the industry attempts to control workers, both inside and outside the plants. Similar tactics are used in meat packing plants and in other low-wage sectors of the U.S. economy. Workers' health, time, movements, living arrangements, their family and friendship ties, their attitudes, and even—through drug testing—their leisure activities have come within the industries' labor control activities. This control is maintained through a combination of scare tactics, or the cultivation of fear among workers, and the manipulation of social relations, resident authority systems, and, in the case of immigrants, control over workers' housing. Such complex, pervasive control over workers' lives certainly contributes to the pressures workers face and the corresponding high labor turnover. In this context, the use and continued dependence on new immigrant workers has emerged as a cornerstone of labor relations in the largest and most powerful of poultry processing plants. While we noted in the last chapter the ways that plant personnel managers have assumed an active role in this increasing reliance on new immigrants, it is useful to consider the same trend from perspectives more in line with new immigrants' and native workers' schedules and lives.

Labor Turnover and the Developing Use of Immigrant Workers

The use of new immigrant workers, particularly those from Mexico and other parts of Latin America, has altered the seasonality of labor turnover in the plants. Many Hispanic workers reported returning to Mexico for either the Christmas or Easter holidays; plant personnel managers who had hired extensively from Latino populations confirmed this. While high labor turnover used to occur as the months grew warmer, with farmers returning to work their land or mothers staying home with their children during summer vacation, it has now shifted toward early winter or spring. A plant manager in Georgia described the situation as follows:

> The Mexicans have filled a gap that always existed in the poultry industry; it used to be that 40 to 50 percent of our workers were transient. They were construction workers who would only work during the winter or mothers who would only work during the school year. Now the Mexicans have filled that gap, or most of it.

If common, this implies that the highly preferred Hispanic workers may be undermining the economic strategies of native households by moving into these jobs when natives leave the plants temporarily to farm, work in construction, or take care of children. As long as labor turnover remains high and comparable jobs are available in the region year-round, this would present no problem. However, with increased local growth in Mexican populations, combined with employers' conscious attempts to replace their "sorry workers" with Mexicans, it becomes more and more difficult for natives to continue to move between poultry work and other economic activities. Such a development may be particularly problematic for farmers who rely on temporary plant employment to endure farm crises, cover farm operating expenses, and so forth, a strategy that has become increasingly common among small- and mid-sized U.S. farmers (Gladwin 1988; Hansen, et al. 1981).

From Mexican workers' perspectives, quitting for the holidays, returning to Mexico, and then returning to the plants makes sense as long as the plants will rehire such workers or there are other plants in the area hiring workers. Few personnel managers reported turning away workers who had quit, although any benefits they may have accrued by virtue of seniority tend not to be reinstated. Nevertheless, both workers and union officials seem unanimous in their belief that the poultry processing industry is so hungry for workers that they will take "any one they can get." Working in the plants for only part of the year also conforms to and continues a well-documented pattern of cyclical migration between Mexico and the United States, one that builds on and takes advantage of complex international households and social networks (Goldring 1990; Reichert 1981; Massey, et al. 1987; Chavez 1989; Griffith and Runsten 1988).

Formal Organizations, Worker Organization Among Immigrants, and the Overlap Between Agricultural and Processing Plant Labor Markets

Labor turnover among Hispanics in the plants is not solely a function of a desire to return to Mexico for the holidays, however. Many Hispanic workers have been recently granted work authorization under the 1986 Immigration Reform and Control Act's highly publicized amnesty provisions. Some of these come into poultry plants from the agricultural labor market, and have not fully divorced this past. As such, they will leave the plants for farm work during certain times of the year when they know, from experience, that they can earn more money than in the plants. For example, the Christmas tree industry in the mountains of Kentucky, Tennessee, and western North Carolina—close to the northern Georgia poultry processing center—can be extremely lucrative for those who know how to prune and harvest the trees. Daily wages in such a harvest can climb as "high" as sixty dollars. Also, agricultural work often pays in cash, without deductions, and includes free housing.

This opportunistic dimension to workers' labor market strategies derives from features of poultry work, too. Particularly in plants where job rotation or utilization of different muscles is not common, working too long in the plants can cripple a worker. Moving out of the plants into agriculture may thus improve the occupational health of workers and prolong their working lives, to say nothing of offering them the relief that must come from leaving the plants. With the option to move back into the plants, moreover, they may also be relieved of exposure to the many occupational hazards of agriculture.

In a related study (Griffith, 1990), a Mexican meat packing worker in Sioux City, Iowa, estimated that between 60 to 70 percent of recent immigrants to Sioux City packing plants came from agricultural backgrounds. In addition, in rural labor markets throughout the United States, affiliates of the Association of Farmworker Opportunities Programs (AFOP) have been actively placing farm workers into both poultry and meat packing plants, using the formal mechanism of the Job Training Partnership Act (JTPA). This program's goal is precisely to place farm workers into more stable, year-round occupations. Similar, government-funded organizations in eastern North Carolina have been active in placing seasonal farm workers in both poultry and seafood houses. In fact, grassroots labor organizers such as the Center for Women's Economic Alternatives object to this practice on the grounds that it undermines not only their organizing efforts but also reinforces ideas that the only jobs former farm workers can obtain are those in low-wage, unskilled sectors of the economy. In areas where plant managers are stepping up their hiring of Hispanic workers, however, relations with these agencies have greatly facilitated recruiting. Since AFOP affiliates also tend to be 402 recipients (the Qualified Designated Entities [QDEs] responsible for helping aliens with the legalization procedures following IRCA), they have direct and ready access to illegal immigrant farm workers and a potential clientele for JTPA programs. Further, the QDEs sometimes work closely with state and local offices of the Employment Service, sometimes inhabiting the same buildings or offices. This effectively broadens the institutional base from which newly legalized farm workers and other illegal aliens can be located and recruited into poultry processing plants. From the employers' side, incentives to hire such workers derive from the fact that JTPA funds pay part of a worker's wage during training, the critical period during which employers estimate a worker's future productivity and worth. This program is similar to another program—the Targeted Jobs Tax Credit (TJTC)—that is popular among poultry processors and administered through the Employment Service.

The focus on this institutional base and the overlap between plant and farm labor markets is important for a number of reasons. First, the formal liaison services provided by QDEs, AFOP affiliates, and Employment Service personnel helps legitimate the recruitment of newly legalized workers by poultry plants. These state and federally funded agencies not only refer workers to the plants, they also make sure the workers are legal by checking identification and keeping files on workers. Meat packing plants achieve similar ends by employing Southeast Asian refugees with the assistance of the Bureau of Refugee Services (Iowa BRS, personal communication; Stanley 1988). The legitimacy this confers on the industry is particularly helpful in communities where the growth of immigrant populations has been met with subtle and open hostility by natives, such as the Ku Klux Klan/Skinhead march discussed in the previous chapter.

Second, industry reliance on these agencies is equally important to the workers. Some workers have used the agency network of AFOP affiliates, QDEs, Migrant Ministries, rural clinics, Legal Aid offices, and so forth to generate community support for Hispanics who have suffered because of the poultry industry. Usually this occurs during a crisis, as when injured workers must leave the plants, or in cases where workers have been lured into regions on the promise of employment in the plants and then not hired, left unemployed in a foreign city.

Third, work in U.S. agriculture, particularly among migrants, selects for specific kinds of social organizational forms and worker strategies. There is some evidence that these forms and strategies have been brought into poultry plants. In agriculture, the most common social organizational form, at least for the past thirty years, has been the crew. This consists of a group of individuals, usually young males, traveling and living together, seeking work together, taking and leaving employment together. Crews vary in size, but the larger crews tend to be composed of small groups of eight to twelve workers. At the core of the crew is the "crew leader," whose authority over the rest of the crew members is highly variable (Heppel 1983). Often, whatever authority the crew leader possesses derives from his being the owner of the car or van that carries the crew from place to place. This agricultural and migratory background also affects family size and household composition. In Sioux City, for example, workers recruited from south Texas generally came to Iowa in smaller domestic units than those they knew in Texas. In detailed studies of farm workers, we have found that migrants' households are extremely fluid, consisting of "anchor" households in the sending communities which some adult members leave and return to seasonally, depending on the migrant streams (Griffith, et al. 1990). These households, in various conditions of composition through the year, also tend to maintain connections with other households in other sending communities, increasing the potential for network recruitment and the plant's access to labor supplies from distant regions. An additional condition of employment that has diffused from agriculture to poultry processing is that of providing workers housing. When the company provides housing (as agricultural employers usually do), the control over workers' lives is further enhanced. Workers in these cases can be relied on to work longer hours and with fewer absences than workers whose jobs do not directly affect their housing.

The social organizational form of the crew or the small domestic unit, especially when combined with housing, influences the nature of the contract between workers and their employers, the propensity of workers to remain on the job, and the general parameters of labor recruitment by personnel managers. The contract between worker and employer is no longer a simple social tie between two individuals. Instead, in the case of the crew, the important tie is between the employer, the crew leader, and a small group of workers, and an important component of the contract is the provision of housing. Again, how much the crew leader acts as a mediator between the employer and the rest of the group is highly variable; however, I encountered case after case of small groups of workers all hiring on with a plant at the same time and all quitting at the same time. In-depth interviews with plant personnel managers yielded the following observations:

The Hispanics live together, travel together, and often work together, and so go to areas like Gainesville where there are a high concentration of jobs.

Among her [the plant personnel manager's] comments were those having to do with group size and the relation between agriculture, holidays, and the poultry industry's work force. Groups are about 8-12 in size, with one who speaks English well and the rest who stay and live with him, working with him as well.

She said she was worried about becoming too dependent on the Hispanics and noticed that their dependence rested on the assumption of a continuous flow of immigrants from Mexico... "But that flow will continue," she said. "Or anyway, it has." So far. This dependence rests on the continued flow hypothesis because she has yet to see one Mexican work a full year at the plant. The industry always has had to deal with seasonal fluctuations in the work force, and the Mexicans have added a new dimension to that (so have the Vietnamese, leaving for shrimp season): they leave, primarily at Christmas, and sometimes at crop time (since most come from "field work" backgrounds). On their applications they write "fields." She said that there was always a drop-off when school let out, because many mothers would quit to stay with kids during the summer (this drop may be compensated for by high school students working at the plants during the summer). Other times of the year there are fluctuations around the holidays and after the first of the year—women work through the holidays for extra Christmas money, then quit after Christmas is over; Mexicans, on the other hand, leave before Christmas and then come back after the first of the year. This may cause severe shortages in the future as they become more dependent on Mexicans. She had observed that the Mexican pattern is to work 4-7 months; return to Mexico for 3-4 months, come back to U.S. Always they give them their jobs back—they've got no choice. (Griffith's field notes, spring and summer, 1989)

Native Workers' Responses to New Immigrants in the Plants

One further dimension of the increasing reliance on new immigrant workers in the plants is how native workers have been responding to their presence, both in their communities and at their work stations. Those farmers and construction workers who worked winters in the plants, or those housewives who worked in poultry plants during the school year, or other workers who simply quit on a seasonal basis to let the wounds of occupational injuries heal, in some areas, now, have seen the erosion of their ability to move in and out of the plants. The active, out-of-state recruitment programs that bring newly legalized and related illegal immigrants into the plants give personnel managers access to networks of Hispanic workers. Workers' responses to questions about new immigrants coming into the plants support comments by plant personnel managers concerning preferences for Hispanic workers. The following observations from the field summarize common worker comments about Hispanics (Vernon Kelley's field notes, winter, 1989-90; the names are pseudonyms).

Worker # 1: Grace, White female, thirty-eight years old

Grace verified that blacks and whites who quit were being replaced by Hispanics, primarily. We get a bunch everyday. It is a strange thing. Hardly any blacks or whites, just Mexicans. It is not a surprise to see 30 to 35 Mexicans a day."
She said originally there weren't many Hispanics working, but that she heard the company paid a Mexican $50.00 a person to bring them here. The recruiter was gone and she was unaware what happened to him. The company purchased 40 acres of land and put a trailer park up. It is mostly Hispanics who live there. "It's a nice trailer park." She feels it is one of the reasons the Hispanics continue to come. Grace has a friend, Maria, who is Hispanic, and Grace complained that the company was taking advantage of the Hispanics in the trailer park. "They take $50.00 a week from a Hispanic family" (man and woman)—total $100.00—and "one has to work night shift." "The company also reserves the right to place other people in your trailer. They wanted to put two men the husband didn't know into the trailer. The husband didn't like it, so they moved."
Grace does not see the Hispanics as a threat to her job or wages. She feels as long as she works she has a job, but she

feels that if she quit, eventually, a Hispanic would have her position. She made the following comments concerning Hispanics:

"The ones in our department is [sic] good workers."

"It's good for the plant. Some people want to work more than others."

"A lot of people in our department feels [sic] that they are taking the jobs of whites and blacks, but I think it is because they are more dependable than the whites or blacks."

"I guess it's the way they are raised in the fields and such."

Grace felt that the community liked having the plant there and the Hispanic population was good for the community. She mentioned that there was prejudice everywhere, but she felt most businesses in the community were glad to have them. They caused no problems and were good customers.

Worker #2: Alice, White female, twenty-four years old

Alice had very little to say that would be considered flattering about Hispanics. She seemed threatened by them. "I don't like it," she said. "They are always staring and whistling, trying to talk to you. You don't know what they are saying no more than a man in the moon."

She did feel, however, they were good workers, "They would work seven days a week, if they could." "When it sleeted last year, some workers couldn't get there. They (Hispanics) worked two straight shifts." "I think they (the plant) want more Mexicans because they work and don't stay out—never complain."

Alice does not feel her job is threatened, but "as long as you do your job, everything's ok. But if I quit, they would probably replace me with a Hispanic."

Alice didn't think too much about the trailer park being there, but told me she heard they took $40.00 a week from their checks and that they stay four to a trailer.

Alice also confirmed they come in large groups. "Sometimes you go in there. [There] are two lines of them waiting to be hired. They can't speak English. They have a girl who translates for them."

Worker #3: Madge, Black female, forty-two years old

The effects on American workers due to the influx of Hispanics is pretty obvious to Madge. "I think if those Mexicans weren't here," she said, "I would make more money."

"If anyone quits, they won't get their job back." She said she had friends who quit and want to come back, but the Mexicans have their jobs.

Madge didn't seem to know much about the trailer park (detail wise), but she knew the "trailers had new everything," and that the money was taken out of their paycheck.

Madge said the Hispanics were showing up and were being hired by the "handful." She did not feel they were recruited, but that "relatives must tell them."

Madge felt the Hispanics were "good workers." "Mexicans are used to hard work, but they stick together. The personnel manager called one in to complain about crop pulling and all four (crop pullers) left."

Worker # 4: Billy, White male, age twenty-seven; USDA inspector

Billy took a civil service test to get his job. He said when the plant first opened, they had a bonus system to recruit (they still do), but "they are not hurting for workers now."

Billy said the Hispanics originally showed up themselves, but that the company quickly saw the advantages. "I think they (the company) realized they had a gold mine." The company then hired a Hispanic as a lead person to recruit. This fellow brought in lots of workers from the agriculture areas in Florida and Texas. Billy does not know what happened to him, but he is no longer there. The Hispanics continue to show up regularly. It seems they find out about the job through "word of mouth." Billy says, "Without them, they would be hurting. I would say 60% at least of work force on second shift is Hispanics."

Billy is also the original informant who mentioned the trailer park behind the plant that is used primarily by the Hispanics, "Little Mexico". Billy felt that they really had little effect on the area, except to spend money in town. They (the Hispanics) have yet to filter into the community life. Billy felt that company was aware of the future in dealing with Hispanics because they were providing classes to teach English. He felt like the Hispanic population would continue to grow and that they would become a larger part of the work force as time went by. He said, "The Mexicans seem to work harder without complaining. They show up regularly."

Worker # 5: Latisha, Black female, thirty-six years old

Latisha did not seem bothered by the influx of Hispanics. Latisha feels the Hispanics are taking jobs that use to belong to black workers, but it was because black workers quit. Latisha did not worry about her job. As long as she works hard, she will have a place.

"These people came to work. They (the plant) just needed someone to do the job." Latisha related the same story about the "Spanish guy" recruiting. Latisha pointed out they got nearly a dollar raise this year, but felt that Hispanics might be holding wages down because everyone else knew they could be replaced.

Living in [town name], Latisha didn't know much about the trailer park. She knew it was mainly for Hispanics, but "they is some black guys who live there, and they say they at least have a place."

Workers # 6 and 7: John, Black male, nineteen years old, and his sister Wilma

He felt the fact that the company had the trailer park for the Hispanics was fair, because they needed a place to stay, although he didn't think they would be doing the same for blacks.

John said he saw "twenty to twenty-five a day in there for an interview." John said of the Hispanics, "Tell you the truth, they are hard workers." "Don't complain much."

John felt things in the plant could be better, but he accepted things as [they were]. He felt it was [plant name] job to look after itself. John told me he felt that Hispanics were keeping wages down, but he felt that it is okay. It's sort of the American way.

Wilma offered a little different perspective on the subjects of job and Hispanics.

Wilma has applied for another job at present. She is not happy with the job at [plant name]. She works nights. She did have a day job, but switched to night to make more money. She has a fairly easy job—cryovac, bag and base bird—yet she hopes to get on at [other job] because they pay more.

There are no Hispanics in her department. They must weight the birds and the Hispanics cannot read the scales. Wilma was very outspoken about the Hispanics. She felt they were given special privileges that were not afforded American workers.

Wilma felt "they get hired quicker than blacks or whites." She said that if a black or white quit, they would not be rehired, but they always rehire Hispanics. She said that the Hispanics sometimes get drunk and miss work, but they get more warnings.

Worker # 8: Linda, White female, thirty-eight years old

Linda had less to say about Hispanics than most informants. It may well be because she was one of the few day shift people I interviewed, and Hispanics are concentrated on night shift. Linda offered both positive and negative comments concerning Hispanics. She said, "They work hard, but we work hard." "Hispanics don't lay out. They come to work." (*Note:* She called them Mexicans at first until she picked up on me referring to them as Hispanics. Then she used that term the remainder of the interview.) Linda felt it was good that they have the trailers for Hispanics to live in because she realized they wouldn't have a place to stay and there are always more Hispanics coming. "There won't be a day that we go to lunch there aren't fifteen to twenty sitting in the lunchroom ready to be hired."

Linda felt they will hire a Hispanic before an American. She based this on "Anna (a Hispanic) told me they paid them less."

These few statements further confirm observations made again and again above: (1) the Hispanic influence in the poultry industry is increasing; (2) this increase seems, to workers, to have been actively pursued by the plant personnel office, which relies heavily on Hispanic networks; (3) workers who quit are replaced by Hispanics; and (4) Hispanics are both more exploited, through housing, and given preferential treatment on the job. Through the same or similar mechanisms, other poultry plants, in other parts of the country, have come to develop similar deepening ties with Hispanic populations, who replace, then displace, other workers in the plants. It remains, or course, somewhat of an open question as to whether or not these other workers are available, ready, and willing to work in the plants. While many workers would like to work in the plants more sporadically than management will accept, this is, because of the Hispanic influx, no longer an option.

Conclusion

Workers in the poultry industry find themselves squeezed between high rates of occupational injury and the continued drive to maintain high productivity. These are, clearly, two sides of the same coin. The rapid lines speeds necessary to maintain high productivity are arguably the most significant contributors to injury. They not only lead to high labor turnover, but also create a social environment where it is crucial to control labor as comprehensively as possible. Without comprehensive control, would it be possible to encourage workers to tolerate minor injuries that could eventually lead to crippled hands? Would it be possible to expect workers to comply with living arrangements in which women were expected to stay at home, at night, with strange men? Would it be possible to keep injured workers at work, all day long, sitting alone in a cafeteria, simply to reduce the number of worker compensation claims?

That plant personnel managers, nurses, and other supervisors can count on workers to go along with such ridiculous suggestions is itself a testament to the comprehensiveness of the industry's labor control. It also suggests a certain complicity on the part of the community, of which the poultry workers form a part. The "intelligence" networks of plant management certainly participate in this complicity, subsisting on workers' fear. Yet equally important have been the general bias against organized labor in the South and other aspects of rural southern culture that discourage workers from collective resistance. The problems encountered by the Center for Women's Economic Alternatives must be understood in this light.

While the Hispanic workers cannot be said to be carriers of the South's anti-union sentiments, they possess qualities, as new immigrants, that feed the continued weak positions of labor relative to capital. As long as new immigrants and undocumented workers permeate their networks, there are few incentives to organize, join labor unions, or resist plant authority in any capacity besides leaving the plant's sphere of control altogether. Again, fear plays an important role in labor control. With new immigrants, however, the mechanisms of labor control need not extensively involve existing community institutions, such as the church or local employment services. Labor control mechanisms assume other concrete forms, such as representing or sponsoring immigrations into rural communities and providing new immigrants housing. These strategies then affect the economic strategies and attitudes of native workers in ways that further subjugate their life spaces and schedules to the organization of time and space in the plant. What this tells us about low-wage labor under advanced capitalism is the subject of the following two chapters.

IV

Conclusion: Case Studies in Theoretical Perspective

9

Towards a Theory of Low-Wage Labor Under Advanced Capitalism

Introduction

Underlying relationships among low-wage labor processes, state policy, and capitalist strategy is the defining feature of a low-wage labor market: low wages. Yet wages are only low *relatively*, in terms of a household's ability to maintain and reproduce itself at a subjectively acceptable level. Traditionally, neoclassical economics regards labor as a commodity like other commodities. According to this view, wage rates fluctuate with the supply and demand for labor, rising and falling because of market mechanisms. In short, labor will be cheap where there are labor surpluses and expensive where there are labor shortages. More detailed case studies question this. Instead, social scientists paying closer attention to local processes have noted the influence of social, cultural, and political phenomena on labor's availability, its propensity to staff certain industries (thus creating surpluses or shortages), and its cost (e.g. Wood and McCoy 1985; Doeringer, Moss, and Terkla 1987; Portes and Borozc 1989). This makes labor far less sensitive to market mechanisms than other commodities. Its cost is affected by such political factors as minimum wage legislation and international terms of trade. Cultural factors, too, enter into negotiations between employers and workers concerning wage rates and working conditions. A black American's definition of subsistence and consequent wage needs are likely to be qualitatively and quantitatively distinct from a new immigrant Mexican's or an Indian fleeing the Central American ethnic wars. In the preceding chapters, we have seen that labor recruitment and retention policies often draw upon workers' networks, families, and sources of authority within the community. In the seafood and poultry processing industries, raising or lowering wages has less influence on attracting and keeping workers than political and sociological means of recruiting, mobilizing, and organizing labor (Wood and McCoy 1985).

The use of kinship, social networks, and community-based social institutions to assure supplies of labor is especially common in rural economic activities that depend on nature. In economies based on gathering, hunting, agriculture, fishing, or a combination of these, the relationship between production and the reproduction of human labor power is readily recognized by the society's members. In such societies, kinship permeates production and operates as the key organizing principle in many other social contexts. This affects relationships of power between the sexes and between generations (Meillassoux 1972; Foucault 1980), making deployment of labor an authoritarian act endorsed by symbolic and social realms:

> Kinship can be understood as a way of committing social labor to the transformation of nature through appeals to filiation and marriage, and to consanguinity and affinity. Put simply, through kinship social labor is "locked up," or "embedded," in particular relations between people. This labor can be mobilized only through access to people, such access being defined symbolically. *What* is done unlocks social labor; *how* it is done involves symbolic definitions of kinsmen and affines. Kinship thus involves (a) symbolic constructs ("filiation/marriage; consanguinity/affinity"), that (b) continually place actors, born and recruited, (c) into social relations with one another. The social relations (d) permit people in variable ways to call on the share of social labor carried by each, in order to (e) effect the necessary transformation of nature. (Wolf 1982: 91, emphasis in original)

In advanced capitalist economies, mobilizing and organizing workers when market forces do not work becomes an economic problem with cultural, social, and political repercussions. It involves, in short, developing a nonmarket labor process such as slavery or indentured servitude. With notable exceptions (Griffith 1986b; Lamphere 1985; Nash 1985; Foner and Napoli 1978), social scientific analyses of these phenomena have been confined primarily to capitalist enclaves in underdeveloped countries. In these contexts, tribal, peasant, and other non-Western cultural features intervene between the expansion of capitalism and its need for a reliable, reproducible supply of wage labor (e.g., Stoler 1985a, 1985b; Worsley 1984; de Janvry 1983). These studies have documented a variety of ways that capitalist industries reduce their reliance on market forces by drawing on resident systems of authority. They range, for example, from studies of tribal villagers and peasants entering labor markets to pay taxes or rents (e.g. Roseberry 1983; Boyd 1981; Ong 1983; Stricter 1985) to studies that show how imperialist, patriarchal, and militaristic social relations aid in the development of a docile, reliable supply of labor (e.g., Froebel, Heinrichs, and Kreye 1977; Portes and Walton 1980; Stoler 1985a; Fernandez-Kelly 1983; Lim 1983; Bolles 1983). Some analysts have also shown how industries rely on sexual, ethnic, and national distinctions between workers to undermine the political power and class consciousness of labor (Gordon, Edwards, and Reich 1982; Mintz 1974; Safa 1983; Saffioti 1980; Bunivic, Lycette, and McGreevey 1983). In the process, these industries reinforce myths about certain groups of people being biologically or culturally predisposed to assuming specific positions in the international division of labor.

The next logical step in expanding this work involves demonstrating how resident systems of authority and mythology are used to assure supplies of workers in advanced capitalist societies. By drawing on kinship, informal social relations, and formal political relations, these labor processes involve redefining power relations between those who demand and those who supply labor. The revised power relations often conflict with prevailing political economic ideologies and ideas of legitimate and illegitimate behaviors. This may create no great problem when mobilizing labor for short-term tasks involving few people. Yet when employers need labor for large-scale economic tasks, redefining power relations becomes problematic and complex. Typically it involves a joint endeavor of attempting to legitimate a nonmarket labor process while developing more comprehensive power relations to assure a supply of labor.

Clearly, at some level, labor supplies can be regulated by wage rates, yet the level at which these market mechanisms take effect is often too high from the employer's subjective and objective notions about the profitability of the firm. Such a situation commonly prevails in industries that produce highly perishable commodities in highly competitive environments, or produce commodities that are extremely sensitive to fluctuations in supply and demand. Food producing industries fall squarely within this category. In addition to producing perishable commodities, these industries are susceptible to the myriad natural phenomena that ripple through the food chain, influencing the supplies and prices of foodstuffs. Commodity subsidy programs, preferential market arrangements, and restrictive trade policies help to reduce this exposure somewhat, yet prices and profit margins can fluctuate so greatly that food producers tend to operate with a "worst-case-scenario" outlook (Hansen, et al. 1981). Their conscious attempts to keep labor costs as low as possible influence their labor recruitment strategies.

In this chapter, I reconsider the labor processes of seafood processing and poultry processing, comparing them to a labor process that depends on legally imported alien farm labor. These three cases share a number of features that make them comparable at a general level of analysis. First, these industries produce perishable commodities. Second, labor recruiters in these industries actively seek workers who are somewhat marginal to the labor market because of gender, ethnic, or national affiliations. Marginality implies workers will have means of support independent of their participation in the labor market. We have seen that workers accomplish this in a variety of ways. They may engage in informal economic activity (babysitting, landscaping, upholstering, etc., for example), rely on transfer payments, or rely on incomes of other members of their households or social networks. We noted earlier that workers in rural areas are likely to have these alternate support systems because of their direct access to low-cost, locally produced foodstuffs and because of the complex of bartering and informal commerce that occurs in the countryside (Gladwin 1988; Hansen, et al. 1981). Whether rural or urban, however, the presence of alternate means of support allows workers to offer their labor for sale to employers at lower rates than workers who have no means of support beyond the labor market. This is not to say that low-wage workers do not seek higher wages or better working conditions; nor are we suggesting that workers with alternate means of support do not really need the low-wage jobs. Often the low-wage job is a crucial part of the total household income, and workers who are dependent on their jobs must exercise care in combining the employer's scheduling needs and tolerance for absenteeism with the needs of the alternate means of support. Combining one's own needs with employers' tolerance levels often forces workers to engage in secrecy, conspiracy, and deception. This enhances divisions between employers and employees in a way that characterizes class struggle under more authoritarian and militarized systems of control.

The negative side of this, from employers' perspectives, is that these alternate means of support contribute to high rates of absenteeism among the workers and to high labor turnover. They contribute, as well, to the erosion of employers' power over workers because workers who engage in a variety of economic activities experience a variety of forms of domination. For example, domination can be rooted in relations between sexes within the household, ethnic relations within communities, or class relations within complex societies. These forms of domination may be justified by not only distinct but contradictory symbolic systems (Griffith 1988). Thus, because workers "have experienced the dominance of different classes in different contexts, they are often able to see [employers'] power—not as a necessary fact of life—but as contingent and contestable" (Collins 1989: 8).

Under these conditions, it becomes advantageous for employers to reduce the training periods in their shops to accommodate a high-turnover labor force, adjusting the technical components of the production process accordingly. This facilitates simplifying and compartmentalizing employee-employer relations to the point that supervision hinges on a few authoritarian mechanisms (e.g., firing, failure to pay bonuses, increased intimidation) rather than rests on a complex symbolic system. It becomes advantageous, in other words, to deskill jobs in low-wage labor industries even further. In industries where some jobs cannot be further deskilled, high labor turnover ranks among the industry's most pressing problems.

Yet even in highly automated environments, high labor turnover remains a gnawing problem for low-wage labor industries, exerting heavy influence on employers' labor strategies. At some level, even authority within the plants must have symbolic backing, if only based on crude notions of law, ownership, and the existence of police. Thus the third, forth, and fifth features common to the three cases discussed in this chapter are that employers' strategies typically combine: (1) the exercise of political power at various levels; (2) the harnessing of informal authority (of the family, ethnic group, community, etc.); and (3) the invocation of myth and symbolic endorsement to justify and lend legitimacy to these behaviors. In concrete terms, employers in low-wage industries actively lobby for political decisions that reduce native low-wage workers' alternate means of support or reduce the extent to which workers can rely on these means. Current welfare reforms that include "workfare" provisions can be interpreted, in part, as the result of such sentiments. The process of reducing workers' alternate means of support is similar to the ways proletarianization displaced or destabilized peasantries in the context of plantation agriculture around the world (e.g. Stoler 1985b; Wolf 1982). Among other things, more relaxed immigration policies would achieve this by increasing the size of the low-wage labor pool and the consequent competition between low-wage native and immigrant workers. As evidence that employers perceive these relationships, we note here the personnel manager who said, "Take a group of black and white workers and bring in Asians or Mexicans and the others will start to work harder and have less absences." Additional legal immigration programs would accomplish this as well, although with a different impact on native workers, since legal immigration programs (e.g. H2a's or SAWs) rest on the premise (itself constructed in legal battles— see Griffith 1986b, 1984) that native workers are not willing to work in the job in question.

Political activity that succeeds in reducing workers' alternate means of support, while assuring greater supplies of low-wage workers, nevertheless runs the risk of contradicting workers' abilities to work for low wages in the first place. Again, this is because their alternate economic activities and survival strategies partially subsidize their wages.

In addition to exercising political power, employers in industries with high labor turnover also rely on systems of informal authority, such as the authority of senior members of a society over junior members or men over women. In low-wage labor processes in advanced capitalist societies, this assumes the concrete form of network recruitment, which shifts responsibility for locating and attracting labor from employers to current workers in the plants. In places where network recruitment has been enhanced or institutionalized with direct payments to workers who recruit new workers, the potential for workers exerting their authority over new recruits increases. In these cases, the recruit's performance—particularly his or her attendance— directly affects the worker-recruiter's pay. In its most insti- tutionalized form, network recruitment amounts to nothing less than subcontracting the social pressures to perform on the job to a portion of the labor force.

Finally, in low-wage labor processes in the culture of late capitalism, where autocracy is politically unfeasible, employers' power over workers cannot be absolute. Hence, employers must marshall myths and symbols toward justifying the labor process. The ways employers draw upon myths of ethnicity, gender, and nationality to justify hiring, job allocation practices, etc., can be extremely subtle. This dimension of employers' behavior has received little attention in the social scientific literature on labor, since it deals with the amorphous symbolic realm of human behavior. In addition to its subtlety, symbolism is difficult to measure. Nevertheless, as we have seen in earlier chapters, it has been common for employers to draw upon myths that certain sexes, ethnic groups, or nationalities are somehow predisposed toward working harder or working specific tasks better than others. Certainly this is not entirely myth, since there is ample evidence that new immigrants will perform better, from an employers' perspective, than U.S. workers. They tend to complain less because of language barriers, and they tend to be more grateful for their jobs than native workers, at least in the short run. Yet there is an equal amount of evidence that, over time, these immigrants shed their pliant reputations and behaviors (Massey, et al. 1987). This suggests that these behaviors are not derived from gender or ethnicity per se but from the historical experiences of specific classes in the international division of labor. Drawing on myths such as these, however, has political implications, aiding employers in their lobbying efforts or their influence over court decisions (Griffith 1984).

The similarities and differences among the cases presented here aid us in teasing apart low-wage labor processes and determining the principles underlying the use of low-wage labor in advanced capitalist culture. The analysis I present in this chapter suggests that low-wage labor processes depend on the organizing principles of kinship and informal social relations, as well as on formal political power. The ways employers combine these three systems of authority vary according to the scale and seasonality of production. However, as the labor processes utilize more formal organizing principles, they do not necessarily involve a corresponding increase in reliance on market forces to assure the supply of labor. Instead, employers have developed political and cultural mechanisms to maintain, extend, and legitimate their

control over the quantity and quality of labor available for commodity production.

I have already fully elaborated my argument for seafood
and poultry processing. Chapters 3 through 8 presented copious
amounts of data illustrating the ways employers and workers in
those industries construct labor processes that rest on labor
control. Both of these industries have been able to rely on local
kinship and ethnic relations to assure supplies of labor to their
industries. Yet the same organizing principles cannot be relied
upon in the production of commodities requiring thousands of
workers for highly seasonal work. Few North Carolina seafood
houses hire more than fifty workers, and most hire fewer than
twenty-five. Some poultry plants hire upwards of 1,000 to 1,500
workers, yet can offer regular work throughout the year. The apple
harvests along the eastern seaboard and the south Florida sugar
harvests, on the other hand, require the mobilization of upwards
of 15,000 men per year for seasonal work ranging from six weeks
to seven months in duration. In this case, both the scale of
production and the length of the harvest season underlie growers'
dependence on a nonmarket labor process that is distinctly
different from that found in poultry or seafood processing.

The mechanisms that growers rely on to recruit, organize,
and deploy labor are clearly more political than economic. The
international transfer of men for the harvest involves the
participation of the U.S. Department of Labor, the Immigration
and Naturalization Service, the British West Indian Central Labor
Organization, and the Ministries of Labor in the participating
emigrant countries (Jamaica, Barbados, St. Vincent, St. Lucia,
and Dominica). Other formal associations involved in this labor
process are growers' organizations such as the New England Apple
Council and the Florida Fruit and Vegetable Association. The
continued reliance on the alien labor program has been characterized by the expansion of political influence of the growers. This
formal political influence precludes any less informal, kinship or
community ties which may exist between workers or between
workers and growers. For this reason, I discuss here growers'
political influence and its repercussions.

Background to the Development of Legal Imported Labor

Both the Bracero and the British West Indies (BWI) programs—two programs that legally imported farm workers—began

in response to real and perceived shortages of farm labor brought about by U.S. involvement in World War II. Between June, 1940, when the defense manpower program began, and October, 1941, five million defense related jobs were created (*Monthly Labor Review* 1945). Responses to farm labor shortages came from a variety of sectors of U.S. society. In addition to hiring more women—a practice common throughout the economy—growers turned to youths, older people, and strange mixes of cooperation and coercion:

> The major source of wartime farm-labor recruits was the local population, either residents or persons from nearby small towns. "Twilight" bands of townspeople, soldiers on special leave, vacationists, high-school students, and college girls temporarily increased the ranks of farm labor. Japanese-Americans and prisoners of war were utilized in some farm areas. (*Monthly Labor Review* 1945: 449)

During the first two years of the war, however, the U.S. Department of Labor (DOL) continued to balk at importing foreign workers to harvest crops. Despite perceived labor shortages and complaints of labor shortages by growers, DOL officials maintained that there were adequate numbers of domestic workers for the harvests. In an attempt to restrain the rhetoric surrounding this issue, the DOL recommended that public documents claiming that a farm labor shortage existed should be reviewed by the Department of Agriculture prior to their release (*Monthly Labor Review* 1945). Writing over ten years later, Rassmussen argued that labor *shortages* were less at issue than the ability of growers to keep paying low wages because of oversupplies of labor (1951). Whether labor shortages were real or perceived during the first two years of the war, there was little dispute that a farm labor shortage was slowly in the making. Comparisons of 1940 domestic employment in agricultural and nonagricultural sectors with the same figures for 1945 are particularly telling. Even with substantial increases in women entering the domestic labor force, agriculture experiences a nearly 10 percent loss of labor power.

The structural changes taking place throughout the economy underlie the development of a variety of labor processes, including the use of foreign labor. Small family farms were especially hard hit. As larger farms attracted more and more workers, smaller farms began to rely more on family labor and other means, as

Wolf puts it (1982: 91), "of committing social labor to the transformation of nature:"

The desire to stabilize the labor force appears to have caused a reversal in the South, since 1940, of the earlier trend from sharecroppers to hired workers. Moreover, some members of farm families who were formerly paid for their work on the family farm became partners or tenants and thus were removed from the hired-worker category. In some cases family workers shifted to paid work on other farms. Increased farm incomes, making possible the payment of a regular wage, caused some family workers to shift to the hired-worker group on the family farms. This change in status sometimes proved to be necessary to induce family workers to remain. Changes of this nature, however, did not prevent a comparatively large decline in the number of hired farm workers. (*Monthly Labor Review* 1945: 447)

TABLE 9.1

Changes in U.S. Agricultural and Nonagricultural
Employment by Sex: March 1940 and March 1945 Compared

Group	Employment		Percent of labor force
	March, 1940	March, 1945	
Agricultural			
Total	8,510,000	7,290,000	−9.3
Male	8,000,000	6,170,000	−20.1
Female	510,000	1,120,000	+72.0
Nonagricultural			
Total	36,550,000	43,540,000	+18.7
Male	25,820,000	27,060,000	+2.3
Female	10,730,000	16,480,000	+63.1
Entire Economy			
Total	45,060,000	50,830,000	+12.5
Males	33,820,000	33,230,000	−3.5
Females	11,240,000	17,600,000	+64.1

Source: *Monthly Labor Review*, September, 1945: 443.

As the farm labor crisis spread, the pressures to import workers grew: in 1942, Mexicans first legally entered the United States for the harvests. In 1943, over 50,000 Mexicans were allowed to work in the agricultural harvest of the Southwest, an 1139 percent increase over 1942. At the same time, a smaller group of alien workers came to the eastern United States from the Caribbean, marking the official beginning of the BWI Temporary Alien Labor Program. In its first year, the program admitted 8,828 men from Jamaica and 4,698 men from the Bahamas to work in agricultural occupations throughout the United States east of the Mississippi River. Throughout the war years, the Mexicans outnumbered the British West Indians by over two to one.

Following the war, the size differences between the Bracero and BWI programs grew, although both had become institutionalized to a degree that growers continued to argue for a need for foreign labor. Growers requesting foreign workers used the same arguments they use today: the threat of crop loss, the high productivity of foreign workers compared to U.S. workers, and the unreliability of U.S. workers to provide labor for the duration of harvests (Martin 1986). Although farm labor shortages were neither as widespread nor acute during the Korean conflict as during WWII, the perceived shortages of domestic farm workers further justified continuing both the BWI and Mexican programs (Rassmussen 1951; U.S. Congress 1978). Western growers took advantage of the accommodative political climate. From nearly 75,000 Mexican workers in 1950, the Bracero program provided the legal framework to import between 400,000 and 450,000 annually during the last half of the decade.

During the 1960s, while the Bracero program came under increasing scrutiny and fire in the U.S. Congress and the courts, the BWI program succeeded in keeping a low profile. Many opponents of the Bracero program praised the BWI program as "a situation that is working out perfectly satisfactorily today" (U.S. Congress 1978: 13). Many of the statements by labor leaders, however indicate they were willing to sacrifice the termination of the BWI program for the termination of the Bracero program, which was considerably larger. Prior to the Bracero program's termination, Congress dissected the BWI program from Public Law 78, the law which guided recruitment and transport of Mexican workers (U.S. Congress 1978).

Discussion

The legal distinction between the two programs reflected concrete differences. Obviously, the Bracero program, especially during the 1950s, was a far larger, more visible, more apparently threatening assault on domestic farm labor than the BWI program. The Bracero program's size dictated more comprehensive government support and regulations, factors which made it more "national" in scope. Involving direct participation by federal agencies and elected officials, it was also more legitimate and more susceptible to higher levels of litigation than the BWI program.

Whereas the Department of Labor recruited and transported Mexicans to work in U.S. agriculture, apple and sugar growers with access to West Indian labor negotiated directly with the governments of the countries that supplied them with workers. In addition, the DOL's role in the BWI program has been advisory only. Whether growers are actually allowed to import foreign workers is decided in the Justice Department, usually at the district court level. The DOL's local and regional offices inspect labor camps, establish wage rates, and certify growers to import labor, but denial of certification does not necessarily mean growers will not receive workers. In fact, certification acted as an endorsement of the program, a means to legitimate it, for nearly thirty years. Only since the early 1970s has the DOL begun, in isolated cases, to refuse to certify growers, and in all cases a district court judge has overturned the DOL's ruling (Griffith 1984; U.S. Congress 1978). The certification door, evidently, swings only one way: legitimating growers' access to foreign labor, but never hampering access in the absence of legitimacy.

Until the 1970s, the BWI program received little opposition from domestic labor groups and their supporters. Since then, however, it has come under increasing political scrutiny as opposition to the program has become more organized, more litigious, and more vocal. The dialogue surrounding the opposition between growers, domestic labor, and the state is indicative of the political and ideological supports that growers draw upon to continue to gain access to Caribbean labor. At the heart of the growers' claim to foreign labor is their insistence that U.S. workers simply will not cut sugar cane or pick apples. To support this claim, growers' associations collect and publish statistics showing attrition rates of domestic workers. In response, the DOL has collected testimonial evidence that capable domestic workers are willing to do the work, producing, for example, affidavits at Senate subcommittee hearings. At other times the DOL has provided Puerto Ricans for apple harvests in West Virginia, and Mississippi farm workers and Cuban (Marielitos) and Haitian refugees for the south Florida sugar harvests, only to have growers shun them for British West Indians. Growers' justifications, in these cases, expand to invoke myths of ethnic or national propensities toward certain behaviors, stating that Cubans "only showed up to the recruiting sessions to see what they could steal" or citing the low productivity of U.S. workers. "There is a social taboo on this kind of work," said a sugar company spokesperson during a labor dispute in 1973 (Shabecoff 1973: 4). "Besides, American people don't like this kind of stoop labor. It's too hard for them. Jamaicans can cut 100 feet an hour all day. That's about eight tons a day. But when we test Americans who come for the jobs they can't even cut 100 feet for an hour." In other cases, growers have charged that the DOL's attempts to get them to hire domestic workers are discriminatory, undermining their abilities to compete with other growers who import Jamaicans (U.S. Congress 1978, 1983a, 1983b). One district court ruling, later overturned at a higher level, maintained that it was "burdensome" to import workers from Louisiana when the DOL found willing, unemployed Louisiana men to pick apples for a Virginia company. Evidently the judge believed it was less "burdensome" to import men from Jamaica.

The BWI program continues in part because of growers' direct access to British West Indians combined with the many local and regional layers of bureaucracy insulating them from the legal attacks of domestic labor and the DOL. The ultimate battles over farm labor are fought at the local (i.e. district court), instead of the national, level, where it is notoriously easier to exercise legal and illegal forms of persuading judges. Eastern growers who import British West Indians control the labor process largely by virtue of their influence at levels of organization below the national level, although they also have lobbyists and others working for them in Washington. Especially in local contexts, drawing on sometimes absurd arguments to justify their control over labor, they are able to muster the kind of support that western growers, battling labor groups in a national arena, were ultimately unable to find.

Conclusion

Clearly, there are distinct differences between processing poultry and seafood and importing Mexican and British West Indian workers to harvest U.S. crops. Nevertheless, at a general level, the cases tell us about attempts to control labor in an advanced capitalist economy when market forces have failed. Their lessons are twofold: First, they offer insight into how labor processes change as the work settings involve different scales of production combined with different seasonal demands and, in this and other ways, diverge from traditional settings such as those found in year-round, urban occupations. Second, they provide interesting commentary on the means employers use to justify the labor process when it diverges from the traditional mold.

In a capitalist political economic system, the so-called "free market" and its brethren concepts (e.g. supply and demand, market mechanism, etc.) exist not only as objective phenomena, but also as symbolic reservoirs, repositories of meaning and ritual that influence thought, opinion, and behavior. The supportive roles they play in prevailing political economic practices are often so great that any political or economic activities that appear to contradict them become objects of hostility and sources of conflict. The apparent failure of market forces in the production of perishable commodities has engendered such conflict. In the cases presented above, people question the legitimacy of the labor process. The cases presented above resemble one another not only because they depend on nonmarket forces to assure supplies of labor, but also because the employers are forced to justify, legally and informally, their reliance on nonmarket forces. Their justifications sometimes serve as legal avenues to actual policy decisions. They also, often, reinforce local myths to legitimate the labor process to those directly or indirectly involved at the local level.

In fact, to some extent, these labor processes depend on myths of ethnicity, gender, nationality: the "nigger-work," "women-are-better-with-their-hands," "Americans-don't-like-this-kind-of-stoop-labor" ideas that certain kinds of people are somehow culturally or biologically predisposed to performing certain tasks. The sugar company spokespeople have always been quick to cite domestic workers' reluctance to cut cane and West Indian rates of productivity as means to further justify their continued access to foreign workers. Yet new domestic workers' productivity rates are compared, somewhat unfairly, with those of long-time, skilled and highly productive West Indian workers (U.S. Congress 1983a; cf. Foner and Napoli 1978). Such comparisons *appear* to give credence to the notion that West Indian are somehow "naturally" better than U.S. workers at cutting sugar or picking apples.

Similarly, owners of oyster and crab processing plants in North Carolina and poultry processors throughout the southeast reinforce myths of sex and ethnicity in many ways. The sections on ethnicity and the work ethic, discussed in chapter 7, more than confirm this in the poultry plants. North Carolina seafood processing plant owners are nearly unanimous in their complaints that they must rely on predominantly Black, female workers because white males just won't do the work. Many also made statements to the effect that men had no patience for this kind of work, implying that even if they did raise wages or improve working conditions they would still have a labor supply problem. Their recruiting efforts, conducted primarily in black settlements and through black contacts, reflect these beliefs. So, too, does the way they allocate tasks in the plants. White women usually occupy the year-round or higher status jobs at the plants, as office employees and clerks at seafood counters. Black women pick the crabs, occupying the lowest positions in the plants. Black men most often fill the trucking, maintenance, and other positions that are more varied and less seasonal than the crab-picking and oyster-shucking jobs. Poultry processors also reported some task allocation by ethnicity, which Walker's study in Utah (1987) more explicitly confirms.

Whether or not the assertions of plant owners are objectively true is an issue that they do not explore. The occasional male or white crab picker, for example, tends not to erode the fact that the primary recruiting practices and task assignments reinforce myths of gender and ethnicity. Plant owners' interactions with their workers confirm the extent to which they have internalized these myths. One day in the field I observed the following confrontation between a white crab-processing-plant owner and one of his black employees. Though laced with jest, the scene depicts the myths and tensions inhabiting relations between White employers and their Black employees. It also makes it quite clear that plant owners may use their power to degrade their employees. The passage, taken from my field notes, uses pseudonyms to protect respondents' privacy.

It was lunchtime. I was interviewing Les, the plant owner, as Black women passed through the office to buy the cans of deviled ham and Vienna sausages or cellophane packs of soda crackers that Les sold from the shelves above his file cabinets, making notes in his ledger about debits and advances. The workers streamed through for about five minutes before settling in for lunch. Just after most of this activity died down, Phil, a Black man, one of Les's mid-level employees, stormed into the office, impatient, dressed to work but tired of waiting. Irritated, he said, "I told Johanessen if he didn't show up [with fish to pack and ship] by noon, I wasn't gonna wait any more."

Les narrowed his eyes at Phil. "You'll wait if I tell you to."

Phil straightened up on that one, immediately defiant, evidently resenting Les's implication. Raising his voice and shaking his head, he said, "I got five dollar in my pocket!" Something like a smile crossed his lips, but whether of pride or humility I couldn't tell.

"How'd you get five dollar?" Les asked him, squinting even more.

Now smiling openly, even victoriously, although still maintaining the defiant stance, Phil said, "I told Peterson I wouldn't deliver no mo' lessen he paid me."

Les looked at him directly, only now joining Phil in the humor of the exchange, yet turning it back on Phil, grinning, saying, "Now don't you go nigger on me," to which Phil shook his head dramatically, still smiling, and stormed back out the door.

What does this confrontation tell us about labor relations? First, Phil obviously earned his "five dollar" from a source other than Les's plant, and that income contributes to his ability to leave Les's plant when scheduling or working conditions don't suit him. He's tired of waiting. He has the means, just then, to go home. How does Les implore him to stay? He tells him not to "go nigger," a verb phrase I take to mean something like: acting in a manner characteristic of a certain stereotypic black person. "Going nigger," evidently, isn't something a processing plant owner likes to see from his employees. It involves becoming independent of work by virtue of having the means, temporarily, to shirk dependence.

But there is something more telling going on here. The ease with which Les insults Phil shows how institutionalized are race relations in the South. These relations entail not only innumerable material conditions but also the ability of whites to degrade and humiliate blacks. The strained humor that characterizes this exchange illustrates how ritualized this humiliation has become. Nor is this restricted to rural or uneducated people of the deep South. Indeed, the frank familiarity of the confrontation reminded me of a famous exchange between LBJ and Thurgood Marshall. When Marshall asked the president why he nominated him for the Supreme Court, LBJ said, "Because I want people to look down that hall and see a nigger sitting in one of those offices." The ease with which Les and LBJ used one of the worst ethnic slurs in America implied an acceptance of racial discord. Its ritualized nature further implies a fatalism toward dispelling myths of ethnicity, and even a willingness to perpetuate and extend such mythologies among those who could probably most effectively promote understanding and cooperation.

In light of the above findings, how can we expect employers to respond when confronted with labor supply problems? Rather than rely on market mechanisms, employers of small labor forces with fluctuating seasonal labor demands rely on the traditional authority that resides in relations of family and community. Employers needing large numbers of workers for seasonal work, however, must draw on the more formal, comprehensive systems of authority of the state. Finally, between these extremes, employers such as poultry processors, who need low-wage labor for onerous tasks on a year-round basis, rely on both formal political authority and the traditional authority found in ethnic groups and communities. They have, moreover, begun to institutionalize the latter through bonus payments for network recruitment. In an advanced capitalist economy, these different kinds of and mixes of authority, which may be legitimately combined and exercised in noneconomic contexts, may be perceived as an illegitimate exercise of authority in economic contexts. Because of this employers invoke myths, and these myths act as justification to politicians and local personnel who can aid in solving the labor supply problem, including the workers themselves.

In widely publicized settings, such as South Africa and Chile, nonmarket labor processes have grown up in heavily militarized, authoritarian contexts. Such potentially explosive cases overshadow the subtler ways that the authoritarian deployment of labor occurs and is supported by resident myths and symbols in advanced capitalist societies. Analyses of these phenomena are increasing in importance as the "new" international division of labor continues along its current course of fragmented industrial production that relies on cheap, malleable, and often female and foreign labor (Gordon, Edwards, and Reich 1982; Edwards, Reich, and Gordon 1973; Worsley 1984; Wolf 1982; Nash 1985; Stoler 1985a, 1985b; Sanderson, 1985; Frobel, Heinrichs, and Kreye 1977). Border industrialization programs, export platforms, and alien labor and European guestworker programs—all symptoms of this new division of labor—exacerbate differences between segments of labor forces and further reinforce the myths that certain kinds of people are culturally or biologically predisposed to performing certain kinds of tasks. At a more abstract level, this implies that specific sexes, ethnic groups, or nationalities are predisposed toward specific class positions in the international division of labor.

The means of ascribing peoples and individuals to class and occupational groups because of their ethnic, gender, or national affiliations may well be undergoing revision in labor's own backyard. This occurs as employers attempt to marshal the authority systems and symbolism that already exist (in workers' households, communities, and political systems) to address their labor problems. The failure of the domestic labor market to provide necessary labor under conditions amenable to maintaining profit margins has led industries to adopt more authoritarian methods of labor control, methods based less on market mechanisms than on formal political power or the informal power that rests within family and community. In some cases, we have seen here, this involves nothing less than tapping the powers that rest within spheres beyond the market: family, community, ethnic group, and nation. The principles by which these practices emerged are the subject of the following chapter.

10

Networks, Reproductive Labor, and the Manipulation of Community in the Formation of Low-Income Populations

> The protests of the workers this time were based on the lack of sanitary facilities in their living quarters, the nonexistence of medical services, and terrible working conditions. They stated, furthermore, that they were not being paid in real money but in scrip, which was good only to buy Virginia ham in the company commissaries.... [T]he workers turned away from the authorities in Macondo and brought their complaints up to the higher courts. It was there that the sleight-of-hand lawyers proved that the demands lacked all validity for the simple reason that the banana company did not have, never had had, and never would have any workers in its service because they were all hired on a temporary and occasional basis. So that the fable of the Virginia ham was nonsense... and by a decision of the court it was established and set down in solemn decrees that the workers did not exist.
>
> —Gabriel Garcia Márquez, *One Hundred Years of Solitude*

The title of this chapter is designed to situate this work in the tradition in anthropology that has documented capitalism's role in the formation, reorganization, and maintenance of specific populations (e.g Collins 1988; Lamphere 1985; Stoler 1984; Griffith 1986a; Wolf 1982; Ong 1987; Roseberry 1983; Nash and Fernandez-Kelly 1983). Unlike the present work, most of these studies focus on regions and communities outside the United States. Most, in addition, come from the "peasant studies" tradition discussed in chapter 2, describing structural features and contradictions of the various processes by which peasants have been incompletely or unevenly incorporated into capitalist political and economic relations. Like the present work, however, most have engaged in documenting the interplay between local and global processes.

By situating this work in this tradition, yet using case material from populations that are clearly not peasantries or other traditional objects of anthropological inquiry, we can begin to establish a connection between capitalist expansion in under-developed regions and capitalist development and change in countries like the United States. This allows us to establish connections, as well, between what has been primarily sociological theory on labor under advanced capitalism and what has been primarily anthropological work on the incorporation of the peoples of underdeveloped regions into capitalist production systems and capitalist circuits of value. Such an endeavor is in the same spirit as the work of Frobel, Heinricks and Kreye (1977), who relate industrialization in the underdeveloped world to the weakening positions of labor in West Germany. They focus on the investment strategies, technological mechanisms, and trade policies by which production can be conducted, globally, through a joint fragmentation/integration process. Here, instead, I am interested in the social and cultural principles by which the construction, reorganization, and maintenance of capitalist labor markets take place, and in what conditions families and communities find themselves as a result of those processes.

Theoretical Representations of Labor

Within advanced capitalist dogma, theories of labor range from neoclassical economic models to segmentation or split labor market models. The former emphasize the free movement of labor according to market mechanisms and the latter emphasize structural barriers constraining the free movement of labor and its ability to respond to wage offers. Each of these positions contains clear lessons for the use of labor in the production process, including how workers are dealt with outside the confines of the production process. Each also has political implications. Finally, each of these positions results in distinctly different popular and intellectual representations of workers. Some portray them as organized political actors, others as rational economic actors, and still others as victims of exploitation. In the case of low-wage, marginal workers, each theoretical position represents their economic functions differently as well.

The Neoclassical Economics Model

In its treatment of labor as a commodity governed by market forces, the neoclassical economic model rests on the central assumption that human economic behavior is ultimately guided by economic rationality. Specifically, individual economic actors are assumed to sort themselves freely in labor markets, or into nonwage economic endeavors, attempting to maximize their incomes. The principal weakness of the model, however, is exactly this emphasis on individual decision making, which colors all empirical work and formal mathematical modeling conducted within this framework. Most importantly, the individual becomes the unit of analysis, thus reducing households, networks, and communities to mere collections of individual behaviors. Usually this is necessary to satisfy analytic criteria of statistical and mathematical modeling, which demand that units of analysis are discrete rather than interconnected, or that observations are independent of one another rather than influenced by one another. Other methodological problems derive from these as well as other traditions of neoclassical economic research. Case studies, for example, tend to be dismissed by economists for their restricted application. In place of case studies, economists usually rely on census data and other large data bases, willing to bury questions of data quality under academic conventions that carry weight among their colleagues and impress policy makers interested in "bottom-line" answers to complex social problems. In the process, economists reify their methods as being particularly objective and rigorous, reinforcing the fiction that phenomena such as "the economy" or "the labor market" exist apart from their social and cultural settings and operate according to the assumptions of economic rationality. If they don't, the economic actors, not the methods, are represented as flawed. As these ideologies are incorporated into the business training of capitalist entrepreneurs and corporate personnel managers, they influence the ways in which such individuals conceive of workers and, by extension, the ways they attempt to conform workers to the expectations and assumptions of economic rationality. In this vein, it becomes something noble or good to manipulate labor to behave as neoclassical economics expects it to behave, encouraging the ergonomic, time-and-motion, and other productivity experiments conducted after the tradition of F. W. Taylor's *Principles of Scientific Management* (1911).

Despite continued analytical, epistemological, and methodological flaws in this approach, understanding individual decision making lies at the heart of neoclassical economic models of the labor market. Specifically, individuals' decisions are assumed to be driven by the desire to maximize utility, which is itself organized or guided by the job market. In a recent article, discussing the concept of an "immigration market," which is essentially a labor market, Borjas characterizes this position as follows:

> It is important to note that although the idea of an immigration market is somewhat novel in the immigration literature, the notion that different agents are considering the allocation of resources among alternative uses and that this allocation is guided by a market basically defines economics.... [I]ndividuals consider a number of options to which they can allocate their time. Firms (or countries) offer different "employment" contracts. Individuals compare these job offers and nonrandomly sort themselves among available jobs (countries). (1989: 461)

The standard objection to the individual decision-making model of economic behavior is that it fails to give any formal recognition to the social and cultural foundations of decisions (Cook 1973; Boyd 1989). Its analytic focus occurs at a level of observation that cannot capture either the individual's social position or cultural heritage. Both social position and cultural background prevent the individual from considering some options in the first place. They also function to narrow the decision maker's range of options. This is not simply saying that a Mexican peasant won't apply for a position as a rocket scientist. Indeed, most economic models account for such things as skills and education, and assume that individuals take these into account when selecting jobs. The inadequacy of these models is that they are designed to observe the results of social and cultural processes— that is, individuals—rather than the processes themselves. Indeed, they treat these individuals as causal agents of some of the very social and cultural processes that influence their decisions.

The neoclassical model is especially inadequate as a guide to understanding *low-wage* labor markets for at least three reasons. First, it implies that individuals are free agents, unfettered by social relationships. Second, it overemphasizes the role of market forces in organizing and driving decisions. Third, it assumes that individuals are faced with a broad range of choices (whether of jobs, regions, countries, etc.), instead of with the restricted choices facing most low-wage workers. Low-wage workers often live in rural towns with few employment opportunities, have family responsibilities that dictate their labor market behavior, or come from educational and linguistic backgrounds that severely restrict their movement in labor markets. It is possible to demonstrate, empirically, that at some point low-wage workers freely choose among alternatives, sorting themselves in job markets, and that at some point the market is involved in this process. Yet such a focus misses the causes of those activities. It thus yields a partial, static, and superficial portrait of a dynamic and complex process (cf. Papademetriou, et al. 1989; Massey, et al. 1987; Portes and Bach 1985). The mechanisms by which low-wage workers' movements and job market behaviors are controlled are varied, numerous, and *common* enough to render the assumptions of utility-maximization misleading. Giving market forces dominance in this process, moreover, diverts attention from historical and experiential factors that surround and penetrate low-wage labor markets. Alternate theories of labor under advanced capitalism, however, recognize the ways in which history, society, and culture influence not only the behavior of workers in labor markets but the compositions of the labor markets themselves.

Segmented Labor Market Models

Theories of labor critical of the neoclassical model emphasize, after traditions established by Marx and Polayni, the social and cultural embeddedness of labor. The most influential models in this vein are the split labor market model, labor market segmentation models, and the dual economy model. While there are important distinctions between these approaches, all recognize that capitalist labor markets are segmented to the extent that mobility between segments of the labor market is restricted by sociologically important attributes of workers. Such attributes include ethnicity, race, gender, legal status, minority status, and socioeconomic background; in non-Western settings, we could add to this list such identifiers as tribes and castes (Vincent 1974). They become sociologically important as capitalist entrepreneurs organize production processes, a point noted by Wolf:

The opposing interests that divide the working class are further reinforced through appeals to "racial" and "ethnic" distinctions. Such appeals serve to allocate different categories of workers to rungs on the scale of labor markets, relegating the stigmatized populations to the lower levels and insulating the higher echelons from competition from below. Capitalism did not create all the distinctions of ethnicity and race that function to set off categories of workers from one another. It is, nevertheless, the process of labor mobilization under capitalism that imparts these distinctions their effective values. (1982: 380)

Segments of the labor market, as Wolf suggests, are structured hierarchically. Distinctions between levels of the hierarchy are functionally important in creating and maintaining key fictions, within working classes, about individual achievement and opportunities for advancement. These distinctions also offer workers psychological satisfaction from comparing their own conditions to those of workers in more hazardous, onerous, and lower paid positions. In addition, particularly from the perspective of the split labor market model, workers in various segments of the labor market can be used against one another, as when black or immigrant workers have been imported into union-organized industries to break strikes or undermine the effectiveness of labor organization (Portes and Bach 1985).

Though viewing the labor market as segmented, the dual economy model differs from the others in that instead of a number of segments, differentiated by ethnicity, gender, and so on, there are only two basic segments differentiated from one another by degree of organization and level of bureaucracy. An oligopolistic sector, sometimes referred to as the primary sector (e.g. Nash 1983), consists of those unionized industries in which labor is highly organized, rules of employer-employee interaction clearly delineated, some measure of job security achieved, and collective bargaining and grievance procedures highly developed. By contrast, a competitive or secondary sector is characterized by lack of labor organization, high degrees of uncertainty, low wages, high labor turnover, situational rules of employee-employer interaction, and so forth. The dual economy model converges with the other segmented models, however, in its observation that the two sectors are *internally* segmented: the oligopolistic sector by a complex, highly organized system of grades and job ladders, and the competitive sector by such factors as capital and labor-intensive technologies, firm size, production units, legal status, ethnicity, gender, and so forth.

While segmented models are preferable to neoclassical models, they still fail to capture the extent to which low-wage labor processes become interwoven with workers' households, networks, and communities. One criticism, coming from neoclassical economics, asserts that the lines between different segments of the labor force have been arbitrarily drawn and that the existence of segments has not been established empirically. More importantly, no one has "proven" the existence of boundaries between the different segments.

These criticisms rest in part on the kinds of proof some social scientists are and aren't willing to acknowledge. At the same time, they point to methodological and substantive weaknesses in segmented labor market models. Ironically, they also point to their strengths: while labor market segmentation theorists understand that labor markets are seated in social and cultural processes, they fall short of the logical extensions of their claims. In other words, the notion that labor markets, and the larger social phenomena of labor processes, become segmented by political, cultural, and social organizational means suggests their embeddedness in a broader social and cultural milieu. Segmentation models, though recognizing some degree of embeddedness, fall short of recognizing the complexity and subtlety of this embeddedness, particularly its relationship to power and labor control. Combined with the processual nature of the construction, reorganization, or maintenance of labor markets, this complexity and subtlety account for the difficulty of establishing, empirically, the existence of boundaries between segments of the labor market.

Reconsidering Notions: An Anthropology of Low-Wage Labor Under Advanced Capitalism

In the chapter that bears the same title as this section, I suggested that it is primarily in the low-wage sectors of the economy that capital experiments with recruitment techniques, methods of exploitation and labor control, and other features of the labor process. This is particularly the case in those onerous, injurious, difficult-to-staff industries such as seafood and poultry processing. In these contexts, low-wage labor, in turn, experiments with resistance, protest, and rebellion. Metaphorically, I refer to this process as workers attempting to pioneer new frontiers after old frontiers have been closed. Both of these positions derive from observations made by anthropologists studying the historical formation of peasant and tribal regions. Particularly relevant to the current work has been their emphasis on mechanisms of labor control, or the relationship between power and economic behavior. In addition to direct, firsthand supervision of workers, labor control also involves closing frontiers, commoditizing labor power, harnessing local patterns of authority, and other more subtle methods. By virtue of these power relations, global political economic processes assume central positions in the small-town, rural theaters of workers' households, networks, and communities.

The interplay of global and local processes has been central to the formation and transformation of low-wage labor markets under advanced capitalism. For example, the migrations of Southeast Asian refugees into the United States, and their subsequent use in poultry and meat packing, derive from geopolitical developments as well as from policy decisions at state and federal government levels. Obviously, the United States first embraced the humanitarian notion that we owed Southeast Asians political asylum following the Vietnam war. This served to relax federal refugee policy for Southeast Asians, as well as elicited impassioned responses from states and communities around the country. In the 1970s, the governor of Iowa, responding to a presidential request for states to come to the aid of Southeast Asian refugees, agreed to take virtually all black Thai that were in Southeast Asian refugee camps. This move, first, resulted in the formation of a large Iowa refugee service bureaucracy, capable of catering to additional refugee flows. At the same time, it encouraged native Iowan support for and tolerance of Southeast Asian refugees. An additional, unanticipated result of the refugee flow was the large-scale placement of Southeast Asian refugees in Iowa meat packing plants, a process aided by the newly established refugee service bureaus. Into the packing plants were thus transferred "old country" divisions along class and ethnic lines from Southeast Asia, which affected union membership, hiring, and promotion practices. Finally, this resulted in 98 percent of all black Thai in the United States living in Iowa, a fact that encourages later waves of black Thai refugees and immigrants to settle there as well (Iowa BRS, personal communication). The class and ethnic dynamics of these refugees' origins have been important because social and cultural backgrounds influence the behaviors of new immigrants in local economies and societies (Benson 1990; Portes and Bach 1985: chapter 2; Bonacich 1982). As such, the geopolitical developments that led to the refugee flow help us make sense of the ways the refugees contribute to the transformation of these small Iowa town's labor markets. This is particularly evident in cases where Southeast Asians have become directly involved in recruitment, establishing the terms by which new workers work in the plants (e.g. on the condition they post bonds or give kickbacks or sexual favors to personnel managers).

In another example, the migrations into the United States from the Caribbean, Mexico, and Central and South America, have been modified by changes in U.S. tariff laws and developments in the international division of labor (Sanderson, 1985; Nash and Fernandez-Kelly 1983). These laws and developments have stimulated industrial development along Mexico's border and in selected locations throughout Latin America and the Caribbean. Such developments tend to be accompanied by the reorienting and reorganizing of village and regional economies in Latin America and the Caribbean, which draw rural dwellers further into systems of taxation and labor and commodity markets (Goldring 1990; Mines and Anzaldúa 1982; Wolf 1982; Roseberry 1983). This contributes to labor flows to urban and industrial centers as domestic production systems become insufficient to meet the consumption needs of the household. In many cases, these domestic production operations have already been destabilized by labor recruitment schemes, agrarian reforms, export agricultural development, or forced resettlement (Hewitt de Alcantara 1976; Hansen and Oliver Smith 1983). Historically, we have seen this occur during the building of the Panama Canal, the Naval shipyards of Bermuda, the railroads of the United States and Central America, or the oil refineries of St. Croix, in plantation agricultural regions, and in the contexts of the Bracero and British West Indian Alien Labor programs (Massey, et al. 1987; Portes and Bach 1985; Papademetriou, et al. 1989; Griffith 1986b; Stoler 1984).

This interplay of global and local processes has resulted in one of the central features of low-wage labor in advanced capitalist economies. Specifically, low-wage labor's recruitment, its organization, and its terms of trade often become deeply interwoven with processes at work in workers' households (broadly defined), networks, and communities. This, in turn, generally results in a few concrete, interrelated practices in low-wage labor industries. All affect how labor is dealt with both inside and outside the production process. They are presented here as general principles of low-wage labor processes, which point to crucial social and cultural arenas where power relationships are negotiated and patterns of labor organization established. We have observed these principles at work in the seafood and poultry industries and in the U.S. farm labor force. This section is thus a summary of some of the more important points raised during the above discussion.

Network Recruiting. First, network recruitment assumes a central position among all methods of labor recruitment. This is an extension of the observation made by Portes and Bach (1985), Massey, et al. (1987), and others (Radcliffe 1990), that labor migrations into low-wage industries are consciously engineered rather than the result of "natural" flows of supply and demand. Those recruiting through network ties also become partially responsible for locating, screening, transporting, training, and controlling new workers. Of course, network recruitment also takes place among workers who are more effectively organized, unionized, and receive higher wages. Yet network recruitment among low-wage workers assumes dimensions that influence the organization of work, the wages and working conditions workers are willing to accept, and the extent to which employers can rely on "traditional" patterns of authority in their systems of labor control (e.g. the authority of parents over children, men over women, patrons over clients, clergy over congregation).

Network recruitment also serves as a tool for specific populations to establish monopolies over certain jobs or certain areas, and sometimes to use this monopoly to negotiate more amenable working arrangements (Martin 1986). In Watsonville, California, for example, a government subsidized labor camp for strawberry workers has been completely "colonized" by residents of a single village in Mexico. Although the camp is supposedly open to any strawberry workers in Watsonville, the residents of one village in Mexico have succeeded in keeping access to housing as well as information about openings of units confined to others from the same village (Goldring 1990; Mines and Anzaldúa 1982).

Once such monopolies have developed, they can serve as bases for labor organization or as social organizations that confine workers to specific regions or segments of the labor market. Indeed, Goldring found that the Mexican villagers with preferred access to cheap Watsonville housing tended to be less likely than other Mexican villagers from similar backgrounds to move out of work in agriculture or to seek work in other regions of the United States. By contrast, villagers from similar backgrounds, but without similar monopolies over housing, have tended to move out of agriculture more frequently and to have settled or found work in more locations throughout the country (Goldring 1990: 19-23).

Worker Self-Subsidization. The second common practice of firms in low-wage labor industries is that they tend to depend on formal and informal social support mechanisms to subsidize the costs of reproducing labor and maintaining labor during off seasons or periods of economic crisis. Particular reliance is placed on unpaid domestic or reproductive labor: through various income-generating activities, household restructuring and reallocation of tasks, or consumer-tightening strategies, workers' households absorb some of the costs of reproducing and maintaining labor. This could take the form, for example, of children assuming part of the household responsibilities at a younger age than would otherwise be the case, or elderly individuals put to work in the household after leaving the formal labor market. Of course, these practices may seem beneficial for their promotion of responsibility in young people or for keeping old people active and full of self-worth. Yet their benefits can also easily become outweighed when children have to leave school because of household tasks or the elderly sicken under increased strain and anxieties of their tasks.

Low-wage industries may also take advantage of unpaid domestic labor through relocation strategies. Since the 1940s, the U.S. poultry and meat packing industries have relocated plants from northern and urban areas to southern, midwestern, and predominantly rural areas. We noted in the above chapters that locating plants in rural areas implies drawing upon a labor force that may also engage in domestic production and independent, small-scale producer activities. Further, many counties that drew meat packing plants out of Chicago and St. Louis three decades ago were and are still predominantly farming counties, where seasonal fluctuations in labor demands on farms make it possible for farmers to work in meat packing during winter months. In urban settings, informal economic activities also include landscaping, masonry, carpentry, artisan production, food processing for street vending, scavenging, and engaging in crime. These other economic activities, whether in rural or urban areas, constitute the raw sociological material for the new frontiers that low-wage workers pioneer.

Again we note that these sorts of formal, informal, or seasonal economic activities can be both beneficial and detrimental to plant labor policy. On the one hand, they allow workers some independence from plants and constitute a basis for rejecting job offers and resisting the extent to which capital can penetrate their households, networks, and communities. On the other, they subsidize workers' wages and lower workers' "living wage" needs and expectations.

The most efficient balance between worker self-subsidization and worker independence of plants is struck when plants use immigrant or refugee populations. This becomes most clear in programs such as the H2a program discussed in the previous chapter and elsewhere (Griffith 1985; U.S. Congress 1978), or in the migrant programs of South Africa. When using immigrant populations in populations such as these, capital is able to separate productive and reproductive labor. Workers are wholly dependent on plants while at the work site, yet may be repatriated during slack seasons, after layoffs, or during economic downturns (Burawoy 1976; Portes and Walton 1980; Griffith 1985). Even in cases where immigrants and refugees bring their families with them, reduced subsistence and reproductive needs may derive from different subjective notions of acceptable levels of subsistence, particularly in the realm of housing. In some cases, the ways households experiment with various forms of coresidence, bringing individuals into households for specific maintenance and reproductive reasons, serves the needs of capital while allowing workers to broaden their economic opportunities (Chavez 1989; Griffith, et al. 1990). More broadly, such experimental coresidence has been identified as transnationalism, which involves designing household survival strategies with reference to the opportunity structures, social constraints, and cultural features of communities, often ethnically based, that span two or more nations (Glick-Schiller and Fouron 1990). In a number of places in this work we have documented cases of households with "anchor" domestic units or residences in two or more countries or regions (see chapters 8 and 2, for example). While such social organizational forms serve capital's needs for an extremely fluid labor force that is able to subsidize itself during layoffs and other periods of economic crisis, these forms may also empower workers against other attempts to control their time and space. Speaking of illegal immigrants,

Chavez notes that, "Coresidential strategies are the undocumented immigrants' first level of defense against the economic and political constraints on their lives" (1990: 31).

Such strategies are not designed in social vacuums, however. Although they may empower workers who are able to transcend national boundaries, they serve to undermine those workers who cannot form and reform households or move between areas with high and low costs of living with each shift of economic growth or decline. The presence of workers so disadvantaged stimulates community groups to establish soup kitchens and friendship houses, as well as provides the state with reasons to institutionalize welfare and unemployment insurance programs. Particularly in the farm labor market, these public and private social funds have partially replaced the domestic or reproductive labor necessary to assure continued supplies of labor. Usually, some combination of relying on such social funds and relying on domestic and reproductive labor has emerged.

Finally, a practice related to taking advantage of social support mechanisms such as subsidies is the increasing fragmentation-integration of the production process through subcontracting. We see this in the poultry industry, where the growing of birds is almost entirely subcontracted, as well as in the farm labor market, with increases in the use of farm labor contractors over the past thirty years. Sharecropping and other arrangements that subcontract parts of the productive process to the workers themselves are also spreading. In the economy at large, we see this occurring with the proliferation of "homework" systems, in which companies offer women bound by childcare responsibilities the opportunity of performing tedious piecework in their homes. Such arrangements serve to transfer risk from the corporation to the individual who raises the birds, harvests the crops, wraps the semiconductor, and so forth. They also relieve industries of much of the responsibility for worker safety, health insurance, unemployment, pensions, and other common features of the wage relationship.

Community Penetration. In addition to relying heavily on network recruitment and domestic and reproductive labor, in low-wage labor contexts, employers and owners of capital use social, cultural, and political features of their host communities and worker populations to assign tasks and control labor. In a recent book, Bailey (1986) acknowledges this with his insistence on looking beyond skill levels and individual economic (human capital) traits to understand differences between immigrants and native workers in low-wage labor markets:

> The conception of the labor process as simply the employment of individuals of various skill levels is a narrow one indeed. For each individual, work is one among a set of competing activities. The mobilization of labor involves more than a technological relationship among skills, machines, and materials; it is fundamentally shaped by the interactions between workers and the broad social and institutional context within which work occurs. Moreover, the labor process not only involves the use of skills in the production of goods and services but is also itself a crucial process in the reproduction of required skills. (1986: 21).

In most cases, these broader social and institutional contexts are entire rural communities or significant neighborhoods and networks within rural communities. The nature of a plant's interaction with the community becomes a central feature of labor relations in the plants and of the ways in which the plants are staffed. These interactions are simultaneously a part of and a result of the condition of the local economy in which a plant operates. Today, poultry, meat, and seafood processing plants are usually located in counties with low population densities and low per capita incomes relative to the rest of the United States. Within these settings, power relations that are established inside low-wage work places become mirrored and reinforced by power relations beyond plant walls.

An important issue here concerns the extent to which plant managers view themselves as part of the community as opposed to the guardians of capital, investing where they will receive the highest returns, with weak links to, or little long-term interest in, the community. In one sense, we can consider the "community"—here usually a small rural town or a county—as the state in microcosm. Communities mediate among capital, labor, and larger regulatory bodies and agencies (especially, in the present case, OSHA) by "translating" regulation into terms which make sense in the local cultural, social, and institutional context. Through mediums of public opinion, communities also assess the relative legitimacy or worth of the respective claims and complaints of workers or managers. While the degree of community involvement or attachment is difficult to quantify, its importance has been noted by many observers of U.S. industry (Bluestone and Harrison 1982; Newman 1988). In meat packing, the development of "corporate mentality," or an attitude of profits over people, generates not only resentment among workers but tends to alienate native workers with regard to the value or place of work in their lives, a development that soon undermines what plant managers see as the "work ethic." In poultry plants, as well, workers reported that they felt like old used up pieces of machinery after occupational injuries: "used up and tossed out the door." At the community level, the high incidence of occupational injury burdens local social services and erodes the productivity of the entire population. During periods of crisis, as in labor disputes or plant closings, the kinds of concessions handed to workers as community commitment dwindles can be drastic, complex, and conscious raising, as I recorded after an in-depth interview with a forty-three-year veteran meat-packing worker and his wife. The interview itself focused on a major strike in the meat packing industry. Throughout the interview, the worker's wife's comments were just as telling and interpretive as those of the worker, indicating that the struggle had been drawn deeply into the home. Both expressed bitterness toward a company to which they had once been extremely loyal. The bitterness arose from the rubble of concessions workers had earlier made to finance the expansion and modernization of the plant. They viewed this as an investment in their future. Along with the concessions, they agreed to an eight-year no-strike agreement to get the plant operational, along with the promise from management that the workers in the new plant would never make less than they had in the old. When the plant went into operation, however, management proposed another pay cut. Moreover, these cuts were only a small part of a complex package handed to workers, demoralizing them, and even reducing pay benefits. Many of the younger workers were working under extremely stressful conditions:

"They worked hard ten hours a day," said the worker, "and then probably couldn't sleep at night from the pain and the stress. One woman worked all day stooped over. Much of this was the result of poor design on the part of the engineers."

According to this worker, all these changes were the result of a new corporate attitude. "It wasn't reasonable," he said. "It used to be that if there was a draft in the plant, they would complain and they'd fix the draft. The new plant was constantly cold, except for the hog kill room. When the workers complained of the cold, they just told them to wear a hooded sweatshirt and a hard hat."

The change occurred when the "Nebraska syndrome" took over. The new corporate mentality couldn't tolerate educated, credentialed people making less money than the workers in the plant. They wanted to transfer wage cuts to management, which they did, raising the CEO's salary from $250,000 to 500k to 919k with Golden Parachutes for all those who might be affected by a hostile takeover. (Griffith's field notes, summer, 1989)

This workers' and my own arguments are supported by the comments of a plant manager of one of the largest meat packing firms in the nation. According to this individual, attachment to the community and capital accumulation directly contradicted one another. He said, "When [company name] was formed, we were determined from the start to get the highest return on invested capital for our stockholders. We weren't going to do any of this goody two-shoes stuff with the community." Indeed, the plant in question has been a major player in reorganizing local labor markets with imported labor, often at the expense of its image in the communities.

In yet another example, that of Hage's and Klauda's work, *No Retreat, No Surrender,* on the Hormel strike, there emerges a clear portrait of a company whose managers and executives once viewed themselves as intimately connected to and deeply rooted in Austin. The Hormel family's commitment to the community was largely responsible for the fifty years of labor peace at the plant before the strike. Over time, however, as the Hormel family withdrew from direct management, this commitment dwindled to the point where, during the strike, executives used the threat of leaving Austin as a means of turning the citizens of Austin against local P-9 (Hage and Klauda 1988). Much of Hormel's original commitment to Austin remained after the strike, at least in a residual form (its chief executive officer is an Austin native). Yet workers who took part in the strike recognize that its altered or diminished commitment to Austin, evidenced by its considering leaving the city during the crisis, ushered in a change in the relations between labor and management in the plant.

We conceive of these relations between plants and their host communities as representing the micro-level parameters of political economic relations between labor, capital, and the state. Where attachment to the community is fleeting and weak, or restricted to taking advantage of resident authority systems to maintain labor control, plants become predisposed to maintaining a high applicant flow—predisposed to expecting high turnover. As various groups of workers are "used up," in the words of the union official quoted earlier, new groups need to be located, drawn to the plants, and encouraged to organize into the networks that create the social momentum needed to keep labor flowing to, and through, the plants.

Conclusion

Network recruiting, heavy dependence on reproductive labor, and the use of cultural, social, and political components of the worker populations to control labor are all interrelated. Their interrelatedness underlies the propensity for low-wage labor markets to become supplied by immigrant populations with enduring international or interregional connections. Specifically, reproductive labor is most efficiently tapped via international migration networks, which are established, maintained, and institutionalized by network recruitment. The use of networks in labor recruitment, moreover, implies social, cultural, and political homogeneity within those segments of the labor-supplying population recruited through the same networks. Within this process, as labor and capital negotiate wages and working conditions, these negotiations become learning experiences for both employers and workers. Both, that is, come to understand key features of one another's cultural backgrounds. In the cases presented here, the particularly important lessons concern such aspects of thought and culture as expectations regarding the availability and reliability of labor, the value of time, definitions of and expectations regarding work, productivity, job safety, task assignment, scheduling, and other features of work environments. Through these lessons, workers participate in the design of their own subordination.

Yet workers tend not to accept subordination passively. Often the social forms most useful to capital contain the seeds of worker resistance and the potential for power. Networks can provide the bare social frameworks for organized resistance. Domestic production operations offer sanctuary to workers wounded at hazardous job sites, sanctuary similar to political asylum. The social forms necessary to bridge the chasms between domestic production and wage labor jobs, reoriented, may become means by which workers pool knowledge, assets, and experiences and reduce their dependence on specific low-wage industries. The growth of transnational households, transnational networks, and transnational communities may prove impossible for even transnational capital to penetrate. The challenge facing low-wage workers today is to recognize these potential sources of power and marshall them toward collective resistance. These are their strength, their hope. These are the new frontiers that low-wage workers can and will pioneer.

Appendix A

Counties Selected for Poultry Processing Study

Region 1: Northeast Texas/Southwest Arkansas
Texas
1. Titus
2. Camp
3. Panola
4. Shelby
5. Upshur
6. Nacodoches

Arkansas
Southwest:
7. Sevier
8. Noward
9. Hempstead
10. Polk
11. Pike
12. Union

Region 2: North Georgia
13. Jackson
14. Elbert
15. Hart
16. Hall
17. Barrow
18. Banks
19. Cherokee
20. Forsyth
21. Cowfta
22. Carroll
23. Whitfield
24. Murray

25. Gilmer
26. Habersham

Region 3: North Carolina
27. Duplin
28. Bertie
29. Martin
30. Pender
31. Hoke
32. Chatham
33. Robeson
34. Richmond
35. Union
36. Cabarrus
37. Moore
38. Durham
39. Surry
40. Wilkes
41. Burke
42. Madison

Region 4: The Delmarva Peninsula (Delaware, Maryland, Virginia's
  Eastern Shore)
Delaware
43. Sussex
Maryland
44. Queen Anne's
45. Talbot
46. Caroline
47. Dorchester
48. Wicomico
49. Somerset
50. Worchester
Virginia
51. Northhampton
52. Accomack

Notes

Chapter 1

1. By using the term "advanced" capitalism, I do not mean to imply superiority or greatness. I simply refer to those societies with long histories of capitalist development, such as the United States, England, and Germany, or societies where most of the underlying assumptions and justifications for capitalism are accepted as "natural" by the status quo. In some passages, I use the term "late" capitalism instead, which is meant to connect this work with other works that use this designation in the context of larger discussions of capitalist hegemony.

2. A labor process includes the locating, recruiting, organizing, transporting, supervising, and reproducing of workers, as well as the methods used to legitimate the means of accomplishing these tasks.

3. Domestic production generally refers to small-scale productive operations that are staffed by household members, are run out of homes as opposed to designated work sites, and produce goods and services that contribute to the maintenance and reproduction of the household rather than generate a profit.

4. Dichotomous models have been extremely influential in the social sciences, opposing not only traditional and modern but also culture from nature, materialist from mentalist, evolutionism from particularism, and so forth. Roseberry (1988) discusses some of the problems with these oppositions in terms of how much they simplify and misrepresent complex realities. Those who defend such models, on the other hand, usually do so on the grounds that abstraction is necessary for theory building; in the process of abstracting, one loses the richness of detail while capturing an essence. In the traditional/modern and other dichotomies mentioned above, however, such abstraction also distorts reality by reifying the modern and defining the traditional in terms of the (reified) modern rather than on its own terms. The most cogent critique of such dichotomous modeling that I have run across comes not from a social scientist but from the poet Elizabeth Bishop, in her poem entitled *Santarem* (1987: 185), written in response to the confluence of the Tapajos and Amazon rivers, where she contemplates whether or not the confluence is symbolic of some of our most fundamental antimonies, such as male

and female, good and evil, and so forth, ending with an image, again, of confluence, of these antimonies being absorbed and "resolved... in that water, dazzling dialectic."

5. Statistical portraits based on the U.S. census and other large data bases are notoriously suspect, especially when it comes to immigrant and minority workers, in whose best interests it is, usually, to remain invisible or to lie.

Chapter 2

1. While this observation seems rather simple, its political, economic, and ideological consequences are actually quite profound, with clear implications for policy and for the ways we interact with foreign powers. If one believes, as modernization theory and classical economic theory would have us believe, that there is a thing called "progress" that is slowly incorporating more and more of the world in its sweep and that, given time, most of the evidently backward nations will progress to our "level," then there is no need to try for structural change, since the structure is basically sound; people need only wait their turn for prosperity. We can speed the process through development programming, but this involves only the pace of change, not the quality of that change. What qualitative changes have taken place (e.g. the Green Revolution being displaced by Integrated Rural Development and then Farming Systems Research/Extension—see de Janvry 1983), have been primarily technical, or social in the sense of recognizing that local-level systems are integrated; these changes, though qualitative in nature, involve no distinct difference in the trajectories of capital accumulation or the balance of power in the international context, though both wealth and power may be redistributed on the national, regional, or local levels in the short term. Indeed, these patchwork qualitative changes, peopled by anthropologists and other scholars who regularly contribute to intellectual discourse, help to mask the true properties of capital accumulation and to keep capitalist expansion an uneven and creatively exploitative process.

2. The official political rhetoric that comes out of South Africa, which justifies apartheid on the grounds of preserving "Christian Nationalism" and the racial integrity of the Afrikaaner people, suggests that these kinds of emotionally stirring justifications are no less functional today in masking relations of dependence and exploitation.

3. As measured by such indices as Gross Domestic Product (GDP), debt levels, balances of payments, trade statistics, and various "human capital" variables (literacy, percent of college and high school graduates,

etc.). These indices were constructed, for the most part, by classical economists of the West, compiled and established in data sets by organizations like the World Bank, and used to guide development planning. Unfortunately, statistics such as these, in addition to being ethnocentric—measuring things primarily of interest to capitalists—were generally flawed in terms of both validity and reliability.

4. A similar manifestation in the United States is the practice among new immigrant groups to form "enclaves" and creative housing and transportation arrangements in order to spread costs of living from the individual or household to the collective. These practices are all the more enhanced among illegal immigrants, who benefit from the protectionist dimension of these practices as well: a houseful of illegal immigrants, for example, need only have one legal individual to answer the knock of an Immigration and Naturalization Service enforcement officer.

5. During the 1980s, the expansion of global control capability has been facilitated by the reluctance, in the United States under the Reagan and Bush administrations, for the Justice Department to enforce antitrust laws, thus allowing capital concentration to progress at a pace that allows for even greater control.

6. This is seen, in particular, in recent programs, such as the Job Training Partnership Act (JTPA), designed to improve the life chances of poor and disadvantaged, often minority, individuals by subsidizing their wages during their training periods. With the fragmentation and deskilling of many jobs, however, the training periods in some industries (e.g. meat packing) has been reduced to a few days instead of the ninety days covered by the JTPA funds. In these cases, the firm makes no investment in the individual's training, nor takes any risk, and thus effectively receives a subsidy for hiring a JTPA worker. There are additional programs, that give companies tax credits, that function in similar ways. Strangely, executives who take advantage of these subsidies are often the first to condemn an individual's receipt of food stamps or other social service benefits.

7. Marx might have called them lumpenproletariat, because of the casual nature of their wage labor activity and their weak ties of class and underdeveloped class consciousness. I avoid this term because of its pejorative connotations.

Chapter 3

1. The thirteen states were Alabama, Arkansas, Florida, Georgia, Kentucky, Louisiana, Mississippi, North Carolina, Oklahoma, South Carolina, Tennessee, Texas, and Virginia.

2. Seven (25 percent) of the twenty-eight eastern North Carolina counties have negative migration rates, with five of these falling within the lowest tenth percentile in relation to all North Carolina counties. Washington County had the hightes emigration rate in the state from 1983 to 1984.

3. I have since determined that the belligerent independnece I noted is in fact common among poor rural folk who live somewhat marginal existences.

Chapter 4

1. The mechanization that has occurred in the processing plants has been oriented primarily toward streamlining processing tasks and making them less difficult; most labor displaced through this process has been relocated inside the plants.

2. Most growers interviewed reported that the designation "part-time" by the industry was misleading. While it is the case that the birds require little attention in terms of hours daily, the flocks nevertheless need constant attention in case of equipment failure (e.g. fans breaking down).

3. According to TPF officials, these operations can use as much as 25,000 hours of labor per acre annually.

Chapter 5

1. Significance levels were derived from two-tailed student's t-tests.

2. Actual criteria used in scoring (unless otherwise indicated, each worth one point) were as follows: (1) no geographical mobility; (2) at least 50 percent of respondent's working years spent in seafood processing; (3) respondent's only job has been in seafood processing; (4) respondent has no skills; (5) respondent was born after 1945 and never graduated from high school (one point for each year less than twelve); (6) respondent was born prior to 1945 and received fewer than six years of formal education (one point for each year under six); (7) respondent had no technical training; (8) seafood processing was the only job respondent held during the year; (9) seafood processing was the only job held by anyone in the household; (10) one point for every ten miles by highway from a population center of 10,000 or more; (11) one point for each capable wage earner in household who has no skills; (12) respondent has no independent economic activity; (13) one point for each

person in the household supported by seafood processing earnings. The resulting scores, then, are ordinal measures that reflect the degree to which households are dependent on the seafood processing industry (not the fishing industry in general) as a source of jobs and income.

Chapter 7

1. A complete list of the counties included in the study can be found in Appendix A.

2. Most of the native Americans in the plants are concentrated in the eastern part of the state, and most of those in turkey processing plants.

3. Chi-square analysis comparing ethnic change by region revealed a significance level of .012 (10.883; df=3).

4. Some editing and paraphrasing of the plant personnel managers' comments has been necessary.

5. Social scientific research supports the success of some Asian populations, although this has not been uniformly distributed among all Asian refugee groups (e.g. Bach and Carroll-Sequin 1986).

References

Abbreviations used in the text

NBC   National Broiler Council.
DPI   Delmarva Poultry Industry.
TPF   Texas Poultry Federation.
PS   Poultry scientists at one or more universities in North Carolina, Texas, Arkansas, Delaware, Maryland, Virginia, and Georgia.

Citations

Acheson, James. 1978 "The Anthropology of Fishing." *Annual Reviews in Anthropology* 10: 275-316.

Algren de Gutiérrez, Edith. 1985 *The Movement Against Teaching English in Schools of Puerto Rico*. New York: University Press of America.

Amin, Samir. 1979 *Accumulation on a World Scale*. New York: Monthly Review Press.

Antler, Ellen and James Faris. 1979 "Adaptation to Changes in Technology and Government Policy: A Newfoundland Example (Cat Harbour)." In *North Atlantic Maritime Cultures*, edited by R. Anderson. New York: Mouton.

Avina, Jeff. 1984 "Mexican Immigration and Labor Market Evolution in Sonoma County." Paper prepared for the Project on Mexican Immigrants in California Industry, Center for U.S.-Mexican Studies, University of California, San Diego, 1984.

Bach, Robert. 1985 "Political Frameworks for International Migration." In *The Americas in the New International Division of Labor*, edited by S. Sanderson. New York: Holmes and Meier.

Bach, Robert and Howard Brill. 1991 *Impact of IRCA on the U.S. Labor Market and Economy*. Final Report to the U.S. Department of Labor. Binghamton, N.Y.: SUNY Institute for Research on Multiculturalism and International Labor.

Bach, Robert and Rita Carroll-Sequin. 1986 "Labor Force Participation, Household Composition, and Sponsorship among Southeastern Asian Refugees." *International Migration Review* 20 (2): 381-404.

Bailey, Thomas. 1986 *Immigrant and Native Workers: Contrasts and Competition.* Boulder, Colo.: Westview Press.

Barnet, Richard. 1981 *The Lean Years: Politics in an Age of Scarcity.* New York: Simon and Schuster.

Bauer, P. T. 1966 *Dissent on Development.* Cambridge: Harvard University Press.

Baumola, W. J. and A. J. Blinder. 1979 *Economics: Principles and Policy.* New York: Harcourt, Brace, Jovanovich, Inc.

Bellow, Saul. 1977 *The Adventures of Augie March.* New York: Penguin.

Beneria, Lourdes and Git Sen. 1981 "Accumulation, Reproduction, and Women's Role in Economic Development: Boserup Revisited." *Signs* 7: 279-298.

Benson, Janet. 1990 "Good Neighbors: Ethnic Relations in Garden City, Kansas." *Urban Anthropology* 20.

Bishop, Elizabeth. 1987 *Selected Poems, 1929-1979.* New York: Farrar, Straus, and Giroux.

Blaxall, M. 1987 "World Trade in Seafood." Paper presented at the Symposium on Marketing of Seafood and Aquaculture Products, Mariott Hotel of Charleston, S.C., August, 1987.

Bluestone, Barry and Bennet Harrison. 1982 *The Deindustrialization of America: Plant Closings, Community Abandonment, and the Dismantling of Basic Industry.* New York: Basic Books, Inc.

Bolles, Lynn. 1983 "Kitchens Hit by Priorities: Employed Working-Class Jamaican Women Confront the IMF." In *Women, Men, and the International Division of Labor,* edited by J. Nash and M. Fernandez-Kelly. Albany: State University of New York Press.

Bonacich, Edna. 1982 "A Theory of Ethnic Antagonism: The Split Labor Market." *American Sociological Review* 37: 547-549.

Borjas, George. 1989 "Economic Theory and International Migration." *International Migration Review* 23: 457-485.

Borjas, George and Marta Tienda, eds. 1985 *Hispanics in the U.S. Economy.* New York: Academic Press.

Borjas, George and Marta Tienda. 1987 "The Economic Consequences of Immigration." *Science* 235: 645-651.

Bort, John. 1987 "The Impact of Development on Panama's Small-Scale Fishermen." *Human Organization* 46: 233-242.

Boserup, Ester. 1971 *Women's Role in Economic Development*. London: George Allan and Unwin.

Boyd, David. 1981 "Village Agriculture and Labor Migration: Interrelated Production Activities Among the Ilakia Awa of Papua, New Guinea." *American Ethnologist* 8 (1): 74-93.

Braverman, Harry. 1974 *Labor and Monopoly Capital: The Degradation of Work in the Twentieth Century*. New York: Monthly Review Press.

Brody, David. 1964 *The Butcher Workmen*, Cambridge: Harvard University Press.

Broidy, Elizabeth. 1987 "Patterns of Household Immigration into South Texas." *International Migration Review* 21 (1): 27-47.

Broiler Industry. 1988 "Pressure to Raise Minimum Wage Continues." *Broiler Industry* 51 (4): 18. Mt. Morris, Ill.: Watt Publications.

Bunivic, Mayra, Margaret Lycette, and William McGreevey, eds. 1983 *Women and Poverty in the Third World*. Baltimore: Johns Hopkins University Press.

Burawoy, Michael. 1976 "The Functions and Reproduction of Migrant Labor: Comparative Material from South Africa and the United States." *American Journal of Sociology* 81: 1050-1087.

Burton, Michael and Douglas White. 1984 "Sexual Division of Labor in Agriculture." *American Anthropologist* 86: 568-583.

California Department of Labor. 1962 *Survey of Cannery Workers*. Report 436G No. 4. Sacramento, Calif.

Chavez, Leo. 1989 "Coresidence and Resistance: Strategies for Survival among Undocumented Mexican and Central Americans in the United States." *Urban Anthropology* 19: 31-61.

———. 1991 "Outside the Imagined Community: Undocumented Settlers and Experiences of Incorporation." *American Ethnologist* 18 (2): 257-278.

Chayanov, A.V. 1966 *Theory of Peasant Economy*. New York: International Publishers.

Clammer, John. 1978 *The New Economic Anthropology*. New York: St. Martin's Press.

———. 1985 *Political Economy*. New York: St. Martin's Press.

Cobb, James. 1982 *The Selling of the South: The Southern Crusade for Industrial Development, 1936-1980*. Baton Rouge: Louisiana State University Press.

———. 1984 *Industrialization and Southern Society*. Lexington: University of Tennessee Press.

Collins, Jane. 1988 *Unseasonal Migrations: The Effects of Rural Labor Scarcity in Peru*. Princeton: Princeton University Press.

———. 1989 "Class Formation and Semi-Proletarianization in the Andes." Paper presented at the Eighty-seventh Annual Meeting of the American Anthropological Association, Pheonix, Arizona, November 1989.

Coltrane, Robert. 1984 *Immigration Reform and Agricultural Labor*. Agriculture Report Number 510. U.S. Department of Agriculture, Economic Research Service. Washington, D.C.: U.S. Government Printing Office.

Comitas, Lambros. 1964 "Occupational Multiplicity in Rural Jamaica." In *Work and Family Life*, edited by L. Comitas and D. Lowenthal. Garden City, N.Y.: Anchor Books/Doubleday.

Cook, Scott. 1973 "Production, Ecology, and Economic Anthropology: Notes Toward an Integrated Frame of Reference." *Social Science Information* 12 (1) 25-52.

Cornelius, Wayne. 1982 "Interviewing Undocumented Immigrants: Methodological Reflections Based on Fieldwork in Mexico and the U.S." *International Migration Review* 16 (2): 378-411.

———. 1988 "The Persistence of Immigrant-Dominated Firms and Industries in the United States: The Case of California." San Diego: Center for U.S.-Mexican Studies, University of California. Working Paper.

Dalton, George. 1968 "Introduction" to *Primitive, Archaic and Modern Economies, Essays of Karl Polanyi*. Boston: Beacon Press.

Daniel, Peter. 1972 *The Shadow of Slavery: Peonage in the South*. Urbana: University of Illinois Press.

David, Adam C. 1981 *The Rural County Seat: A Study of Locality-Oriented Activity Patterns*. Raleigh, N.C.: Department of Sociology and Anthropology, Agricultural Research Service, N.C. State University.

Davis, John E.. 1980 "Capitalist Agricultural Development and the Exploitation of the Propertied Laborer." In *The Rural Sociology of the Advanced Societies*, edited by Frederick H. Buttel and Howard Newby. Montclair, N.J.: Allanheld, Osmun.

de Janvry, Alain. 1983 *The Agrarian Question and Reformism in Latin America*. Baltimore: Johns Hopkins University Press.

Deere, Carmen and Alain de Janvry. 1979 "A Conceptual Framework for the Empirical Analysis of Peasants." *American Journal of Agricultural Economics* 61 (4): 601-611.

Doeringer, Peter, Philip Moss, and David Terkla. 1986 *The New England Fishing Economy: Jobs, Income, and Kinship*. Amherst: University of Massachusetts Press.

Dostoyevsky, Fydor. 1968 [1866] *Crime and Punishment*. New York: Signet.

Economics, Statistics and Cooperative Service. 1980 *Twenty-fourth National Conference of Bargaining and Marketing Cooperatives, January 10-11, 1980, New Orleans, Louisiana: Proceedings*. Washington, D.C.: U.S. Department of Agriculture.

Edwards, Richard, Michael Reich, and David Gordon. 1973 "The Labor Process." In *Labor Market Segmentation*, edited by R. Edwards, M. Reich, and D. Gordon. Lexington, Mass.: D.C. Heath.

Ember, Carol. 1983 "The Relative Decline in Women's Contribution to Agriculture with Intensification." *American Anthropologist* 85: 285-305.

Erickson, Ken and Donald Stull. 1988 "Immigrants and Refugees in the U.S. Meatpacking Industry." Washington, D.C.: Paper presented at the Eighty-eighth meeting of the American Anthropological Association.

Faris, James. 1971 *Cat Harbour: A Newfoundland Fishing Settlement*. St. John's: ISER. Newfoundland Social and Economic Studies No. 3.

Faulkner, William. 1939 *Light in August*. New York: The Modern Library.

Federal Register. 1977 "Contents of Fishery Management Plans." *Regional Fishery Management Councils*. 602.3. Vol. 42, No. 137 (Monday, July 8, 1977). Washington, D.C.: U.S. Department of Commerce, NOAA.

Fernandez-Kelly, Maria Patricia. 1983 *For We Are Sold, I and My People: Women and Industry in Mexico's Frontier.* Albany: State University of New York Press.

Floyd, Jesse. 1987 "Recent Development of International Tuna Industries and the Asian Pacific Trade." In *Proceedings of the Symposium of Markets for Seafood and Aquacultured Products,* edited by David Liao. International Institute of Fisheries Economics and Trade and the South Carolina Wildlife and Marine Resources Department. Charleston, S.C.: 214-232.

Fogel, Walter A. 1970 *The Negro in the Meat Industry.* Report no. 12, The Racial Policies of American Industry. Philadelphia: University of Pennsylvania.

Foner, Nancy and Richard Napoli. 1978 "Jamaican and Black-American Migrant Farm Workers: A Comparative Analysis." *Social Problems 25* (4): 491-503.

Foucault, Michel. 1980 *The History of Sexuality. Vol. 1.* New York: Vintage Books.

Frank, A.G. 1967 "The Development of Underdevelopment." In *Capitalism and Underdevelopment in Latin America,* edited by A. G. Frank. New York: Monthly Review Press.

Fricke, Peter. 1980 "Socioeconomic Aspects of the Bay Scallop Fishery in Carteret County, North Carolina." Raleigh, N.C.: UNC Sea Grant College Program Working Paper 81-12.

Friedland, William and Dorothy Nelkin. 1971 *Migrants: Agricultural Workers in America's Northeast.* New York: Holt, Rinehart, and Winston.

Frobel, Folker, Jurgen Heinrichs, and Otto Kreye. 1977 *The New International Division of Labour: Structural Unemployment in Industrialised Countries and Industrialisation in Developing Countries.* Cambridge: Cambridge University Press.

Fuchs, Victor R. 1986 "Sex Differences in Economic Well-Being." *Science 232* (April 26, 1986): 459-464.

Furtado, Celso. 1973 *The Economic Development of Latin America.* London: Cambridge University Press.

Garrity, Barbara. 1991 *The Meaning of Work for Black and White Fishermen of the U.S. Menhaden Fish Meal and Fish Oil Industry.* Ph.D. dissertation, Department of Anthropology, University of Virginia.

Gladwin, Christina. 1988 "The Case for the Disappearing Mid-Size Farm in the U.S." In *Food and Farm: Current Debates and Policies*, edited by C. Gladwin and K. Truman. Lantham, Md.: University Presses of America.

Glick-Schiller, Nina and Georges Fouron. 1990 "'Everywhere We Go, We Are in Danger': Ti Manno and the Emergence of a Haitian Transnational Identity." *American Ethnologist* 17: 329-347.

Godfrey, D. 1975 *Utilization of Social Services by White and Black residents of Region Q, North Carolina*. Ph.D. dissertation. University of North Carolina.

Goldoftas, Barbara. 1989 "Inside the Slaughterhouse." *Southern Exposure* 17 (2): 25-29.

Goldring, Luin. 1990 *Development and Migration: A Comparative Analysis of Two Mexican Migrant Circuits*. Working Paper No. 37. Washington, D.C.: Commission for the Study of International Migration and Cooperative Economic Development.

Gordon, H. Scott. 1954 "The Economic Theory of a Common-Property Resource: The Fishery." *Journal of Political Economy* 62: 124-142.

Gordon, David, Richard Edwards, and Michael Reich. 1982 *Segmented Work, Divided Workers: The Historical Transformation of Labor in the United States*. Cambridge: Cambridge University Press.

Griffith, David. 1983 *The Promise of a Country: The Impact of Seasonal U.S. Migration on the Jamaican Peasantry*. Ph.D. dissertation, Department of Anthropology, University of Florida.

———. 1984 "International Labor Migration and Rural Development: Patterns of Expenditure among Jamaicans Working Seasonally in the U.S." *Stanford Journal of International Law* 19 (2): 357-370.

———. 1985 "Women, Remittances, and Reproduction." *American Ethnologist* 12 (4): 676-690.

———. 1986a "Social Organizational Obstacles to Capital Accumulation Among Returning Migrants: The Case of Jamaicans Working Seasonally in the United States." *Human Organization* 46 (1): 34-42.

———. 1986b "Peasants in Reserve: Temporary West Indian Labor in the U.S. Labor Market." *International Migration Review* 20 (4): 875-898.

———. 1987a "Nonmarket Labor Processes in an Advanced Capitalist Economy." *American Anthropologist* (89) 4: 838-852.

———. 1987b "Labour Migration and Changing Peasant Agriculture in Jamaica." In *Peasant Resources and Small-Scale Farming in the Caribbean*, edited by H. Rubenstein. Manitoba, Canada: Department of Geography, University of Manitoba.

———. 1988 "Enhanced Recruitment Demonstration Project." Project funded by the Office of the Assistant Secretary of Labor, U.S. Department of Labor, Washington, D.C.

Griffith, David and Jeff Johnson. 1988 *Social and Cultural Dimensions of Seafood Consumption*. Greenville, N.C.: East Carolina University. ICMR Technical Report 88-04.

Griffith, David, Ed Kissam, David Runsten, Anna Garcia, and Jeronimo Camposeco. 1990 *Assessing the Availability and Productivity of U.S. Farm Labor Under Enhanced Wages and Working Conditions: an ethnographic approach*. Washington, D.C.: Second Interim Report to the Office of Policy, U.S. Department of Labor.

Griffith, David, Manuel Valdes Pizzini, and Jeff Johnson. 1987 "Wage Labor and Small Scale Fishing in Puerto Rico." Project funded by the National Science Foundation.

Griffith, David and David Runsten. 1988 *The Impact of Immigration Reform and Control Act on the U.S. Poultry Industry*. Report prepared for the U.S. Department of Labor's International Labor Affairs Bureau. Washington, D.C.

Guyer, Jane. 1988 "The Multiplication of Labor: Historical Methods in the Study of Gender and Agricultural Change in Moder Africa." *Current Anthropology* 29 (4): 247-272.

Hage, David and Paul Klauda. 1988 *No Retreat, No Surrender: Labor's War at Hormell*. New York: William Morrow and Co.

Hansen, Art, David Griffith, John Butler, Sandra Powers, Elon Gilbert, and Masuma Downie. 1981 *Farming Systems of Alachua County, Florida: An Overview with Special Attention to Low-Resource Farmers*. Gainesville: Center for Community and Rural Development, Institute for Food and Agricultural Sciences, University of Florida.

Hansen, Art and Anthony Oliver Smith, eds.. 1983 *Involuntary Resettlement and Relocation*. Boulder, Colo.: Westview Press.

Hardin, Garret. 1969 "The Tragedy of the Commons." *Science* 162: 1243-1248.

Heffernan, Bernard. 1987 "World's Largest Turkey Plant Takes Leading Role in Industry." *Turkey World* 63 (3): 24-38.

Heilbroner, Robert and Lester Thurow. 1968 *The Economic Problem.* Englewood Cliffs, N.J.: Prentice-Hall, Inc.

Heppel, Monica. 1983 *Harvesting the Crops of Others.* Ph.D. dissertation, Department of Anthropology, American University, Washington, D.C.

Hewitt de Alcantara, Cynthia. 1976 *Modernizing Mexican Agriculture.* Geneva: UNRISD.

Howe, Walter. 1986 "Temporary Help Workers: Who Are They, What Jobs Do They Hold." *Monthly Labor Review* 109 (11): 45-47.

Jamison, John. 1960 *Grower-Processor Coordination in the California Broiler Industry.* Giannini Foundation Report No. 239. Berkeley: Division of Agricultural Sciences, University of California.

Johnston, Gary W. 1976 *Personnel Management on California Egg Ranches.* Master's thesis, Colorado State University, Fort Collins.

Johnson, Jeff and David Griffith. 1985 *Perceptions and Preferences for Marine Fish.* Raleigh, N.C.: UNC Sea Grant Technical Report 85-01.

Kaufman, Michael. 1984 Report on Sonoma County Poultry Interviews. San Diego: Center for U.S.-Mexican Studies, University of California. Working Paper.

Kearney, Michael and Carole Nagengast. 1988 "Anthropological Perspectives on Transnational Communities in Rural California." Working Papers on Farm Labor and Rural Poverty No. 3. Davis: California Institute for Rural Studies.

Keesing, Roger. 1987 "Anthropology as Interpretive Quest." *Current Anthropology.* 28 (1): 27-52.

Kember, Robert. 1977 *Migration and Adaptation.* Beverley Hills: Sage Publications.

Kennedy, Theodore. 1980 *You Gotta Deal With It: Black Family Relations in a Southern Community.* Chapel Hill: University of North Carolina Press.

King, Gordon A. 1980 "Trends in California Livestock and Poultry Production, Consumption, and Feed Use: 1961-1978." Giannini Foundation Information Series 80-5, Bulletin 1899. Davis: University of California.

Kim, Kwang Chung and Wan Moo Hurh. 1985 "Ethnic Resources and Utilization of Korean Immigrant Entrepreneurs in the Chicago Minority Area." *International Migration Review* 19 (Spring): 82-111.

Kopytoff, Igor. 1986 "The Cultural Biography of Things: Commoditization as Process." In *The Social Life of Things,* edited by Arjun Appadurai. New York: Cambridge University Press.

Lamphere, Louise. 1985 "From Working Daughters to Working Mothers: Production and Reproduction in an Industrial Community." *American Ethnologist* 13 (1): 118-130.

Lasley, Floyd. 1980 "The U.S. Poultry Industry: Changing Structure and Economics." Agricultural Economic Report No. 502, U.S. Department of Agriculture, Economic Research Service. Washington, D.C.: U.S. Government Printing Office.

Lehmann, Nicolas. 1986 "The Underclass." *Atlantic Monthly.* August, 1986.

Levine, David, Kenneth Hill, and Robert Warren, eds. 1985 *Immigration Statistics: A Story of Neglect.* Washington, D.C.: National Academy Press.

Lewis, Oscar. 1966 "The Culture of Poverty." *Scientific American.* 215: 19-25

Liebow, Elliot. 1967 *Tally's Corner: A Study of Negro Streetcorner Men.* Boston: Little, Brown and Company.

Lim, Linda Y. C. 1983 "Capitalism, Imperialism, and Patriarchy: The Dilemma of Third-World Women Workers in Multinational Factories." In *Women, Men, and the International Division of Labor,* edited by J. Nash and M. Fernandez-Kelly. Albany: State University of New York Press.

Lomnitz, Larissa. 1977 *Networks and Marginality.* New York: Academic Press.

Lukacs, Georg. 1968 *History and Class Consciousness: Studies in Marxist Dialectics.* Cambridge, Mass.: MIT Press.

Maril, Robert. 1983 *Texas Shrimpers: Community, Capitalism, and the Sea.* College Station: Texas A&M Press.

Martin, Philip. 1985 "Review of Bohning's *Studies in International Labor Migration.*" *International Migration Review* 19 (4): 774-775.

———. 1986 *Illegal Immigration and the Colonization of the American Labor Market.* Washington, D.C.: Center for Immigration Studies.

Marx, Karl. 1967 *Capital.* Vol. 1. New York: International Publishers.

Massey, Douglas. 1985a "Understanding Mexican Migration to the United States." Chicago: University of Chicago, Department of Sociology. Manuscript.

———. 1985b "The Settlement Process Among Mexican Migrants to the United States: New Methods and Findings." In *Immigration Statistics: A Story of Neglect,* edited by D. B. Levine, K. Hill, and R. Warren. Washington, D.C.: National Academy Press.

Massey, Douglas, Rafael Alarcon, Jorge Durand, and Humberto Gonzalez. 1987 *Return to Aztlan.* Berkeley: University of California Press.

Maurius, Robert. 1984 "Musings on the Mysteries of the American South." *Daedalus* 113 (3): 143-176.

McCay, Bonnie. 1981 "Optimal Foragers or Political Actors?: Ecological Analyses of a New Jersey Fishery." *American Ethnologist.* 356-382.

McCay, Bonnie and James Acheson. 1989 *The Question of the Commons.* Tempte: University of Arizona Press.

McCay, Bonnie, James Gatewood, and Carolyn Creed. 1989 "Labor and the Labor Process in a Limited Entry Fishery." *Marine Resource Economics* 6: 311-330.

McCoy, Terry and Charles Wood. 1982 *Caribbean Workers in the Florida Sugar Cane Industry.* Occasional Paper No. 2 of the Caribbean Migration Program. Gainesville, Fla.: Center for Latin American Studies, University of Florida.

Meillassoux, Claude. 1972 "From Reproduction to Production: A Marxist Approach to Economic Anthropology." *Economy and Society* 1 (1): 93-105.

Mid-East Commission. 1974 *An Examination of the Mid-East Region's Population and Socioeconomic Base.* Washington, N.C.: Mid-East Commission.

Migdal, Joel. 1979 *Peasants, Politics, and Revolution.* Princeton: Princeton University Press.

Miller, T. M., W. B. Webb, F. B. Thomas, and J. E. Easley, Jr. 1975 "Proceedings of the Workshop on Seafood Processing and Marketing in the Coastal Plains Area." Raleigh, N.C.: UNC Sea Grant College Publication UNC-SG-75-24.

Mines, Richard and Ricardo Anzaldúa. 1982 *New Migrants vs. Old Migrants: Alternative Labor Market Structures in the California Citrus Industry.* San Diego: Monograph No. 9. U.S.-Mexican Studies, University of California.

Mines, Richard and Philip Martin. 1983 "Immigrant Workers and the California Citrus Industry." Giannini Foundation Paper. Davis: Department of Agricultural Economics, University of California.

———. 1986 *A Profile of California Farm Workers*. Giannini Foundation Information Series No. 86-2. Davis: University of California.

Mines, Richard and David Runsten. 1985 "Immigration Networks and California Industrial Sectors." Paper prepared for the Project on Immigration Workers in California Industry, Center for U.S.-Mexican Studies, University of California, San Diego.

Mintz, Sidney. 1974 "The Rural Proletariat and the Problems of Rural Proletarian Consciousness." *Journal of Peasant Studies* 1 (3): 291-325.

Model, Suzanne. 1985 "A Comparative Perspective on the Ethnic Enclave: blacks, Italians, and Jews in New York City." *International Migration Review* 19 (1): 64-81.

Monthly Labor Review. 1945 "Wartime Changes in Agricultural Employment." *Monthly Labor Review* 61 (3): 442-451.

Mortimer, D. M. and R. S. Bryce-Laporte, eds. 1981 *Female Immigrants to the United States: Caribbean, Latin American, and African Experiences*. RIIES Occasional paper no. 2. Washington, D.C.: Research Institute of Immigration and Ethnic Studies, Smithsonian Institutions.

Murray, Merill G. 1972 *The Treatment of Seasonal Unemployment Under Unemployment Insurance*. Kalamazoo, Mich.: W. E. Upjohn Institute for Employment Research.

Nash, June. 1983 "Introduction." *Women, Men, and the New International Division of Labor,* edited by J. Nash and M. Fernandez Kelley. Albany: State University of N.Y. Press.

———. 1985 "Segmentation of the Work Process in the International Division of Labor." In *The Americas in the New International Division of Labor*, edited by S. Sanderson. New York: Holmes & Meier. 253-272.

Nash, June, and M. P. Fernandez-Kelley, eds. 1983 *Women, Men, and the New International Division of Labor*. Albany, N.Y.: State University of New York Press.

National Commission on Food Marketing. 1966 Organization and Competition in the Poultry and Egg Industries Technical Study No. 2, Washington, D.C. June 1966.

National Fisheries Institute. n.d. *America's Most Fabulous Fish: Menhaden*. Washington, D.C.: the National Fisheries Institute.

National Marine Fisheries Service. 1985 *Fisheries Statistics of the United States*. Washington, D.C.: U.S. Government Printing Office.

———. 1983a *Processed Fishery Products, Annual Summary, 1982.* Washington, D.C.: U.S. Department of Commerce, NOAA/NMFS.

———. 1983b *Fisheries of the United States, 1976.* Washington, D.C.: U.S. Department of Commerce, NOAA/NMFS.

———. 1980 *Fisheries Statistics of the United States, 1976.* Washington, D.C.: U.S. Department of Commerce, NOAA/NMFS.

Newman, Kathy. 1988 *Fall From Grace: The Experience of Downward Mobility in the American Working Class.* New York: The Free Press.

Nie, Norman, C. H. Hull, J. G. Jenkins, K. Steinbrenner, and D. H. Bent. 1975 *Statistical Package for the Social Sciences, Second Edition.* New York: McGraw-Hill.

North Carolina County Profiles. 1985 *North Carolina County Profiles.* Raleigh: North Carolina Department of Statistics.

North Carolina Department of Commerce. 1983 *1983-84 Directory of North Carolina Manufacturing Firms.* Raleigh: N.C. Department of Commerce.

North Carolina Department of Labor. 1978 "The Wanchese Harbor Marine Crafts Skill Training Proposal." Raleigh: N.C. Department of Labor.

North Carolina Department of Labor. 1989a Occupational Safety and Health Administration Document No. 1, Robersonville Purdue Plant Violations. Raleigh: N.C. Department of Labor.

North Carolina Department of Labor. 1989b Occupational Safety and Health Administration Document No. 2, Lewiston Purdue Plant Violations. Raleigh: N.C. Department of Labor.

Ong, Aihwa. 1983 "Global Industries and Malay Peasants in Peninsular Malaysia." In *Women, Men, and the International Division of Labor,* edited by J. Nash and M. Fernandez-Kelly. Albany: State University of New York Press.

Ong, Aiwa. 1987 *Spirits of Resistance and Capitalist Discipline: Factory Women in Malaysia.* Albany: State University of New York Press.

Orbach, Michael. 1989 "Of Men and Menhaden." *Journal of Ocean and Shoreline Management.* 4: 32-45.

Overby, Margaret. 1988 "Self-Regulation Among Fishermen of the Gulf of Mexico." In *Marine Resource Utilization: A Conference on Social Science Issues,* edited by S. Thomas, et al. Mobile, Ala.: University of South Alabama.

Packers and Stockyards Administration. 1967 *The Broiler Industry.* Washington, D.C.: U.S. Department of Agriculture.

Painter, Michael. 1985 "Changing Relations of Production and Rural Underdevelopment." *Journal of Anthropological Research* 40: 271-292.

Pamlico County Human Services Department. 1985 *Annual Report: FY 83-84.* Bayboro, N.C.: Pamlico County Courthouse Publication.

Papademetriou, Demetrious, Robert Bach, Kyle Johnson, Roger Kramer, B. Lindsay Lowell, and Shirley Smith. 1989 *The Effects of Immigration on the U.S. Economy and Labor Market.* Immigration Policy and Research Report No. 1. Washington, D.C.: U.S. Department of Labor, Bureau of International Labor Affairs.

Perry, Louis B. and Richard S. Perry. 1963 *A History of the Los Angeles Labor Movement, 1911-1941.* Berkeley: University of California Press.

Pessar, Patricia. 1982 "The Role of Households in International Migration and the Case of U.S.-Bound Migration from the Dominican Republic." *International Migration Review* 2 (16): 342-364.

Peters, Thomas and Robert Waterman. 1982 *In Search of Excellence.* New York: Warner Books.

Pico, Fernando. 1985 *Los Gallos Peleados.* Rio Piedras, Puerto Rico: Ediciones Huracan, Inc.

Polanyi, Karl. 1947 "Our Obsolete Market Mentality." *Commentary* (3): 109-117.

Popkin, Samuel. 1981 *The Rational Peasant.* Berkeley: University of California Press.

Portes, Alejandro. 1979 "Illegal Immigration and the International System: Lessons from the Recent Illegal Mexican Immigrants to the U.S." *Social Problems* 26 (4): 425-438.

Portes, Alejandro and Robert Bach. 1985 *Latin Journey: Cuban and Mexican Immigrants in the U.S.* Berkeley: University of California Press.

Portes, Alejandro and Jozsef Borocz. 1989 "Contemporary Immigration: Theoretical Perspectives on its Determinants and Modes of Incorporation." *International Migration Review* 23 (3): 606-630.

Portes, Alejandro and John Walton. 1980 *Labor, Class, and the International System.* New York: Academic Press.

Radcliffe, Sarah. 1990 "Between Hearth and Labor Market: the Recruitment of Peasant Women in the Andes." *International Migration Review* 24 (2): 229-249.

Rassmussen, Wayne. 1951 *A History of the Emergency Farm Labor Supply Program: 1943-47*. Agricultural Monograph No. 13. Washington, D.C.: USDA, Bureau of Agricultural Research. September, 1951.

Rebel, Hermann. 1989a "Cultural Hegemony and Class Experience: A Critical Reading of Recent Ethnological-Historical Approaches (Part One)." American Ethnologist 16 (1): 117-136.

———. 1989b "Cultural Hegemony and Class Experience: A Critical Reading of Recent Ethnological-Historical Approaches (Part Two)." *American Ethnologist* 16 (2): 350-365.

Reichert, Joshua. 1981 "The Migrant Syndrome: Seasonal U.S. Wage Labor and Rural Development in Central Mexico." *Human Organization* 40 (1): 56-66.

Reichert, Joshua and Douglas Massey. 1979 "Patterns of Migration from a Mexican Sending Community: A Comparison of Legal and Illegal Migrants." *International Migration Review* 13: 599-623.

Reimund, Donn, J. R. Martin, and Charles Moore. 1981 *Structural Change In Agriculture: The Experience for Broilers, Fed Cattle, and Processing Vegetables*. Technical Bulletin No. 1648.

Rogers, George B. 1976 "Changes in Regional Self-Sufficiency in Egg and Poultry Supplies, 1955-75." *Poultry and Egg Situation*. Washington, D.C.: U.S. Department of Agriculture, September 1976.

———. 1963 "Credit in the Poultry Industry." *Journal of Farm Economics* 45 (2) (May 1963).

Rogers, George, et al. 1976 "Shell Egg Packing and Broiler Processing Costs in Major Regions." *Poultry and Egg Situation*. Washington, D.C.: U.S. Department of Agriculture, September 1976.

Roseberry, William. 1983 *Coffee and Capitalism in the Venezuelan Andes*. Austin: University of Texas Press.

Rosenberg, Howard R. and Jeffrey M. Perloff. 1988 "Initial Effects of the New Immigration Law on California Agriculture," *California Agriculture* (May-June 1988).

Rosenfeld, Stuart, Edward Bergman, and Sarah Rubin. 1985 *After the Factories: Changing Employment Patterns in the Rural South*. Research Triangle Park, N.C.: Southern Growth Policies Board.

Rouse, Roger. 1987 "Migration and the Politics of Family Life: Divergent Projects and Rhetorical Strategies in a Mexican Transnational Migrant Community." San Diego: Center for U.S.-Mexican Studies, University of California.

Rungeling, Brian, L. H. Smith, V. M. Briggs, and J. F. Adams. 1977 *Employment, Income, and Welfare in the Rural South.* New York: Praeger Publishers.

Runsten, David. 1985a "Mexican Immigrants and the California Seafood Processing Industry." San Diego: Center for U.S.-Mexican Studies, University of California.

————. 1985b "Mexican Immigrants and the California Poultry Industry." Center for U.S.-Mexican Studies, University of California at San Diego.

Sabella, James, Anthony Paredes, and Marcus Hepburn. 1975 *An Ethnographic Analysis of Indian Rocks, Florida.* Unpublished technical report. Tallahassee: Florida State University.

Safa, Helen. 1983 "Women, Production, and Reproduction in Industrial Capitalism: A Comparison of Brazilian and U.S. Factory Workers." In *Women, Men, and the International Division of Labor,* edited by J. Nash and M. Fernandez-Kelly. Albany: State University of New York Press.

Saffioti, H. I. Bongiovani. 1980 "Relationships of Sex and Social Class in Brazil." In *Sex and Class in Latin America: Women's Perspectives on Politics, Economics, and the Family in the Third World,* edited by J. Nash and H. Safa. New York: J. F. Bergin Publishers, Inc. 147-159.

Sahlins, Marshall. 1972 *Stone Age Economics.* Chicago: Aldine.

Sanderson, Steven, ed. 1985 *The Americas in the New International Division of Labor.* New York: Holmes and Meier.

Sassen-Koob, Saskia. 1985 "Capital Mobility and Labor Migration." In *The Americas in the New International Division of Labor,* edited by S. Sanderson. New York: Holmes and Meier. 226-252.

Scott, James. 1985 *Weapons of the Weak: Everyday Forms of Peasant Resistance.* New Haven: Yale University Press.

Shabecoff, Philip. 1973 "Alien, Poor, and Afraid: Workers in the Florida Sugar Industry." *New York Times,* March 12, p. 4.

Sider, Gerald. 1986 *Culture and Class in Anthropology and History: A Newfoundland Illustration.* Cambridge: Cambridge University Press.

Sinclair, Peter. 1983 "Fishermen Divided: The Impact of Limited Entry Licensing in Northwest Newfoundland." *Human Organization* 42 (4): 307-313.

Smith, David and Philip Daniel. 1987 *The Chicken Book*. New York: Atheneum.

Smith, Estellie, ed. 1977 *Those Who Live from the Sea*. New York: West Publishers.

Sowell, Thomas. 1981 *Markets and Minorities*. New York: Basic Books.

Stack, Carol. 1971 "The Kindred of Viola Jackson." *Afro-American Anthropology,* edited by Norman Whitten. New York: The Free Press.

Stanley, Kathleen. 1988 "Immigrant and Refugee Labor in the Restructuring of the Midwest Meatpacking Industry." Proposal submitted to the Bureau of International Labor Affairs, U.S. Department of Labor.

Steinbeck, John. 1939 *The Grapes of Wrath*. New York: Penguin.

Stichter, Sharon. 1985 *Migrant Laborers: African Society Today*. London: Cambridge University Press.

Stoler, Ann. 1985a "Perceptions of Protest: Defining the Dangerous in Colonial Sumatra." *American Ethnologist* 12 (4): 642-658.

———. 1985b *Capitalism and Confrontation in Sumatra's Plantation Belt, 1870-1979*. New Haven: Yale University Press.

Taylor, F. W. 1911 *Principles of Scientific Management*. Norwood, Mass.: Plimpton Press.

Texas Employment Commission. 1988 "Employment, Hours, and Earnings." Austin: Texas Department of Labor.

Thomas, F. B. and S. D. Thomas. 1983 *Technical Operations Manual for the Blue Crab Industry*. Raleigh, N.C.: UNC Sea Grant College Publication UNC-SG-83-02.

Thomas, F. B., T. M. Miller, N. B. Webb, and J. E. Easley, Jr. 1980 *Manual of Seafood Processing and Marketing in North Carolina*. Raleigh, N.C.: UNC Sea Grant College Publication UNC-SG-80-04.

Thomas, Robert. 1985 *Citizenship, Gender, and Work: California Lettuce Workers*. Berkeley: University of California Press.

U.S. Bureau of the Census. 1987 *Statistical Abstract of the U.S.* Washington, D.C.: U.S. Government Printing Office.

U.S. Congress. 1978 *The West Indies (BWI) Temporary Alien Labor Program.* Study prepared for the Subcommittee on Immigration of the Committee on the Judiciary, U.S. Senate, 95th Congress, 2nd session.

———. 1983a *A Summary of Hearings Held by the Senate Judiciary Subcommittee on Immigration and Refugee Policy.* Washington, D.C.: U.S. Government Printing Office.

———. 1983b *Job Rights of Domestic Workers: The Florida Sugar Cane Industry.* Study prepared by the Subcommittee on Labor Standards of the Committee on Education and Labor, U.S. House of Representatives. Washington, D.C.: U.S. Government Printing Office.

———. 1984 Hearing about "a Bill to Ammend the Packers and Stockyards Act, 1921, to Remove Processes Poultry Marketings From the Coverage of Such Act." September 20, 1984. 98th Congress. U.S. Printing Office: Washington, D.C.

———. 1986 "Immigration Reform and Control Act of 1986." Public Law 99-603. Nov. 6, 1986. 99th Congress. Washington, D.C.: U.S. Government Printing Office.

U.S. Department of Agriculture, Economic Research Service. 1988 Interview with Lee Christiansen, April 28.

U.S. Department of Labor. 1988 Solicitation dated April 15, 1988. Washington, D.C.: Bureau of International Labor Affairs.

U.S. General Accounting Office. 1988 *Illegal Aliens: Influence of Illegal Workers on Wages and Working Conditions of Legal Workers.* GAO Briefing Report to Congressional Requesters. March, 1988. Washington, D.C.: U.S. Government Printing Office.

———. 1986 *Illegal Aliens: Limited Research Suggests Illegal Aliens May Displace Native Workers.* GAO Briefing Report to Congressional Requesters. Washington, D.C.: U.S. Government Printing Office.

University of North Carolina Sea Grant College Program. 1988 "Red Tide" *Coastwatch,* (February, 1988.) Raleigh, N.C.: UNC Sea Grant College Publication.

Valdes-Pizzini, Manuel. 1990 "Fishermen Associations in Puerto Rico: Praxis and Discourse in the Politics of Fishing." *Human Organization* 49 (2): 164-173.

Vass, Tom. 1979 "Low Wages and Industrial Development: North Carolina's Economic Predicament." *Carolina Planning.* (5) (Fall, 1979): 14-21.

Villarejo, Don. 1988 "The Changing Structure of California Agriculture and Its Impact on Farm Labor." Davis: Working Group on Farm Labor and Rural Poverty, California Institute for Rural Studies. May 1988.

Vincent, Joan. 1974 "The Structuing of Ethnicity." *Human Organization* 33: 375-379.

Walker, John. 1987a "Stability in Production and the Demand for Mexican Labor: The Case of Turkey Processing in Rural Utah." Paper prepared for the workshop "Mexican Immigrant Labor in the U.S. Economy: Sectoral Perspectives." Center for U.S.-Mexican Studies, University of California, San Diego.

————. 1987b "Stability in Production and the Demand for Mexican Labor: The Case of Turkey Processing in Rural Utah." Utah: Department of Economics, University of Utah. August 1987.

Wallerstein, Immanuel. 1976 *The Modern World System.* New York: Academic Press.

Weiner, Annette. 1980 "Stability and Banana Leaves: Colonization and women in Kiriwina, Trobriand Islands." In *Women and Colonization,* edited by M. Etienne and E. Leacock. New York: Praeger.

Whyte, W.F. 1978 "Organizational Behavior." In *Applied Anthropology in America,* edited by W. Partridge and E. Eddy. New York: Columbia University Press.

Wilkinson, Alex. 1988 *Big Sugar.* New York: Alfred Knopf.

Wissman, Paul Pence. 1950 *The Nature of the Labor Force of a Rural Industry in Virginia: A Case Study of the Stonewall Plant of Merck and Company, Inc.* M.A. thesis, University of Virginia.

Wolf, Eric. 1982 *Europe and the People Without History.* Berkeley: University of California Press.

Wood, Charles. 1982 "Equilibrium and Historical-Structural Perspectives on Migration." *International Migration Review* 2 (16): 298-319.

————. 1981 "Structural Change and Household Strategies: A Conceptual Framework for the Study of Rural Migration." *Human Organization.* 4 (40): 338-344.

Wood, Charles and Terry Mccoy. 1985 "Caribbean Cane Cutters in Florida: Implications for the Study of the Internationalization of Labor." In *The Americas in the New International Division of Labor,* edited by S. Sanderson. New York: Holmes and Meier. 125-144.

Worsley, Peter. 1984 *The Three Worlds: Culture and World Development.* Chicago: University of Chicago Press.

Index

Sexism, 130-32
Sinclair, Peter, 140-41
Skinheads. *See* Klu Klux Klan
Slavery, 12, 16-17, 58; and Christianity, 17
Social Interdependence, 78-80
Social Services, 12, 34-35; use by seafood processing workers, 57-58, 63-64, 129
South Africa, 5, 17, 216, 238n.2
South, The, 16-17, 58-59, 120-21, 208
Southeast Asians, 152, 224-25; use in poultry industry, 153-54; attitudes toward, 155-57
Steinbeck, John, 16
Subcontracting—Labor Contractors, Contracting, 37; in broiler production, 86
Subsidies, informal economy as, 65-67; commodity, 85-86; and workers, 227-29; public programs as, 239n.6. *See* also Social Services
Supervision, supervisors, 177-81
Surimi, 76

T

Taylor, F.W., 127, 219-20
Texas, 4, 10, 15; union activity, 93-96

Transnationalism, 27. *See also* Immigrants, adaptive social structures of

U

Unemployment, influence on labor supplies, 89-93; among seafood workers, 116-19
Union Activity, in the poultry industry, 93-96; alternatives to 95-96, 182-83
United Food and Commercial Workers Union (UFCW), 19-21
United Packing House Workers of America. *See* United Food and Commercial Union
United States Department of Agriculture inspections, 108

V

Vertical Integration, 87-88, 106-08

W

Welfare. *See* Social Services
Wolf, Eric, 31, 37, 92, 200, 216-17, 221-22
Work ethic, 7, 22, 120, 213-16; among Southeast Asians, 155; among Hispanics, 156-59, 166-67